P9-BYX-888

THE
AGENT

ALSO BY LEIGH STEINBERG

Winning with Integrity

ALSO BY MICHAEL ARKUSH

The Big Fight: My Life In and Out of the Ring
By Sugar Ray Leonard with Michael Arkush

The Fight of the Century: Ali vs. Frazier March 8, 1971

The Last Season: A Team in Search of Its Soul
By Phil Jackson with Michael Arkush

Getting Up & Down: My 60 Years in Golf
By Ken Venturi with Michael Arkush

*My Greatest Shot: The Top Players Share Their Defining Golf
Moments*
By Ron Cherney and Michael Arkush

*I Remember Payne Stewart: Personal Memories of Golf's Most
Dapper Champion by the People Who Knew Him Best*

*Fairways and Dreams: Twenty-five of the World's Greatest Golfers
and the Fathers Who Inspired Them*

Tim Allen Laid Bare

Rush!

60 Years of USC-UCLA Football
By Steve Springer and Michael Arkush

THE
AGENT

*My 40-Year Career Making Deals
and Changing the Game*

LEIGH STEINBERG
with
MICHAEL ARKUSH

Thomas Dunne Books
St. Martin's Press
New York

THOMAS DUNNE BOOKS.
An imprint of St. Martin's Press.

THE AGENT. Copyright © 2014 by Leigh Steinberg. Foreword copyright © 2014 by
Warren Moon. All rights reserved. Printed in the United States of America. For
information, address St. Martin's Press, 175 Fifth Avenue, New York, N.Y. 10010.

www.thomasdunnebooks.com
www.stmartins.com

Library of Congress Cataloging-in-Publication Data

Steinberg, Leigh.
    The agent : my 40-year career making deals and changing the game /
Leigh Steinberg, Michael Arkush.
        p. cm.
    Includes index.
    ISBN 978-1-250-03042-9 (hardcover)
    ISBN 978-1-250-03043-6 (e-book)
    1. Steinberg, Leigh.   2. Sports agents—United States—Biography.   I. Arkush,
Michael.   II. Title.
  GV734.5.S75 2014
  338.47796092—dc23
  [B]
                                                                2013031041

St. Martin's Press books may be purchased for educational, business, or promotional
use. For information on bulk purchases, please contact Macmillan Corporate
and Premium Sales Department at 1-800-221-7945, extension 5442, or write
specialmarkets@macmillan.com.

First Edition: January 2014

10 9 8 7 6 5 4 3 2 1

To the joys of my life, my children—Jonathan, Matthew, and Katie— and my loving brothers, James and Donald

CONTENTS

ACKNOWLEDGMENTS

The process of summarizing sixty-four years of an eventful life was lengthy and arduous and could never have occurred without the skills and dedication of my gifted coauthor, Michael Arkush, who insisted on excellence and who I gave his first grey hairs. Mel Berger, my agent, cared about the quality of the work, not simply the economics, a man of principal. To our editor, Rob Kirkpatrick, who kept us on track, and his assistant, Nicole Sohl, who guided us so wonderfully from start to finish.

The only way I was able to escape the grip of crippling addiction was with an amazing support system. My extended family stuck with me through the worst of times—my brother James literally saved my life; he is a special soul. My wonderful mother, Betty, and her giving companion, Alicia Balthazar, let me come home, when I had none. I have had the privilege of two fathers in my life—my uncle Larry has inspired me and supported me since birth. My aunt Anita and activist aunt Eleanor and cousins like Bob, Jay, and Amy Steinberg, Richard and Joan Blumenberg, and David and Robert Hoffman have always been there. My daughter, Katie, was a constant ray of sunshine who never stopped believing and filled me with hope and optimism. My son Jon set an example of enormous courage and strength.

There is a unique fellowship that formed the key to my recovery; I can never repay my debt to this group and the higher power it introduced to my life. I have the wisest and most visionary of sponsors who calls himself a ditchdigger but quotes Shakespeare, Dwight Heitman, who has guided me through thick and thin. Bill Long, loving mentor, started me on the path. Lee Bouder helped me refocus along with Adam Copenhaver, Roger Holmes, Zach Martin, Meredith Roundtree, Mike Hanrahan, Kent Benson, Tom Overett, Chip Gendreau, Tom Lord, Shawn Mitchell, Bryan Broadbent, Brad Elligood, Curtis Waldschmidt, and countless others. Don Peters gave great insights, Barton Blinder was another font of wisdom, and Kurt Rouzanian helped me probe new depths.

My old friends stepped in and supported me—George Horioka, Ken Abrahamian, John Rosenbaum, Jeff Moorad, Jack Friedman, Bruce Oppenheim, Dennis Gilbert, Richard Gilliam, Megan Bennett, Scott Bogdon, Mary Mckay, and Paul Majors. Tom Van Voorst has played an unparalleled vital role as roommate and terrific friend, and our great friend Terri West.

Dr. Kristin Willeumeir has been a gifted doctor and master of multiple disciplines who helped restore hope and endless opportunity in my life. Nicole Glatman whipped my body back into shape, a surrogate daughter. Dean Erwin Chemerinsky gave me my first Law School Professorship. Alex Assante has been a great lawyer and a caring friend. Compassionate Donna Gugliotta kept me on track with the assistance of astute Robert Gastelum.

Alex Sohailli and David Braun have been super assistants and spent long nights helping with the manuscript. Amanda Gunville and Chris Koras showed me dedication and selflessness.

To Amy Stoody who showed me the meaning of unselfish love and made my soul sing. Cynthia Deatrick reignited my belief in myself and put love back in my heart in the darkest of times—a true giving force for good. Jenni Hogan is my long distance soul mate.

The future looks bright. I am blessed with a loyal friend, the next great superagent, my trusted alter ego Justin Greely. Dave Blanchard was there with optimism in tough times, and he and Scott Irwin entered my life like guardian angels. Scott's amazing wife, Marilyn, has been a great friend, as well as new partners William Dore and Andy Priest.

Troy Aikman and Earl Campbell never wavered in their support. June Jones is an extraordinary human being who has enriched my life in so many ways for so many years, my foxhole buddy to the end. Two of the most impactful people in my life have the name Warren. My deceased father lives in my heart as do his admonitions: first, treasure relationships, especially family, second, make a positive difference in the world and help people who can't help themselves, and third there is no "they" to fix problems—the they is you son! Also Warren Moon, who I grew up with over the last thirty-seven years and whose strength and values and constant impact has made my life so much better! Thanks to you all.

FOREWORD

Roughly thirty-five years ago, when I had just finished my senior year at the University of Washington, I received a letter from Leigh Steinberg introducing himself as a sports agent, mentioning that we shared a high school alma mater, Hamilton High in Los Angeles, and indicating that he would like to meet. Thus began my relationship with an extraordinary man that continues to this day.

I knew Leigh was someone special early on, that his depth of character far exceeded the title later bestowed upon him by the media as the world's first "superagent." Many sought out Leigh and he easily could have concentrated his attention elsewhere, but he so believed in me and my future that he stuck with me after I signed with the Canadian Football League, bypassing the 1978 National Football League draft. We became good friends. He became someone who I could talk to about any subject, good and bad, inside and outside of sports. We talked about life and gave each other good advice. A believer in human rights and highly conscientious himself, he stressed the value of giving back to one's own community and how he found it imperative that I, along with the rest of his clients, start charitable foundations.

He taught me that football was a stepping stone for the rest of my life. He had me network, collect business cards, and memorize names, emphasizing that the relationships I made would carry me forward once I stopped playing the game I loved. All the while, he continued to espouse the fundamental need for a charitable component to one's life work.

I helped Leigh recruit players when I was still playing because I believed in him, so much so that I worked for Leigh for four years after I retired from football. I continued to recruit players, but as head of new business development, I was also able to mentor clients. So, even with my position in Leigh's agency, Leigh had me giving something back to others.

Do you know what? I am involved in a multitude of endeavors, but it is the charitable work that brings me the greatest reward. I can only hope that by example, I am passing on Leigh's insight into how each of us can create a truly meaningful legacy.

Leigh is also one of the most, if not the most intelligent individual I have ever met. Needless to say, his visionary attributes and the respect he deserves and has garnered stem from this intelligence. Beyond his recognition of the need of athletes to give back to the community, he identified the need to protect athletes as the first to highlight, among other things, the dangers of concussions. A man of integrity and foresight, he also transcended and supplanted the "agent" stigma of the time by empowering his clients so they would not be manipulated nor taken advantage of.

I believe his extreme intelligence also weighed heavily in his success and proved the proverbial double-edged sword. For a time, I believe Leigh's intelligence hindered him from combatting a problem with alcohol, not recognizing it as the disease it was and believing that he could handle it by himself. I could not, however, be more proud of Leigh, now sober for over three years after recognizing that he, in fact, needed help from experts and having undergone the rehabilitation process. I hope that my unwavering friendship, care, and support during this period helped in some

small way. After all, Leigh helped show me how to overcome adversity in my life. Still, those of us fortunate enough to know
Leigh knew that he would always come out on top.

I am honored that Leigh asked me to write this foreword and
am privileged to call Leigh a friend, while, in fact, he has been so
much more than that.

Thank you, Leigh. Thank you for everything.

Warren Moon
Canadian Football Hall of Fame Inductee 2001
Professional Football Hall of Fame Inductee 2006

THE
AGENT

PREFACE

The day was unlike any other, before or since. I wished it would never end.

The place was Canton, Ohio, where, on August 5, 2006, Warren Moon and Troy Aikman, whom I represented for their entire careers, were formally inducted into the Pro Football Hall of Fame.

To me, Warren and Troy were much more than clients. They were family. I shared with them their greatest triumphs, on and off the field, and their roughest trials, as they struggled to find success at the most demanding position in American sports. No athlete is asked to do more than a quarterback in the National Football League, and no athlete is criticized more harshly when he fails to perform at a high level. Warren and Troy won games and admirers and grew into men of honor and virtue who gave back to the game, and to their communities, which had given them more than they could ever imagine.

I was used to delivering speeches, hundreds of them, but the speech on this particular afternoon, to introduce Warren, was different. I was not thinking about the crowd in Canton or the people watching on television. All I really cared about was trying to do justice to the magnificent accomplishments of my dear friend Warren.

Warren asked me a few months earlier to be his presenter. We were in the backseat of a limousine heading to the airport. I figured he might ask, yet when he did, I was touched. Agents did not introduce players at the Pro Football Hall of Fame. Fathers or coaches or teammates did, those who taught them how to play the game and act like men.

For weeks, I struggled to fit twenty-three years of a career on and off the field into five minutes. I read my speech over and over to myself, and to friends, timing its length to be certain it did not run one second longer. I mailed a copy a month in advance to the Hall staff in Canton, who were quite strict. "We are timing it to the second," they kept telling me. "Don't ad-lib." I could just picture myself being ushered offstage like one of those long-winded winners in the lesser categories at the Oscars, any final thank-yous drowned out by the orchestra.

I never forgot what happened to Howard Slusher, the only other agent to be a presenter. I looked up to Howard, known as "Agent Orange" for his wave of red hair. He took advantage of the only leverage available to agents in the 1970s, holding his players out of training camp. Unfortunately, Howard, who represented a number of the great Steelers from their golden era, got off the point a bit when he introduced cornerback Mike Haynes in 1997. He was booed off the stage. "Whatever you say," people warned, "don't do what Howard Slusher did."

Once satisfied with the final version, I memorized it.

Upon arriving in Canton, there was so much to be grateful for, in football and the rest of my life:

- Representing sixty first-round picks in the NFL, including the No. 1 pick a record eight times, and securing record-breaking contracts.

- Representing All-Star players in Major League Baseball and the NBA.
- Helping athletes establish charitable programs at the high school, collegiate, and professional levels that raised more than $700 million.
- Assisting San Francisco mayor Frank Jordan and Oakland mayor Elihu Harris to keep the Giants and A's from fleeing the Bay Area.
- Writing a bestselling business book, *Winning with Integrity*.
- Serving as a consultant on *Jerry Maguire*, *Any Given Sunday*, and *For Love of the Game*.
- Training thousands of young volunteers nationwide to combat racism through the Anti-Defamation League and running camps to teach human relations to high schoolers.
- Setting up Adopt a Minefield, with Secretary of State Madeleine Albright, and programs to aid earthquake victims in Haiti.

Altogether, I had received four presidential commendations, six keys to cities, and thirteen Man of the Year awards.

Yes, indeed, there was a great deal to cherish.

The weekend, however, was most of all an opportunity to reflect on my long relationships with Warren and Troy.

I recalled the horrible insults Warren endured at the University of Washington in the '70s. He was from Los Angeles, black, and not Sonny Sixkiller, the school's star quarterback from earlier in the decade. The fans in Seattle did not give Warren a chance. Yet after he became their hero and led the Huskies to an upset in the 1978 Rose Bowl over No. 4 Michigan, he didn't utter a single derogatory word about how they had treated him. Warren had too much class.

I recalled the disappointment on his face only a few months

later when I told him it was unlikely any franchise would select him in the early rounds of the NFL Draft. He played in a rollout system rather than the NFL's drop-back style, and this was during the time when scouts and general managers still believed a black quarterback simply didn't possess the requisite intelligence and leadership skills to succeed in professional football.

I recalled the tour around the country the two of us took in late 1983 and early 1984 when Warren, the first legitimate star to become a free agent, looked to jump from the Canadian Football League to the NFL. Franchises in both those entities and in the United States Football League made efforts to sign him. The doubts over whether he could be an NFL QB were gone forever, the dollars rising by the day. His childhood dream of competing on the sport's grandest stage was about to come true at last. He proceeded to sign the largest NFL contract in history.

I recalled the numerous occasions when he came to my aid, whether lending me money for a down payment on my first home, defending me when another agent implied I was a racist, or phoning prospective new clients to vouch for my integrity. No one was more loyal than Warren Moon.

I recalled our work on his Crescent Moon Foundation, which we created to send hundreds of students to colleges on scholarships. One student told me, "I would never have been a doctor without Warren."

Most poignantly, I recalled the sobering evening in the summer of 1995 when I arrived at his house in suburban Houston after his peaceful world had been shaken with the news he was being charged with domestic violence against his wife, Felicia. Here was my friend, the epitome of coolness—I called him Dark Gable—fearing his marriage and reputation would never be the same. The timing could not have been worse, coming just a year after O. J. Simpson was accused of double murder, but Warren and I came up with a plan, and he, Felicia, and the family got through the ordeal.

I knew him as well as anyone, and I knew the man wasn't capable of harming a soul.

I thought about Warren a lot in the summer of 2006, about what the two of us achieved together, and it wasn't just because I was composing a speech. It lifted my spirits enormously to reminisce about the past. The present was too upsetting, especially after the year had gotten off to such a promising start.

In February, one of my prized clients, Pittsburgh Steelers quarterback Ben Roethlisberger, in just his second year, led his team to a Super Bowl victory over the Seattle Seahawks. The apex of achievement for a football agent is having a winning quarterback in the Super Bowl, the first overall pick in the NFL Draft, and a client elected to the Hall of Fame. Experiencing two of these thrills on the same weekend, and knowing that in August I would have *two* clients—Warren and Troy—going into the Hall, made me optimistic about the future.

Next would be the draft in April, when another client, USC quarterback Matt Leinart, would possibly become the top overall pick. Others close to Matt, however, decided he would be better served by another agency.

It wasn't as if I hadn't suffered my share of setbacks in the past. In 2000, after selling our firm, I lost the autonomy I valued so much during my first twenty-five years as an agent, and soon was unable to stop agent walkouts, lawsuits, and the painful exodus of many clients.

This time, though, losing a client only added to the sense of powerlessness I felt after all the losses I had experienced in my personal life.

My wife, Lucy, and I lost two houses to mold, two children were diagnosed with severe vision problems, and I squandered a fortune in the Internet crash. By 2006, Lucy and I, who had been drifting apart, were on the verge of breaking up for good, depriving me of being around the three kids I loved so dearly. Most crushing of all was the loss of my father in 2004 after a long bout with cancer.

I turned to alcohol when these losses began to pile up. I didn't drink in the day, at least not until I lived on my own, but that's because I knew the reward for my patience, a late-night drink, was waiting for me at home. I tried to keep the alcohol a secret from my friends and co-workers, but that was a lost cause from the start. Many were quite embarrassed or angry, or both. I could not blame them.

The festivities got under way in Canton with a lunch on Friday in a log cabin reserved for members of the Hall and presenters, where I was privileged to sit next to Merlin Olsen, the defensive tackle who was part of the "Fearsome Foursome," the front four that captivated me and countless other Los Angeles Rams diehards in the 1960s. Merlin and I talked about his plans to do more broadcasting and acting. I would later testify about our conversation when his family filed for damages after he died of mesothelioma, caused by exposure to asbestos. Looking around that cabin was like walking through NFL history.

At night, I went to a dinner at the Canton Memorial Civic Center emceed by sportscaster Al Michaels.

I spent at least a few minutes with one legend after another, each beaming once more, grateful to be back, if only for one weekend a year, in the world they sorely missed. Nothing in their lives could ever match the joy they experienced every Sunday afternoon. They took pride in their manhood and their determination to play through any amount of pain, yet in catching up years later with the men they'd battled, partners now instead of enemies, the emotions came easily, and often.

I noticed something else that evening, however, and it hit me very hard.

Perhaps the most moving moment in each Hall of Fame weekend is when the members walk up a ramp to the stage where the new inductees first wear their official yellow jackets. I put the jacket on Warren. This is when it sinks in they have joined the club. Only instead of focusing on the Class of 2006, I couldn't keep my eyes off the players from the past.

Their bodies, which served them so well for so long, had let them down. Quite a few required assistance just to reach the stage, and they were still relatively young men, in their forties and fifties. I had been around pro football for more than thirty years, seeing plenty of players in tremendous agony in their locker rooms after every game, but by the following week they were ready to place their bodies on the line again. The men in Canton would not get that chance. It was not the first time I saw the toll pro football takes on a human being—one of my clients lost a kidney, another a foot—but observing these wounded warriors together, in one place, made me more aware of that toll than ever.

On Saturday morning, after signing dozens of footballs, Warren and I sat in an open convertible as the Class of 2006 cruised through downtown Canton. The streets were lined with thousands of fans taking part in another Hall of Fame tradition, the Timken Grand Parade. It felt like the Fourth of July, with marching bands and helium balloons and gorgeous floats. Warren could not stop smiling and waving the entire ride. Me, too.

After resting at the hotel for a few hours, we took a limo to Fawcett Stadium for the official ceremony. There was so much I wanted to say to Warren, about how proud I was of what he had achieved, and the person he became, but it was not the right moment. The speech, I hoped, would say it all.

"You ready?" I asked when we stepped out of the limo.

He didn't hesitate for one second.

"I'm ready," he said.

He always was.

I headed toward the stage, grateful to be seated next to Al Davis, the longtime owner of the Oakland Raiders, who did as much for pro football as anyone in history. Al was on hand to present his ex-coach John Madden, who, of course, became more familiar as the lead analyst for CBS.

In his late seventies, Al was quite frail, requiring a walker to get around, but the keenness of his mind reminded me of our fascinating chats in the old days when he often called me at my house in Berkeley, usually around midnight, to discuss topics as diverse as the Civil War and ancient Greek history. There was no owner in pro football, or any sport, for that matter, like Al Davis. The fact that the two of us, vastly different in our politics and temperament, could be friends spoke volumes about our passion for the game.

"Al," I told him, "you know your Raiders are still the only team I ever bought season tickets for." He smiled.

The ceremony got under way. Warren was the fourth of six inductees to be introduced. The others were linebacker Harry Carson, defensive end Reggie White, who had passed away not quite two years earlier at the age of forty-three; offensive tackle Rayfield Wright; Madden, and Troy. When the first presenter went way over the mandated five minutes, it was clear it would be a long afternoon.

I gazed behind me at the dozens of Hall veterans I spoke to the day before. They were glowing. The day belonged to them as well, an opportunity to welcome new members to their club. I then focused on the front rows on the floor of the stadium, at Warren's family and Troy's family, people who had been part of our collective journey. I could only imagine the enormous pride they were feeling. They were easily identifiable in the crowd, wearing AIKMAN and MOON T-shirts and hats that the players provided them. I also spotted my wife and three children; I was so happy they were there.

I gazed up at the people in the stadium. They were excited, too. The crowd provided another reminder of how this once-obscure sport had long ago replaced baseball as America's true national pastime.

The heat on the floor of the stadium was quite oppressive, and people were sweating profusely. I often heard from clients about the difference between the temperature in the stands and on the field. Now I knew what they were talking about.

Troy walked slowly to the podium. Just as with Warren, there was so much history to reflect on:

My first visit to his apartment in West Los Angeles when, as a senior at UCLA, he lived only a few blocks from my parents.

The magical day in April of 1989 when the Dallas Cowboys made him the No. 1 pick in the land.

The time he asked me to get him traded from a team that finished a pathetic 1-15.

The limousine ride back to the hotel in Santa Monica, California, in 1993, after he was the MVP in his first of three Super Bowl triumphs. He tossed 4 touchdowns in a 52–17 rout of the snakebitten Buffalo Bills.

"Troy," I asked, "do you realize what has just happened?"

"Yeah, we won the game," he said.

"No, not that," I said. "I mean the fact that your life will never be the same. You just lit up the field in front of a billion people. Just think about that for a few seconds, because the onslaught will come the moment we open this door."

Troy did not realize it—until moments later, when the limo door swung open and the entrance to the hotel was jammed with fans trying to get close to him.

Now, here he stood, a Hall of Famer, an honor richly deserved.

His speech was everything I expected, expressing gratitude to the members of his family and coaches who helped him attain his dreams. His voice cracked at times, which surprised those who always saw him as cool and detached. Not me. I knew the passion he felt for the game, and the people in it.

At last, it was my turn. I took a deep breath and began.

I reflected on those difficult early days when a number of general managers told me Warren should consider changing positions if he hoped to play in the league. "Never," Warren said without the slightest hesitation. "I was born to play quarterback." He was, indeed.

I spoke about how Warren took his talents to the Canadian Football League, and then I explained the powerful impact he had on black youngsters everywhere. In the living room of one black quarterback I met preparing for the NFL Draft, hanging on the wall next to the family photos and trophies were pictures of two heroes who offered him hope and inspiration no matter the barriers for men of his race: Martin Luther King Jr. and Warren Moon.

I closed by stating he was making history as the first black quarterback in the modern era to enter the Hall of Fame, and due to his courage and perseverance, he wouldn't be the last.

The speech was over before I knew it, and, to the Hall's satisfaction, I finished in less than five minutes. The fans applauded as did the members.

After I left the podium, Warren gave me a hug.

"I love you," he said.

Neither of us had to say another word.

I went to bed in peace that evening, rehashing the events from the whole weekend, believing my worst days were behind me.

How wrong I was.

1

LIKE FATHER, LIKE SON

It did not take me long to make the papers for the first time.

"Warren and Betty Steinberg presented John Steinberg with his first grandchild yesterday, a boy, at Cedars," it was reported in the March 29, 1949, edition of *The Hollywood Reporter,* the popular daily trade publication for the movers and shakers in show business.

"He's happier about that than the opening of the swank new Hillcrest."

If that were, indeed, the case, then Grandpa must have been overjoyed, for he was totally committed to his job managing the mostly Jewish Hillcrest Country Club, the answer to decades of discrimination by those who belonged to the older, Waspy Los Angeles Country Club. Hillcrest was also a haven for people in the entertainment community denied membership in other clubs.

Grandpa was never afraid to take a risk. In the early '30s, he owned an upscale restaurant on Long Island called the Pavillon Royal, which attracted some of the biggest acts in entertainment. Ethel Merman, the legendary Broadway singer, who often performed there, credits him with her first big break. Another to benefit was FDR, who held major campaign events on the grounds. In 1936, like so many others in his generation, Grandpa made the move out West, taking over the Café Trocadero, a posh club on the Hollywood Strip that was a hangout for Bing Crosby, Fred Astaire, Judy Garland, and Cary Grant.

Years later at Hillcrest, the regulars were just as impressive, featuring the likes of Jack Benny, George Burns, Bob Hope, Groucho Marx, George Jessel, Danny Kaye—they called it the comedians' table—and a buxom blonde named Marilyn Monroe whose lap I sat on one day. I went to the club once a week, sitting on Grandpa's lap—I'm guessing I enjoyed Marilyn's more—as he played gin rummy. Another time, I was introduced to a singer who had established quite a following, Elvis Presley. He gave me an autographed guitar.

I began to believe the entire world was filled with Jewish comedians. It was Burns, in fact, along with Grandpa, who took me to my first professional baseball game, about three years before the Dodgers arrived from Brooklyn. We saw the Hollywood Stars, the minor league outfit that competed in the Pacific Coast League at old Gilmore Field on Beverly. To me, while there couldn't have been more than maybe 10,000 spectators in the stands on any given night, it seemed like the big leagues. Thus began my childhood love affair with baseball.

Grandpa enjoyed the finer things in life, wearing the most expensive suits and Bay Rum Cologne. His fingernails were manicured every day, and he went on gambling trips to Havana. Grandpa had what they used to call "style." On Monday nights, he took the family out to one of the old, classic L.A. restaurants. Our favorite was Lawry's, a prime rib palace on La Cienega. Spending time at his home in Beverly Hills felt like entering a universe that did not exist anywhere else. He owned every state-of-the-art gadget, even a machine that squeezed real oranges.

On my mother's side, I never knew either grandparent. My grandmother, Florence, died in 1937 from a brain tumor. She was thirty-nine. My grandfather, Leo Blass, somehow found time to take care of three young daughters, including Betty, my mom, who was only nine, while maintaining a medical practice and assuming an active role in the local Jewish community and in the City of Hope. In 1948, he helped found City of Hope National Medical Center, and when the new State of Israel was fighting for its survival against several Arab countries, he went there to help assess the nation's medical needs and treat the wounded soldiers. He didn't think about the risk he was taking, only about the good he might accomplish. Grandpa remains an inspiration to this day.

He was shot by a sniper, and he died a few days later. He was buried in Safed, a city in the northern part of the country. Once the war was over, his three daughters decided to keep him there. My mother was devastated to lose another parent at such a young age—she was twenty—but there was little chance to grieve. She was about to become a parent herself for the first time.

My parents proudly named me after Grandpa Leo. As for the unique spelling of my first name, it depends on who I choose to believe. According to my dad, Leigh came from James Henry Leigh Hunt, a nineteenth-century English poet, essayist, and critic. Mom, meanwhile, attributed it to the actress, Vivien Leigh, immortalized in film history as Scarlett O'Hara from *Gone With the Wind*. I suppose I'll never know the true story—or both versions might be accurate. Either way, my lifelong love for the written word and the cinema were clearly ordained from the start.

I was only ten when I worked on my first publication, *The Corinthian,* named after our residence on Corinth Avenue in a section of Los Angeles adjacent to Culver City. Culver City was home to MGM Studios, and we snuck over fences on back lots to play on Western, Mexican, and South Sea sets.

Assembled with the use of a regular typewriter, the paper chronicled such earth-shattering events in the neighborhood as a mouse we found in our house; the visit to the Marchewka family from Aunt

Blanche, coming all the way from Canada; and the breaking news that the Eschners were selling their house. Our one block certainly felt like a separate world to my friends and me. Everything seemed bigger in those days.

My parents were progressive on every issue that mattered. Both were terribly sad on election night in 1956 when Adlai Stevenson lost for the second time to Dwight D. Eisenhower. There was one political figure, however, they disliked more than any other, Richard Milhous Nixon. They called him "Tricky Dick." They weren't alone.

To my father, being passionate about one's opinions was not sufficient. Each person had a moral obligation to do something about them. It was a lesson I never forgot.

"When you're looking for someone to solve problems in the world, there is no *they*," he said. "The *they* is you, son."

Dad was eternally optimistic, preferring to see the good in human nature. I adopted the same attitude, though it would sometimes later be to my detriment. He was even-mannered, fair, and consistent.

While he was in the Marine Corps, before he was shipped off to the Pacific theater in 1942 or 1943, Dad wrote an editorial for the *Daily Trojan,* the USC student newspaper, criticizing the relocation of Japanese residents in internment camps. By the mid-1950s, after a series of temporary jobs, Dad discovered his true calling as an English and social studies teacher and athletic director, starting out at Jordan High School in Watts. Dad eventually became the vice principal at University High and Crenshaw High, and principal at Le Conte Junior High and Fairfax High.

His father was not very pleased, to say the least, with his career choice. Just a few decades after the Great Depression, Grandpa was more interested in his son making money, as he had done very successfully, than in making a difference. One night, though, he went to a school function at Jordan and was amazed at the effect Dad had on his students, the love they showed him. Grandpa never brought up his son's choice of career again. My father cared deeply about other people and served on the Human Relations Commission in Los Angeles for thirty years, multiple times as its president.

Grandpa was right about one thing: We struggled to get by. In those early days, the five of us, which included my brothers, Don and Jim, shared one bathroom. The three boys slept in one room on bunk beds. When our jeans wore out, we didn't purchase new ones. We put patches on them. Our shoes had taps to preserve the soles. We watched cartoons on a tiny black-and-white television.

Yet we never thought of ourselves as deprived. There were many other riches to savor—simple ones, such as our dog, Harry, named after the book *Harry the Dirty Dog*, or playing hide-and-go-seek or staging rubber-band wars or my favorite, going around the block to Henry's Market for a candy bar and a large bottle of pop and then hanging out by the railroad tracks to throw rocks and talk about comic books or who owned the best baseball card collection. We used our imaginations to make games out of ordinary objects.

For me, as much as I adored Superman, the greatest heroes in my early youth called themselves Dodgers. I'd rooted for them when they were in Brooklyn and can still recall watching on our Emerson as they beat the dreaded Yankees in Game 7 to win the 1955 World Series, their only title in New York. I was in heaven when they moved to Los Angeles in '58 and was lucky enough, thanks again to Grandpa, to be at the Coliseum for the very first home game against the Giants, the good guys prevailing, 6–5. He got me out of school with a note claiming "urgent family business." Urgent it most definitely was.

I saw the Rams play in person at the Coliseum, as well. I cheered wildly as their outstanding running back, Jon Arnett, a local kid, sprinted the length of the field for a touchdown. Ironically, given how I'd eventually make my living, it was baseball, not football, that meant more to me growing up. I continued to root for the Hollywood Stars and was drawn to Gene Autry's Los Angeles Angels when they joined the American League in 1961 as an expansion team, but nothing matched my love for the boys in blue.

One of my favorite players was shortstop Maury Wills, who would become, in 1962, the first to steal more than 100 bases in a season. There was something so wonderfully daring, almost subversive, about the "stolen" base, and no one was a better thief than Wills. I also yearned for him to swing for the fences, as Dad promised to pay me twenty-five cents for every Wills home run. My father was no fool. Over Wills's fourteen-year career, he hit a grand total of 20. I was mesmerized, as well, by the soothing voice of Dodgers play-by-play man Vin Scully. He painted a picture of each ball game more vivid than the one we observed on TV in our living room. To hear Vin as an adult—in his mideighties, he is still going strong—is no less mystical.

The main reason, though, for my attraction to the Dodgers was Sandy Koufax, the superb left-handed pitcher born and raised in Brooklyn. Sandy struck hitters out like no one else in the game, and I loved strikeouts even more than stolen bases and home runs. He was also Jewish, and for Jews growing up in the late 1950s and early 1960s, I cannot possibly overstate how crucial that was. Anti-Semitism was everywhere, in comments that were far from benign—"You killed Christ" or "Don't Jew me down"—and it had been less than two decades since the Holocaust.

Sandy proved that Jews could excel in the most innately American of pursuits, our *national pastime,* and instead of attempting to conceal his rich heritage, he celebrated it. His decision to sit out Game 1 of the 1965 World Series against the Minnesota Twins because it fell on Yom Kippur, the holiest of Jewish holidays, generated even more admiration than anything he did on the diamond. If not for Sandy, I might not ever have become so enamored with sports and drawn to their potential to impact society at large.

I grew up in an area with few Jewish families. From the first day I can remember, I played with the blacks and Mexicans and Asians in our neighborhood, sleeping at their homes so often I felt like part of their families.

Mar Vista Gardens, a housing project for low-income residents, was across the street from my school, Stoner Avenue Elementary. If there were any differences among us, I either didn't notice or didn't care. At home, we put a decal on our front door to welcome neighbors from any race, religion, or nationality. Decades later, I blended in easily with the athletes I represented from various ethnic and religious backgrounds. Blacks can usually tell when a white person is uncomfortable around them, and vice versa.

At the same time, I never let the peer pressure on the street compromise the core principles I inherited from my parents. One afternoon, when I was about eight or nine, as I was walking home from school, I saw a handful of gang members torturing a small mutt. I can close my eyes and still visualize each of them burning the dog with their cigarettes. I could not understand why people kept walking by and no one stopped them. Finally, with no one else daring to intervene, I scooped up the poor thing and ran as fast as I could till I was in the clear. They got in their share of punches, but I rescued the dog. Safe to say, I kept my distance from those young punks from that point on.

I was no hero. I was merely doing what my dad would expect me to do. We were on vacation in Chicago in 1960—the little extra money we did have went for annual trips around the United States and Canada—when we observed a man being a little rough with one of his girls who worked the street. Dad did not hesitate.

He stopped the car, jumped out, and practically ordered the stranger to leave her alone. More startled than angry, the man did exactly that. Dad was not the only person to show me the difference one man can make. So did actor Henry Fonda, who played a juror in the 1957 film *12 Angry Men*. Watching Fonda's character stubbornly search for the truth against eleven other jurors anxious to convict the defendant and be sent home made me think about going into law someday. I was inspired, as well, by my aunt Eleanor who worked for the Anti-Defamation League of B'nai B'rith, and my uncle Larry, an attorney who spent his life fighting for justice, in and out of the courtroom. He was like a second father to me.

A career in journalism was another possibility, although as much as I loved to write, I realized early on I would not be satisfied with reporting on the key events of the day, whether on Corinth Avenue or in the wider world. I needed to *take part* in them. My parents understood this, too, which is why they organized a political club for my brothers and me called the Muttonheads. We selected a president, vice president, and treasurer, and conducted our meetings according to *Robert's Rules of Order*. In retrospect, I'm not certain whether we were truly dedicated to the ideals of democracy or just interested in the dessert we received at the end of each meeting.

Another highlight of my youth came before a slightly larger gathering, and the odds of it occurring were one in a thousand.

My classroom at Braddock Drive Elementary, which I attended before Stoner, was picked among the dozens in Los Angeles to be a source for the popular CBS daytime show *Art Linkletter's House Party*, and then I was one of the fortunate four chosen randomly for the segment "Kids Say the Darndest Things," in which the host interviewed youngsters between ages five and ten. When Mr. Linkletter asked who I thought was the smartest person in the world, I didn't hesitate.

"Myself," I told him.

It sounds, despite our financial difficulties, like the typically idyllic *Leave It to Beaver* childhood from the '50s, and in so many ways, it was.

My brother Jim and I fought all the time as kids—what brothers don't?—but as adults we grew quite close, and I rely on him to this day. The same goes for my other brother, Don, an outstanding athlete in his youth. I also benefited enormously from a large, loving extended family. Aunt Eleanor, Uncle Chuck, Uncle Larry, Aunt Anita, Uncle Arthur, and Aunt Milly each played significant roles in my upbringing. I have such fond memories of the summer we spent with Uncle Arthur, a colonel in the air force, and his family at Wright-Patterson Air Force Base in Dayton, Ohio; my cousin David became an older brother to me. Speaking of family, that is how I felt about our next-door neighbors, Alma, Adolph, Peter, and Margaret Landsberger. We ate together at each other's homes constantly.

Yet life was complicated, even then.

Take my mother, for example. She was an amazing woman, possessing a wit and intelligence that would have taken her a long way in another, more liberated era. She introduced me to movies and books, could solve a double-crostic puzzle at the speed of light, and could be the life of the party like no one else.

Unfortunately, for three or four days each month, she would check out. She would go into her room, shut the door, and start to sob.

"I'm coming down with the flu," she'd say.

Every time this took place, Dad asked my mother's sister Aunt Eleanor, who lived a few miles away and became another mother to me, to watch over her as the rest of us left the house for a break from the tension. Dad could do little except make sure Mom had enough to eat. Then suddenly, almost mysteriously, the episode would be over and she would again be the mother we needed her to be.

I wonder if she was similar to many women of her generation, trapped at home with three children by the age of twenty-five, not able to pursue her own lofty dreams, whatever they may have been. Mom, though, would not be denied forever. She went back to school years later, received her master's degree, and became the city's first audiovisual librarian.

No matter the cause of her behavior, the effect on me was profound—then and forever. I couldn't completely trust her. I didn't know when the loving mother might turn into the absent one.

Even when Mom was doing better, I still felt at times like the odd man out in my own home. She would work on a puzzle with Jim while Dad participated in sports with Don. That spurred me to charge out into the world and accomplish as much as possible.

First came the news we were leaving Corinth Avenue.

My parents decided to move to nearby Cheviot Hills, which presented both opportunities and challenges.

On the plus side, our new house would be much larger. My brothers and I would each enjoy our own room for the first time. We would even own the true barometer of success in the promised land of California, a swimming pool. We weren't rich—we were *never* rich—but we were now members of the middle class. Our good fortune came when our stock in Avnet, an electronics company owned by a friend of our uncle, suddenly went up about fifty points. Another advantage was that Hamilton High School, which I would be attending, was close to MGM Studios, where a number of television shows were filmed.

On the other hand, we were moving from an area where I knew everyone—I had been class president and editor of the school newspaper in junior high—to a section of Los Angeles where I knew no one. The families in this new neighborhood were wealthier and the kids were cliquish.

From my first day at Hamilton, I could see it was a place where students were very serious about their education. I have never been in a more competitive academic environment, and that includes the University of California, undergrad and law school.

I picked three activities I knew I could thrive in: the school newspaper, student government, and the forensics team, where I wrote and delivered a speech on social responsibility that won state-wide awards. I also ran cross-country. I loved playing all sports, but it seemed like I could run forever.

I wrote columns, editorials, and features for *The Federalist*. In one column, I urged the administration to eliminate fraternity- and sorority-type social clubs. I felt they were elitist and excluded too many students. Members of one club seized a huge stack of the papers and burned them in the lunch area.

In the spring of 1965, my senior year, I ran for student body president, and it wasn't just my parents who urged me to make a difference. So did my social studies teacher, Blanche Bettington, who had been at Hamilton since the dawn of time, if not before. Ms. Bettington spoke in a high-pitched voice and dressed rather plainly even as styles grew more modern, but there was a passion in this woman that could not be stifled. She didn't believe only in textbooks. They revealed what someone else felt. She wanted to see what *we* felt—and there was no institution in America, political or religious, we did not have an obligation to openly question.

"You're a leader," Mrs. Bettington used to tell me. "You have a responsibility. Other kids follow you. What are you going to do with that? Are you just going to be another wealthy, unfeeling power broker when you grow up?"

Heavens, no, I told her, not me. I would never become one of *them*.

I won the election, serving until I graduated in June of 1966. It was impossible to ignore the major issues of the day, of course, such as the war in Vietnam or the war over civil rights. Between the footage on the evening news and the gruesome images in *Newsweek, Time,* and *Life,* we certainly were not in the dark about what was going on around us. At school, though, we were mainly occupied with such life-and-death matters as whether we could eat lunch on the front lawn on Friday afternoons and what the theme should be for the prom.

Even so, my education in the art of politics at Hamilton was quite extensive, preparing me well for the intense negotiations I'd conduct years later. We formed the Beverlywood Young Democrats— Beverlywood was our district on the west side of Los Angeles—with dozens of us vying for control, and not everybody playing by the rules. One kid got his tires slashed in a particularly nasty campaign. We counted votes and packaged slates of candidates, assembling our own machine. Two members, Henry Waxman and Howard Berman, would become U.S. congressmen; another, Michael Berman, a top political strategist.

Before I knew it, summer was around the corner, and so, suddenly, was life after high school. Leaving Hamilton, as it turned out, would be as difficult as it had been to leave Corinth Avenue. I had made many friends and accomplished a great deal, making my parents prouder than ever, and now, yet again, I would have to start over.

I assumed my choices for college would be fairly limited. In our family, I wasn't the smart Steinberg (that was Jim) or the athletic one (that was Don). I was the handsome and popular one, which works for the self-contained, insular world of high school but does not guarantee a successful college career.

"I guess I'll have to go to Santa Monica College," I told my father, referring to a small junior college a few miles from home.

"What are you talking about?" he asked.

"I'm not as intelligent as the other kids in my classes," I said.

Dad, who by now had become a high school vice principal, stared at me for the longest time and then set me straight.

"You know I have access to certain IQ information," he said, "and son, I have seen your numbers. They are not any different from Jim's."

"Do you mean I might have an IQ of about 120?" I asked. I shouldn't have been shocked. My grades were excellent, and I had been reading at an extremely high level since elementary school. I'd even been moved up a grade, and could have moved up another if my parents hadn't been concerned about the effect on me socially.

Dad paused again. "Son, your brother is in the Einstein category, and so are you," he said.

I didn't believe him. How could I? To believe him would mean the narrative I had framed in my head for years was flawed. I could write convincing editorials, win debating contests, become student body president, and date the most beautiful girls, but to possess an IQ like Einstein? Me? Please.

Yet I did agree with his encouragement to broaden my search beyond Santa Monica College. My first choice was several hours up the coast, the University of California at Santa Cruz, a brand-new campus with pass/fail classes.

The school, not surprisingly, was bombarded with a massive number of applicants and I didn't get in. I was redirected to UCLA, which pleased two proud alums, Warren and Betty Steinberg, who met when Dad was the sports editor and Mom the managing editor of the *Daily Bruin*. Dad earned three degrees from UCLA; Mom, two.

I was looking forward to it. I'd grown up a "Bruin Baby," being taken to the Coliseum to watch Red Sanders coach two-way single-wing football, and to Venice High and the Sports Arena to see basketball games. In basketball, the Bruins had already won two NCAA crowns (1964, 1965) under legendary coach John Wooden and were on the verge of becoming a dynasty. My father was even more fanatical. He did not miss a single home game between 1947 and when he passed away in 2004.

The only drawback was not being able to participate in a more authentic college experience, as my family didn't have the resources to place me in a dorm. Staying in the same room I had occupied for three years, I almost felt as if I were back in high school.

One solution was to join a fraternity. I went through rush and chose Pi Lambda Phi, a predominantly Jewish house, which was every bit as rowdy as the frat in *Animal House,* complete with toga parties.

Then came Hell Week, and that is putting it mildly. The brothers woke us up every hour to do push-ups and sit-ups and if we didn't execute them properly, they swatted us in the butt with wooden paddles that stung for days. They forced us to wear the same clothes every day for the whole week, and we were fortunate to squeeze in a meal or two. I remember asking myself, How could these brothers, mostly Jewish, be so sadistic? It must not have bothered me too much, though. I was soon one of them and proud of it.

At UCLA, I enrolled in anthropology, not knowing what the word meant, because it was the last class available. I was late one day and took the only seat left. When I looked up, I couldn't see the professor because of a massive head and Afro in front of me.

After class ended, the student turned around.

"Sorry if I blocked your view," Bruins basketball star Lew Alcindor said.

The fate of the football team led to my first march. Political or not, we strongly believed in the cause.

Fresh from a 14–7 triumph over archrival USC, the higher-ranked Bruins were unfairly denied an invitation to the 1967 Rose Bowl. Hundreds of us marched in Westwood down Gayley Avenue, cut over to Wilshire Boulevard, and actually stopped traffic on the 405 freeway, the busiest in the United States.

About six months later, the cause was a bit more serious, and what I witnessed that day changed me forever.

LBJ was in town for a Democratic Party fund-raiser. While the president was dining inside the Century Plaza Hotel with the donors at $1,000 a plate, we assembled outside to protest the war in Vietnam.

There was no reason to believe it would be a violent demonstration. The crowd was filled with plenty of regular folks expressing their constitutional rights, along with my idol, the fighter Muhammad Ali, who had already been stripped of his heavyweight crown for refusing induction into military service.

Then the police, who feared we'd gotten too close to the hotel and might try to take over the building, suddenly began swinging billy clubs. I was in shock. I had grown up in awe of the police, no doubt from seeing them on TV every week putting the bad guys away. Now *they* were the bad guys, clubbing anybody who stood in their path. I also received a crash course in the power of the media and how it can alter the entire perception of events. The coverage on television focused mostly on the angry demonstrators, suggesting, in a not too subtle way, that the cops were fully justified in their excessive actions. I was appalled.

Once again, like father, like son.

The next day, I wrote a letter to the *Los Angeles Times* sharply criticizing the police. The paper ran it.

Several days later, there was a knock at the door. It was an FBI agent. He wanted to know why I wrote the letter and interrogated me about my political views. I got the feeling I was being put on notice, and it would not be the last time.

I didn't care. I was making plans for a new life in Berkeley.

It started with a visit to campus a few months earlier. I was walking down Telegraph Avenue, the main drag, when I fully took in for the first time the smells, sights, and sounds of the 1960s—dope and incense, tie-dyed shirts, beautiful braless women in bell-bottoms, the music of the Beatles and the Stones coming out of speakers in every window. I put headphones on later that afternoon at a friend's fraternity house and went into a trance as I listened to the Doors' "Light My Fire." I took the headphones off and realized, as the Buffalo Springfield song so accurately put it, "there's something happening here"—and, whatever it was, I needed to be in the middle of it. Berkeley was the center of the counterculture in the world.

I felt a tremendous sense of liberation as I headed up north, leaving home for the first time.

2

BERKELEY

I arrived on campus in the fall of 1967 as, essentially, the same person I was at Hamilton High and UCLA. I was, according to the jargon of the times, a bit of a "square."

In my defense, we were not that far removed from the days when students weren't allowed to wear jeans in high school and when the proctor used to place a ruler between boys and girls at dances to keep them from getting too close.

Berkeley, despite its reputation as one of America's most liberal institutions, actually was more traditional than one might imagine. The home of Mario Savio and the Free Speech Movement in 1964, the university also dedicated benches to men such as newspaper magnate William Randolph Hearst. That was about to change, as the school offered countless opportunities for individual growth and exploration, drugs being one obvious example. There were, I kid you not, dorm rooms designated for specific substances—601 for Maui Wowie, 602 for Panama Red, and 603 for Thai sticks.

Back then, you never knew who was going to try what or exactly where it would lead.

I attended a Rams game in Los Angeles late one summer with Howard Resnick, one of my closest friends from Hamilton and

Berkeley, along with good buddies Buddy Epstein and Bruce Oppenheim. We talked about the usual topics: girls, the war, and the Rams.

A few weeks later, back at school, I was walking down the street when I was stopped by a stranger with a bald painted head in a Hare Krishna outfit, wearing the familiar saffron robe and holding incense. I took a quick glance and kept walking.

"Leigh, it's me," Howard said.

I was taken aback. It was Howard, all right, but no longer the Howard I knew. I realized then we were truly living in a different time. Last I heard, Howard was still with the Krishna. Lots of young people went off in different directions like that in the '60s, in search of something, anything, to lend meaning to their lives, and never returned to their former worlds again.

Many, of course, found meaning in the music of that generation. We often trekked to the famous Fillmore auditorium in San Francisco for concerts featuring such great performers as Janis Joplin, Cream, Country Joe and the Fish, and Jefferson Airplane. Books were another source of exploration. *Siddhartha* by Hermann Hesse, *The Teachings of Don Juan* by Carlos Castaneda, Herbert Marcuse masterpieces, and *The Hobbit* were required reading.

The deepest growth, however, came in the classrooms and cafés, where we learned who we were and what we willing to fight for. At one point there were three straight quarters of protests and police occupation, the most traumatic being what took place at the People's Park in May of 1969 as I was wrapping up my junior year.

Just a few weeks earlier, a combination of students and street people had begun erecting a gorgeous new park with trees, flowers, and shrubs on vacant land belonging to the university. We felt the park now belonged to us—hence, the "People's Park."

The governor of California, Ronald Reagan, felt differently. Cracking down on student protestors was a proven technique for

Reagan to enhance his popularity. He sent several hundred California Highway Patrol officers and campus police to quickly install a chain-link wire fence and dismantle practically everything in the park. Soon came backup from Alameda County sheriff's deputies, whom we labeled the Blue Meanies from the 1968 movie *Yellow Submarine* for the giant blue jumpsuits they wore.

We were outraged and, in the spirit of the times, were not to be defeated without a fight.

"Let's go down there and take the park," shouted Dan Siegel, the newly elected student body president during one of the daily noon rallies at Sproul Plaza, the main outdoor area on campus, and that's exactly what we did—or, at least, tried to do.

The police, in all their regalia (helmets, gas masks, and shields) were ready for us, firing shotguns and swinging their nightsticks. They fired tear gas from their guns, threw it, sprayed it out car exhausts, and dropped it over campus via helicopters. We had no chance.

To the police, we were as dangerous as the Vietcong. One student was killed, another blinded, and hundreds wounded, including my roommate, who was hit in the eye with a pellet, and a friend three doors down who suffered a collapsed lung. I wandered into the lounge of the dorm next to ours and saw students lying on the floor and on couches, blood everywhere. This went on for days, with Reagan declaring a state of emergency and sending in the National Guard, a long line of soldiers carrying bayonets positioned in front of the cafeteria. One morning, I heard loud groans from someone on the street in front of our dorm. His arm was broken, the bone sticking through the skin. He had been beaten up by a cop or a Guardsman, he couldn't be sure.

The authorities claimed at first they were using rock salt, but as was later proven, it was something more lethal. It made me realize we needed to change our tactics if we ever hoped to change our country. Asking unarmed college students to encounter officers with bayonets and tear gas and rubber bullets was no solution, as the murders at Kent State would illustrate once again on that terrifying day in May of 1970. Our generation might have believed in entrusting power to the so-called people, but the truth was that most of the "people" wanted to see us marched away in handcuffs, and many in Richard Nixon's "Silent Majority" weren't so silent.

When it came to being arrested, I had my own run-in with the police after I joined a large sit-in in front of the army's induction headquarters in Oakland during Stop the Draft Week in 1967. I was lucky. I was wearing a motorcycle helmet. My friend wasn't as lucky. He got his skull clubbed repeatedly by a billy club. I jumped over a wall in an attempt to stop the officer who was beating him, although it did no good and got me taken away in a van. I didn't regret it for a second. I've always been a bit hesitant to defend myself, physically or in print, but whenever I see anybody I care about in danger, I get very protective.

I was released from jail after a few hours and was pretty disillusioned—until I received a telegram from my parents:

"We hope you are okay . . . We're proud of you."

Many parents during the '60s practically disowned their rebellious sons and daughters. Not Warren and Betty Steinberg. They brought their kids up to question injustice, and I cannot stress enough how much their support bolstered me.

Another day on campus I will never forget was in December of 1969 when the government, having eliminated student deferments, held a lottery to determine the order of who would get called up for military duty. That meant one thing, of course—the possibility of fighting in Vietnam. So it was no huge shock when those who were selected resorted to desperate measures to avoid service. Some, incredibly enough, even shot off one of their toes or put on lace underwear to pretend they were gay or ate potatoes in hopes of causing an unsightly skin rash—anything to avoid dying for a cause they didn't believe in. Quite a few, of course, moved to Canada. I always supported the troops themselves for their courage and valor, as they didn't set policy. It didn't seem fair to blame them for being involved in a senseless war.

We sat in front of a large television set downstairs in the dorm, roughly 150 of us, everyone terrified. One by one, the 366 days of the year (including February 29) were read from little slips of paper placed in a glass jar. Those whose birth dates were called early raced out of the room in panic. The rest prayed they wouldn't be next.

I was fortunate and drew 268, a relatively safe number, and I was never called up. I must confess I had a backup plan, the Air Force Reserve.

During the spring of 1970, I ran for student body president representing the newly formed Nonviolent Action Party. We subscribed to the basic tenets of the progressive agenda—stopping the war, fighting for racial justice, giving students a more influential say in campus decisions—but we believed in working *within* the system, not tearing it apart.

"It is time we recognized . . . our mothers and fathers as potential allies and stopped calling them pigs," I said back then.

Judging by the reaction of those on the far left, it was as if I had joined the John Birch Society. There were some radicals who truly expected the Red Chinese to come to our rescue to overthrow the establishment. Many of them meant well, but many were phonies, worried mainly about saving their own hides and sleeping with as many girls as possible. I wasn't surprised when, once the war ended, quite a few were the first to sell out and *join* the establishment.

I won the election by a 3–1 margin and went right to work. Part of my job was to meet with celebrities who, with very little advance notice, showed up on campus, and it turned out to be quite a list. Having spent much of my childhood with famous comedians at my grandfather's country club, that seemed normal.

Jim Morrison came by the office one day. He wanted to know what students were reading and where they stood in terms of their spiritual consciousness. For someone known for taking a lot of drugs and checking out, the Doors' lead singer was as focused as anyone I had ever met.

"This place is f——ing awesome," he said.

Jimi Hendrix showed up on campus in the summer of 1970.

"You're the student president, right?" Hendrix asked. "Can you tell me what the scene is here?"

I took him to see Lower Sproul Plaza, Upper Sproul Plaza, and Telegraph. Not wearing his familiar military jacket, Hendrix blended in easily.

When Timothy Leary, the well-known LSD advocate, paid a visit, I asked him one question after another about the possible lasting consequences of acid and the revelations that might appear during a typical trip. Leary's insights did not exactly make me want to give it a try. Like everyone else, I believed in exploring new things . . . within reason.

On another occasion, Gloria Steinem dropped in. Although she had yet to launch *Ms.* magazine, she was already a leader of the feminist movement in America. After a tour of campus, I took her to my dorm. Besides her intelligence, I was struck by her beauty.

Taking away our park was not the first thing Governor Reagan had taken away. In the fall of 1968, he shut down the Independent Studies School, which removed any credit from two classes I'd been taking, one of which was taught by Black Panther Eldridge Cleaver. This led to another protest, which led to the Highway Patrol occupying the campus for weeks.

Later in the spring of 1970, while running for reelection, he wanted to take away our chancellor, Roger Heyns. Reagan went after Heyns for allowing the faculty, which was mostly liberal, to hold classes off campus in support of students protesting Nixon's bombing of Cambodia and the murders at Kent State. Nixon was supposed to end the war with his secret plan, not expand it. We met at restaurants, professors' homes, even churches, anywhere that was not official university property.

Soon afterward, Reagan came to a Board of Regents meeting on campus to explain his case. As student body president, I was selected to present the opposing side. A duel between the two of us, from vastly different generations, with vastly different views of a country we both loved, was inevitable.

I pointed out that the chancellor was doing a remarkable job under extremely trying conditions. Students were still being graded, and class attendance was still being taken. We were upholding the integrity of the university, even as we were fighting for our principles.

I was making some genuine headway, which was why, I believe, Reagan, an astute politician, abruptly changed the subject.

"Aren't you the same Mr. Steinberg who was arrested in Oakland in 1960 for sitting in front of troop trains?" he blurted out.

What was he talking about? For a moment, I was too astonished to respond.

"Governor," I finally replied, "I was ten or eleven years old in 1960. I was much closer to playing with toy trains than sitting in front of troop trains."

I didn't stop there. "That question is very consistent with your typical nonadherence to the facts," I said.

Reagan was furious. That was no way, in his view, for a college student to speak to the governor of California. He and I exchanged a few more barbs before the regents moved on to other business.

"I'm sure we'll see each other again," I told him.

"Son, I can't wait," he said.

Years later, as president, he honored me with a Presidential Commendation for Community Service and sent letters congratulating me on the birth of my first two kids. After he left the White House, I visited him at his office in Century City, and we laughed about the old days.

I made a much bigger mistake that spring, and the lesson I learned was one I would never forget.

Because I was not exactly the most adept at picking up languages, I asked a girl I knew to take a French placement exam for me so I could fulfill a requirement I needed to graduate with my class in June. I thought nothing of it. Everyone found a test taker. To us, the foreign language requirement was basically another ridiculous rule made by "the Man," and thus we were justified in doing whatever we could to get around it. I was a political science major. What did I need French for?

I was very excited about pursuing a career in law. Deeply influenced by *Perry Mason, Judd for the Defense,* and *12 Angry Men,* I would stand up for the little guy, just like my father and my uncle Larry.

First, I had to stand up for myself.

One day, a fierce radical who had opposed me in the spring election showed me what hardball in politics was all about.

"Unless you quit as president, I will tell the administration that you had someone take your French exam," he promised. I could tell he was not bluffing.

I was crushed. I'd always been proud of myself for following the example set by my father, the most ethical man I knew, and now I would be exposed for what I truly was: an arrogant twenty-one-year-old who believed the rules did not apply to him.

There was only one thing to do: come clean. It couldn't make up for cheating, but it would launch me on a new, more ethical path, one I told myself I must stay on for the rest of my life. I went to the authorities immediately. In addition to resigning as president, I was placed on disciplinary probation.

That was not the worst of it. The worst was the phone call home.

I still cringe when I recall the words and the tone in my dad's voice. How could I have been so stupid?

I was fortunate. The administration at Berkeley permitted me to pursue my law studies. My fate could have been a lot worse.

There was, however, one other consequence to my actions. The student who replaced me as president was not quite as effective. As a result, the movement we'd started to build of nonviolence groups on campuses across the nation stalled. I felt guilty for the longest time, always wondering how events might have unfolded if I had served my full term.

Law school was not what I imagined. Instead of learning how to become the next Clarence Darrow or Perry Mason or Henry Fonda, I took Civil Procedure and Real Property and other stimulating classes.

I loved the environment, though. I had wanted to be a lawyer for as long as I could remember. I was also now a dorm counselor in Norton Hall, which took care of my room and board.

Norton, an all-male dorm, was packed with athletes, and, well, they tended to enjoy a little adult refreshment or two. Or three. A favorite prank was to combine surgical tubing with water balloons and shaving cream, then wait for someone to occupy the phone booth across the street. From a window on the eighth floor, they fired away, one balloon after another, trapping the unfortunate victim inside. I don't believe they ever missed. They once dropped a bowling ball out the window. The ball shattered, sending little pieces in every direction. It was a miracle nobody was seriously hurt. One of their regular targets was a kid they thought was a nerd from San Jose, though I believe Steve Wozniak turned out just fine. Another athlete, star runner Brian Maxwell, later started the PowerBar company.

I set them up in rooms at opposite corners of the hall, but when three or four joined forces, as they invariably did, the inmates were definitely running the asylum. I will never forget when my friend Mark, the other dorm counselor, and I found the room the balloons were coming from and decided to investigate.

"Who should go in first?" Mark asked. He stood 6'4".

I was 5'10". "Are you kidding me?"

Mark went in. Seconds later, his body came out flying, headfirst. Most of my job, thankfully, had little to do with discipline and, while I did not know it at the time, a lot to do with preparing me for the job ahead.

Students often came to me with their problems—with girlfriends, teachers, parents, anyone. Being three or four years older lent me a lot of credibility, yet I was not *too* old and thus was not one of the authority figures their (my) generation was rebelling against. I listened and helped them resolve their difficulties just as I'd listen years later to the athletes who relied on me to preserve the life they worked so hard to acquire.

One Saturday at a Cal football game in the fall of 1973, I saw her.

Her name was Lucy Semeniuk. She was Homecoming Queen, and she had the most striking almond-shaped eyes I had ever seen. As Lucy waved to the crowd from a car chauffeuring her around the stadium, all I could think was *I have to meet this girl, and soon.*

A week or two later, at another football game, I made my move. Lucy was sitting in the stands just a few rows away, looking even more beautiful than before.

We talked. About what, I have no idea. She was so smitten with my charm and good looks she left at halftime.

I was not going to give up.

As I left the stadium, I approached a friend, Harry Sherr. Harry knew everyone at Berkeley. Every college in America has a Harry Sherr.

"You are a fixture at all of the sorority houses. Do you know how I can find this Lucy?" I asked.

Harry sure did, and in no time I got her number and she agreed to go out with me. I took her to a local Kip's burger and pizza restaurant. We spent most of the evening debating the merits of rent control—what a romantic, huh?—and it became obvious Lucy was as brilliant as she was breathtaking. We could talk about anything.

We had a great deal in common. She also grew up in Southern California and attended UCLA for two years, and we both loved the beach. We dated for a while.

After graduating from law school in the spring, I stuck around campus to take a few extra classes.

I told myself it was because I had been elected to the new position of student advocate and felt a responsibility to assist those who might approach me with any grievances.

The truth was I'd been in love with the campus from the afternoon I walked down Telegraph and put the headphones on, listening to "Light My Fire," and I was not prepared to say good-bye just yet. Come to think of it, who ever is ready to leave Berkeley?

In February of 1974, I took the California Bar but once again found an excuse to hang around, this time until July to see if I passed.

Also, for the first time, I gave serious thought to other careers besides law. I received plenty of offers, including one from Jerry Brown, the son of the former California governor Pat Brown, about to launch his own bid for the position. Acting was another option. I'd done a little in L.A. and was the token white actor in a black drama ensemble at Berkeley.

I heard about one job that sounded perfect: working for ABC Sports as a sideline reporter at college football games, a totally new concept in the early '70s. I knew the sport, obviously, and felt at ease in front of the camera; I had already received an offer from a

TV station in San Francisco to cover news. I made it down to the final few but lost out to Jim Lampley, who would have the ABC job for years and become an accomplished professional in the field. No matter. I was not suffering from a lack of options, including a number in corporate litigation.

First there was another exciting adventure to embark on: to trace the evolution of civilization in Greece, Israel, Egypt, France, Italy, and England. In Greece, a friend and I arrived on the day in July of 1974 that the U.S.-backed military junta collapsed. On the way from the airport into downtown Athens, we saw American flags being burned on the streets.

After seeing the sights in Italy, I flew to Israel, where I was taken around by Aunt Milly, Uncle Arthur, my cousin Michael, and my cousin Bobby, who had moved there after he retired from the air force. Aunt Milly was in charge of educating Russian immigrants. I was inspired everywhere I went in this magical part of the world; perhaps my grandfather, Leo Blass, felt this way when he came to help out during the War of Independence in 1948. I visited his grave in Safed, which was quite moving. I was in awe of the sites of the three great religions—Christianity, Judaism, and Islam. I then headed by myself to Egypt, while my friend, also Jewish, stayed behind, as it had been less than a year since the end of the Yom Kippur War. I couldn't blame him, but I was fascinated by Egyptology—the pyramids, mummies, wall paintings, and the gods.

It *was* dangerous in Egypt, only not in the way I envisioned.

I took a ride down the Nile with an Egyptian family I got to know. The kids jumped in the river. I did, too. What harm could there be?

Plenty. Within a couple of hours, I began to have severe lower intestinal symptoms.

No guts, no glory. I ignored the pain and visited the ancient city of Luxor. I figured I'd eventually forget I had been sick but would never forget seeing those remarkable ruins.

Well, as I once told my father, I never claimed to be the smartest one in the family. The pain became overpowering, and to this day, I'm not certain how I made it on my own to England. I recall waking up in Central Middlesex Hospital one afternoon and doing nothing but running back and forth to the bathroom. A microbe had apparently triggered acute colitis in my system.

Six weeks later, finally healthy enough to travel, I flew back to California. Tracing the history of Western civilization is worth any minor inconveniences, but I sure was glad to be home. I had no idea how much weight I had lost because in England the weight was measured in stones. When Dad put me on a scale, he couldn't believe I weighed only 128 pounds. I was at 170 when I left the States.

I stayed home for months, slowly regaining my strength and stamina. I accepted a job in the Alameda County District Attorney's Office in Oakland and looked forward to a future in criminal law, and perhaps politics. I would make a difference just as my father taught me.

Then, one night in the spring of 1975, I went to dinner in the Bay Area with a good friend from Norton Hall. He also happened to be the school's star quarterback.

My life would never be the same.

3

BART

Steve Bartkowksi, or Bart, as his friends called him, and I got along from the start. He stopped by my room many evenings to talk sports and girls. The more I got to know Bart, who was three years younger, the more I was impressed with how he had harnessed his God-given talent to make himself among the best players in college football. The journey was never easy. His father, Roman, spent nine years in the Chicago Cubs minor league system and wanted him to focus on baseball.

"Play that game," Roman said, referring to football, "and they will take your knees, and if they take your knees, you will lose your athletic career."

Bart loved his father, but he loved football, too, so he enlisted the support of his mother, who forged her husband's signature on the parental consent form that allowed him to suit up for his freshman year at Buchser High School in Santa Clara, California.

At Berkeley, Bart faced another obstacle, sharing time with highly regarded Vince Ferragamo, who would later play in the NFL. As a senior in 1974, however, the job was his alone after Ferragamo transferred to Nebraska. Bart didn't waste his chance, leading my beloved Golden Bears to a 7-3-1 record, including a tie versus the mighty USC Trojans. In January 1975—the NFL Draft was held earlier in those days—the Atlanta Falcons made him the No. 1 pick, three slots ahead of a running back from Jackson State named Walter Payton.

Bart and I met for dinner at a restaurant on the Bay with a gorgeous view of Alcatraz and San Francisco. I could not wait to hear how his negotiations with the Falcons were proceeding, and how excited he must be on the verge of fulfilling the dream he and I talked about night after night in Norton Hall. I never doubted it would come true.

It wasn't too long before I realized I'd never seen my friend this agitated.

"What's wrong?" I asked.

"Leigh," he said, "how difficult can it really be to get a deal done? I need to get signed so I can get to work. I am losing valuable time."

For months, Bart had put his trust in Wayne Hooper, a well-respected lawyer who negotiated contracts for many of the top players in the Bay Area. He was a close friend of Cal football coach Mike White and was the program's go-to guy in those days.

According to Bart, though, Wayne Hooper was not making enough progress with the front office in Atlanta, led by general manager Pat Peppler.

"I don't know what to do," Bart went on. "I've run out of ideas."

We moved from appetizers to the main course, and it was probably around that time when Bart popped the question.

"Can you take over for Hooper?"

I wasn't shocked. Bart had casually mentioned the possibility several weeks earlier, but I hadn't taken him very seriously. I had told him to go back to Hooper and find a way to make the relationship work. I had tremendous regard for Hooper and saw no reason Bart should get rid of him.

This time, though, Bart made it clear sticking with Wayne

Hooper was no longer a viable option, and if I didn't take the job, he'd find someone else.

"I'll do it," I said.

We shook hands, and that was enough. As a matter of fact, I didn't ask for a signed contract with any clients in the early days. People could not believe it, but I always felt that if a player was not satisfied with my services, he should feel free to leave at any moment. I didn't ask them to sign anything until many years later when the National Football League Players Association (NFLPA) made it mandatory.

Bart phoned Hooper the next day to give him the news. He told me it was the most difficult call he had ever made. I could not imagine how Hooper must have felt. One day I would find out.

Splitting time between Berkeley and my parents' home in Los Angeles, where I turned their tiny card room into my office, I went to work. Needless to say, I did not have the resources to assemble a very intricate operation. A secretary? You have to be kidding. I was my secretary. I answered the phone. I typed the letters. I kept running to Kinko's to make copies. If I was on the phone, it would ring busy forever. The one luxury I could afford was extending the phone cord outside to make calls by the pool in the backyard.

I was thrilled beyond belief. It was not just that Bart was the No. 1 pick in the draft, which meant the rest of the league was anxious to see what type of contract he would receive. It was the fact he was a player from *my* school. Wherever I went around campus, I ran into friends seeking the latest updates on the talks with Atlanta. They were almost as engaged in the process as I was.

It would be natural to ask if I ever worried I was in over my head.

The answer was no, and that was because of the lessons I absorbed with the Beverlywood Young Democrats, in student government at Hamilton, and especially at Cal, when rarely a day passed when I wasn't engaged in politics or intense negotiations that drew their share of press coverage. I just saw the negotiations with Atlanta as a political problem.

The key to dealing with Pat Peppler was to put myself in his heart and mind, see the world the way he saw it, and try to craft an outcome that would allow both sides to emerge feeling victorious. I enlisted friends Buddy Epstein, Jack Flanagan, Dave Bateman, and Brian Kahn as sounding boards. Brian actually took part in several conversations with Peppler.

Among my first tasks was to grasp Bart's priorities and goals for his career and his life. I also needed to determine why the negotiations had stalled and what I might do to get them moving again. I understood from Bart that Atlanta's best offer was about $400,000 over four years, and that was back in March.

It didn't take very long to locate the problem. It can be summed up in the one word that is essential in any successful negotiation: leverage. Bart did not appear to have any, and that was why the Falcons showed little flexibility.

Peppler and his staff figured once training camp approached, Bart would be forced to accept the team's best offer. He could play quarterback for the Atlanta Falcons or play for no one. The team would survive just fine, but what would the player do during the football season? He had no other financial offers. Would he go back to campus and develop a new theory for the next Super Collider? Play cello in the Berkeley Philharmonic? Before adjustments in the salary structure, in fact, teams preferred to negotiate with the top overall pick before the draft, when they enjoyed the advantage. If they couldn't come to terms with the player, they'd simply choose someone else.

Fortunately, when it came to Bart, I knew exactly where we would find the leverage we needed, and it changed everything.

The leverage was the WFL—the World Football League. The

league wasn't around long—just two seasons (1974 and 1975), to be exact—but for Bart and me, it was around just long enough. The WFL fielded franchises in about a dozen cities, places like Memphis and Birmingham and Shreveport, and signed a number of top collegiate prospects including Anthony Davis, the star running back from USC, who received a sizable deal from the Southern California Sun, most of it deferred. Still, if AD could pocket an impressive sum—he was just a second-round pick in the NFL—Bart stood to earn a fortune. With his remarkable arm—in high school, legend has it, he threw a pass from one end zone in the L.A. Coliseum to the other—and his blond, blue-eyed matinee-idol looks, Bart was the rare player who would be a major coup for a league striving for legitimacy. It did not hurt he hailed from California, which always carried an extra level of mystique.

No doubt there were would be tons of skeptics, the Falcons among them, who would suspect that we were bluffing, that Bart would never sign with a risky outfit such as the World Football League when he could follow instead in the footsteps of Otto Graham, Bart Starr, Johnny Unitas, and Terry Bradshaw.

I would have three words for them: Joe Willie Namath.

In 1965, Namath, a sensational rookie QB from the University of Alabama, spurned the established NFL to sign with the New York Jets of the upstart American Football League for an unprecedented $400,000. No one took the AFL too seriously at first, either, but as early as the mid-'60s, the NFL realized a merger was better for their bottom line than a war between the two leagues, each trying to snatch players from the other. Namath became Broadway Joe, a counterculture icon, leading the Jets to an upset Super Bowl victory. If Namath could have that much impact, why couldn't Bart?

I made a few calls and found two franchises, the Shreveport Steamer and the Chicago Winds, who appeared interested in signing Bart. How interested, I couldn't be sure, but enough to achieve two purposes: getting the Falcons to recognize that Bart would seriously consider taking his talents elsewhere, and giving us a chance to see if there was a viable opportunity, however unlikely, for Bart to be a pioneer.

At the same time, I did a prolific amount of research. I began with an overview of the team's revenue and expenses. When I attempted, however, to discover how well the Falcons had compensated their players in the past, I was not very successful, as teams closely protected such information back then, which left players at a disadvantage. The ultimate goal was to determine how important Bart was to the future of the franchise.

The answer: *very* important.

The team was coming off a woeful 3-11 campaign, scoring only 111 points, its fewest ever. In four of those fourteen games, the Falcons failed to reach the end zone. Their quarterback was Bob Lee. Bob was a solid player who hung around the league for more than a decade, but he had as much chance of taking his team to the Super Bowl as Robert *E*. Lee.

The poor offense resulted in poor attendance—the last game in 1974 barely cracked the 10,000 barrier—and that's where bringing in Bart would really pay off. Conversely, failing to sign Bart, thus wasting the No. 1 pick, which they'd acquired by trading All-Pro offensive tackle George Kunz and their own first-rounder to Baltimore, would be a public relations disaster for the Falcons, and the fans in Atlanta would not recover from it for years. I kept this potential scenario in mind throughout the negotiations, and I made certain the other side didn't forget it, either.

When it came time for me to make an official offer, our first since I took over, I proposed $750,000 over four years. The Falcons suggested there was a private and embarrassing place I could insert my proposal. Peppler, who helped build dynasties in Green Bay and Miami, was known as a tough negotiator, and he certainly would not change his style for a novice like me.

Prior to the negotiations with Peppler, I had asked Bart if he wanted a blow-by-blow report or a condensed version.

"This is your life and I'm your representative," I said, "so you are obviously entitled to hear every single thing that goes on."

Bart preferred the complete story. I soon realized I'd made a mistake when the Falcons resorted to a tactic I would come to expect in just about every negotiation: They criticized Bart. Only four months earlier, they chose him over any other college football player in America, and now they disparaged him as if he could not make first team in Pop Warner.

"Steve doesn't have a ton of mobility," Peppler argued. "We're taking a risk on his knees. He played baseball as a catcher, and we have the medical reports on that."

Once I shared those comments with Brad, he went ballistic. "Screw them," Bart said. "I never want to play for that team. Get me traded."

I spent the next half hour or so trying to calm him down.

"Bart, they have to justify their position somehow," I explained. "We are asking for the largest amount of money any football player has ever been given. It's going to be a headline event. Remember, they picked you first in the whole draft and traded an All-Pro offensive lineman to get you, which proves how much they love you. This is just how people negotiate. It's business, Bart. It is not personal."

I vowed to never again give a full, word-by-word account if I were to represent other players. This is another reason agents are indispensable. They keep their emotions out of the equation.

I was still learning what not to do as an agent, like agreeing to take on Bart in a friendly Ping-Pong match. I picked up the game from my father, a Marine Corps champion and a gritty competitor. Like father, like son. After I beat Bart, he did not talk to me for the rest of the day. Nice going. I had one client and I just alienated him. Bart got over it, of course, but from then on, I made a habit of not competing with clients in anything. You can't win no matter what you do. They are so competitive that they'll try to beat you at tiddlywinks, and if you lose or, worse yet, look foolish, they'll never let you forget it.

Meanwhile, with the Falcons and us far apart, I looked for any creative argument.

One was checking into the percentage of people of Polish descent who lived in Atlanta and the suburbs. Bart, in fact, had already acquired the nickname of "the Golden Pole," as well as "Peachtree Bart." Peachtree was a major street in the city. Another was figuring out how many Cal alums resided in the metropolitan area. Neither figure proved substantial enough to make a difference.

Another idea I developed was suggesting to the Falcons that if they would reduce ticket prices, we would reduce our salary demands. Some perceived it as a publicity stunt. It was not.

The offer came from the simple fact that I viewed the game as a fan, not an agent, and felt strongly that too many hardworking middle-class folks could not afford to take their families to a game.

That had not been the case in the late 1950s and early 1960s. My parents were not wealthy, and yet I attended many games in the Coliseum, even if we were so far up in the open end of the stadium that we needed a telescope to really see the action.

I worried that football was in danger of not building an audience for the future, and I've always been convinced kids need to play the game or watch it in person to sustain a long-term interest. A team could charge a large amount for tickets, which enough people would pay, but would the sport later suffer for shortsightedness? Each team would merely have had to set aside 5,000 inexpensive seats per week so that by the end of the season, about 35,000 people would attend games who would otherwise have missed out.

The Falcons did not share my concern.

"We appreciate the sentiment," a team official told me, "but ticket prices are not a function of players' salaries. They are a function of supply and demand."

Soon it was early June, and training camp in Greenville, South Carolina, was just a few weeks away. Bart was eager to start working with his receivers, but the passage of time was more of an issue with the Falcons than with us. Bart, after all, was enjoying his last days in Berkeley, cruising around in a Porsche. He was, as usual, the object of every coed's fantasies.

The Falcons, on the other hand, could not afford to alienate their supporters, who saw Bart as their long-overdue savior, and while the press remained skeptical he'd ever suit up for the vastly inferior WFL, the team could not take that chance. If Bart were to miss a substantial portion of camp, he would fail to get in enough reps to replace Bob Lee as the starter, and a whole year might be wasted. No other position in professional football requires as much tutelage as the quarterback, and for Bart, migrating from the dry climate of Northern California to the humidity of Georgia, the period of adjustment was bound to be longer.

Pat Peppler flew to Los Angeles for a few days, and we followed up over the phone. Peppler took our battle to the press, as a lot of general managers would do in those years. They were aware that the average person, struggling from paycheck to paycheck, would not be overly sympathetic to coddled athletes complaining they would not accept many millions of dollars as opposed to even more millions.

"We're not trying to close any doors," Peppler said, "but it's getting to the point where we're going to have to start working around the thing. We can't commit financial and moral suicide."

His comments did not shock or dissuade me in the least. I knew Bart and I were the ones in control, and more importantly, I knew *the Falcons* knew it.

Finally, on June 13, we reached an agreement for four years at $600,000, the most lucrative rookie contract in NFL history.

Bart was set for life. To me, there was no doubt he would be a Hall of Fame quarterback. The fact that he didn't make it to Canton is due to his frequent knee problems. Quarterbacks can rebound from multiple arm and shoulder injuries and even neck ailments— Exhibit A: Peyton Manning—but if a weakened knee limits their mobility, they become sitting ducks.

I just wish I could have enjoyed Bart's big moment more than I did. After all, I had accomplished something rather significant when you think about it.

Only twenty-six, barely out of law school, working in the card room at my parents' house with no assistants, not even a secretary, I had held my own with the general manager of a professional sports franchise with years of experience. So why didn't I rejoice in my own success?

The reason is I have never celebrated success. I didn't celebrate it when I got Bart his huge payday, and I didn't celebrate it a decade later when I struck gold for Troy Aikman, Steve Young, Warren Moon, and the rest of my millionaire clients. I worried that if I were to celebrate and become self-absorbed, I would become vulnerable and lose focus on the next task. I could read the newspaper clippings in retirement. I made the choice to live life, not memorialize it.

Bart, sitting in first class for the first time, and I flew the next day to Atlanta. We spoke for most of the flight about the adjustments he'd have to make in the pros. I took him through the contract word for word. We were relieved the negotiations were over and Bart could now get on with the business of learning how to play quarterback in the National Football League. We expected to meet with a few reporters and sign a few forms, nothing special.

How wrong we were. When we landed at the airport close to midnight, there were people everywhere, and the entire sky was lit up by dozens of TV cameras. I remember hearing one animated correspondent break the news to his viewers: "We interrupt the

Tonight Show Starring Johnny Carson to present the arrival in Atlanta of Steve Bartkowski and his attorney, Leigh Steinberg."

I looked at Bart and said, as Dorothy did to Toto when they got to Munchkinland, "I guess we're not in Berkeley anymore."

The celebration in the city went on and on. Bart was treated as a conquering hero wherever he went. Any bitterness that may have existed because of our salary demands was forgotten, as was any trepidation I might have felt about Bart leaving Berkeley for the Deep South, with its reputation for bigotry. Not much time had passed, really, since as a teenager, from the comfort of our living room in Los Angeles, I saw police set dogs on black protestors in Georgia and Mississippi and elsewhere to impose "law and order." The horror I felt led me to volunteering at a local office for CORE, the Congress of Racial Equality.

This was a new Atlanta in 1975, though, more cosmopolitan than ever, and a bustling center of commerce for the whole Southeast. More important for Bart, the fans in Atlanta were crazy about their football. They had suffered long enough and now had their quarterback for the next decade.

Another reason the response in Atlanta made such an impression was that I had never seen anything quite like it in Los Angeles or, for that matter, Berkeley. In Los Angeles, as deeply as we love our sports teams, professional and college, the highest adoration is reserved for movie stars, while in Berkeley we treasured a more balanced life, not the culture that revered celebrities.

Nowhere was the hysteria in Atlanta more apparent than in the discos Bart and I visited over the next several days. Disco was big, as were leisure suits, platform shoes, and puffed-up hairdos.

"Ladies and gentlemen, we have to stop the music," the DJ at one club after another said. "Put your hands together for a special guest . . . Steve Bartkowski!"

Bart would then be mobbed by girls who had their own idea of the forward pass.

I thought they went wild over him at Cal. That was nothing compared to the scene in Atlanta. They left flirtatious notes on the windshield of his Porsche with their phone numbers. He could have had anyone he wanted.

There are certain athletes, even Hall of Famers, who can almost go unnoticed in a crowd. Steve Bartkowski, 6'4", with massive shoulders, was not one of them. He and I would be having a polite conversation in public when, out of nowhere, strangers would push between us to get Bart's attention. I saw the same pattern later with Aikman, Young, Moon, and Roethlisberger. There was no clearer sign the player had reached a whole other level of fame. Finding each other in the scrum and escaping to safety was a never-ending challenge.

Being in his company for most of the day, I received my share of proposals, as well, though I was careful to remind myself that when I was around Bart, he was the star, not me, a lesson I learned early on when I visited the Jewish comics at Hillcrest. Too many agents don't grasp this distinction and end up living vicariously through their clients. I may have my own identity away from working with players, but my role is to enhance them and their lives.

Something else occurred to me while I watched Bart receive all this attention, and it's the reason I became a sports agent. It wasn't about the money. It was recognizing I could make a difference. Prior to those four days in Atlanta, I assumed I'd have to go into law or politics or perhaps the media to affect people's lives, which was why Bart's contract figured to be my first and last.

It was quite a revelation. What could ensure a more lasting impact, after all, than giving fans in cities across America role models who could make a positive impact in their communities? I knew, even back in 1975, that as the years would wear on, no matter how many six-figure deals I might put together or accolades I'd receive, any sense of satisfaction would be fleeting. If, however, I could help the athletes set up charitable programs, I would fulfill the values I was raised with by my parents and make the world a better place. Athletes, I realized early on, could break through the screen people normally use to tune out commercial pitches.

In Bart's case, the charity was the United Way. He got behind the concept 100 percent. Bart and I met Jimmy Carter, and the fact that my client happened to end up in the city that was home to the campaign of the eventual president was just one of a series of crazy coincidences over the course of my life that would make me sometimes feel like Forrest Gump. Bart would become cochairman of Athletes for Jimmy Carter, and the president sent him a personal thank-you for his help in the 1976 campaign.

By mid-July, Bart was at training camp in South Carolina and I was home in California, answering calls around the clock from reporters and other agents.

I was happy to accommodate the members of the press, who were eager to find out how some young first-time lawyer had accomplished this feat. I was not as willing to satisfy the agents who wanted to work with me or buy my practice. What *practice* they were referring to, I did not have a clue.

I didn't know where I was headed in this exciting new enterprise. Wherever it was, and however long it took, I would head there on my own terms. Of that much I was certain.

4

FITTING THE PROFILE

For months, Steve Bartkowski was my only client, and, believe me, that was enough to keep me busy.

As I would discover again later, with Moon, Aikman, and Young, one superstar generates greater interest from the press, corporations, and the public than the next fifty players combined. The key was signing potential superstars.

With Bart, I did what we now refer to as "branding," attempting to build a distinctive recognition factor so that the public would know who he was and be able to attach specific adjectives or attributes to him. I was amazed at the range of fascinating possibilities, including a small part in an upcoming James Bond movie. As for Bart playing the hero or villain, my talks with producer Albert Broccoli never got that far. Bart eventually appeared in TV commercials for car dealerships and camera companies in the Atlanta area and hosted a pregame radio show. His face popped up everywhere—on T-shirts with a picture of him holding a peace sign with one hand and making a fist with the other, on a 200-foot-high billboard along I-285 on the way to Fulton County Stadium, and on the cover of *Atlanta Magazine*.

On the field, he performed quite admirably for a rookie quarterback. I monitored Bart's progress on the phone—my first attempt at what I called "client maintenance"—and by subscribing to the two major Atlanta dailies, the *Journal* and the *Constitution* (they have since merged), which is what we did before the Internet. I became acquainted with the newspaper beat reporters who covered the team and also attended a few games. I personally kept Delta solvent, staying with Bart at his apartment in a swinging-singles part of town.

I spent a lot of time in Berkeley, as well, building what every agency needs, an infrastructure. This means getting to know the trainers, assistant coaches, office secretaries—anyone who could create a greater probability of meeting the right type of athletes. I became friendly with Mike White and the rest of the Cal staff, including Walt Harris, Al Saunders, and Paul Hackett, who each went on to be head coaches themselves, in college and the NFL. All an agent has to do is focus on one staff and wait a couple of years—another future pro coach, Dom Capers, joined Cal in 1978—and it is remarkable how wide your network will spread.

With help from Bart, I brought aboard my second client, Pat McInally. Bart and Pat became friends by playing on the same team in college All-Star games, which was how a lot of players bonded back then. He was drafted by the Cincinnati Bengals as a punter/wide receiver. Pat was the ideal client for me: smart, individualistic, witty, engaged in a wide array of interests beyond sports. He remains, to this day, the only athlete to record a perfect 50 score on the Wonderlic test, which measures problem-solving capabilities. Pat later became the company's director of marketing.

As intelligent as Pat was, there was a problem he could not solve—nor could I, for that matter—and that was Mike Brown.

Brown, son of the legendary Cleveland Browns coach Paul Brown, one of the most influential people in pro football history, was the assistant general manager of the Bengals and my perpetual nemesis. After every draft, or so it seemed, I had to deal with him regarding a client of mine, and those talks were often hostile. If I had represented astronauts, I'm sure Mike Brown would have owned the franchise on the moon.

In fairness to Mike, who took over the Bengals in 1991, he had a more daunting task than most NFL owners. The Bengals operated in a small market with a small stadium, so each dollar mattered if they were to remain solvent. He didn't own other revenue sources. The Bengals were *the* family business.

In 1987, we met in his office to put what I figured would be the final touches on a contract for Cincinnati's No. 1 pick, Jason Buck, a defensive lineman from BYU. Mike Brown clearly had a different purpose in mind.

"Leigh," Mike said, leaning across his desk, "sometimes in life you win and sometimes you lose. You lose." He didn't say another word, and as he closed a book he had opened in front of him, it became clear the meeting was over. (Jason did sign about a month later, for four years and about $1.5 million, and he played in the league for seven years.)

No wonder that in 1992, when I learned one of my quarterbacks, the University of Houston's David Klingler, had been selected by the Bengals, my immediate response—which, unfortunately, was caught live on ESPN—conveyed my honest feelings.

"Oh my God, it's Mike Brown."

Brown was a passionate Republican, and I once saw exactly how passionate. We were in the stadium parking lot shortly before the Ohio presidential primary in the spring of 1976 when we saw a man walking around with a large Jimmy Carter sign. Brown swerved his car wildly to scare him. The fellow was scared, all right.

When it came to working out a rookie contract for Pat Mc-Inally, Brown never gave me a chance.

"We don't deal with agents," he said and hung up.

Brown was simply reflecting how a lot of management felt in the mid-'70s, that the right of representation had not been established. It would not be until 1977 when the owners and players signed a new collective bargaining agreement.

Pat was left with no choice but to ask his father to make a deal with Brown, which was common in those days, just as it was in baseball before big-time agents such as Dennis Gilbert, Dick Moss, the Hendricks brothers, and my eventual partner, Jeff Moorad, entered the scene. Fewer than half of the first-round picks in the NFL were represented by agents.

I was able to offer several contractual suggestions to Pat. He put ten good years into the league, all with the Bengals, mainly as their punter. Pat didn't fare too poorly after football, either; he sold an idea for a series of sports action figures to Kenner, a major toy company.

In the spring of 1976, I also took on Jeb Blount, a quarterback from the University of Tulsa referred to as "the Tossin' Tulsan."

I liked his father, Peppy, who played football at the University of Texas, was elected to the state's House of Representatives after he returned from the war, and later became a county judge. The problem was that Peppy wanted to sit in on our talks with Al LoCasale, an executive with the Oakland Raiders, who selected Jeb in the second round. I couldn't imagine a worse idea.

"Peppy," I explained by the pool at the Beverly Hills Hilton Hotel, "I learned in my first negotiation with Steve Bartkowski it is extremely difficult for a player or his parents to listen to the negative things a team will say to defend its position. You should let me handle it. I will not let it affect what we are trying to achieve."

"I understand," he said. "I've been a judge. I just want to be supportive."

I was not convinced.

"They will tell you your son is not very mobile," I went on, "or he is injury prone. You have to know they are not going to just roll over and give us the money we're asking for. That's not how the process works."

"I know," Peppy continued, "but I want to be there."

I still was not convinced, but there was nothing more I could say. This was Jeb's dad and he wanted him to be there.

So we were maybe three minutes into the conversation when Al LoCasale behaved precisely as I anticipated.

"We took a chance on drafting Jeb that high, and obviously every other team passed on him. The vote in our draft room was 8–1 with everyone preferring (placekicker) Chris Bahr, but that one vote for Jeb was Al Davis," LoCasale said. "We're not sure how soon he'll get a chance to start."

It didn't matter to Peppy whether LoCasale might be telling the truth. The Raiders had a terrific quarterback already, Kenny Stabler, who was still only thirty years old and would propel his team to a Super Bowl title in the upcoming season. What mattered to this proud father, who was getting angrier and angrier, was that somebody was putting down the son he loved, and he would not stand for it.

"Oh, yeah, Al," he said. Peppy, who was maybe 6'6" and 275 pounds, suddenly reached across the table and tried to strangle LoCasale, who was 5'5". I used every ounce of strength I could muster to squeeze in between them, and it was barely enough.

LoCasale was not injured, thank goodness, and after everyone took a short break, Peppy, to his credit, apologized.

In the same class as Jeb, I represented Steve Rivera, an All-American receiver from Cal, who was picked in the fourth round by the San Francisco 49ers. Also, again with assistance from Bart, I took on my first veteran, Dave Hampton, who had rushed for just over 1,000 yards a year before with the Falcons. I hit the club scene in Atlanta with Dave and other members of the team regularly after games that season. One night, he, Atlanta mayor Maynard Jackson, and I got to talking about Dave's future, and before I knew it, he asked me to be his agent. Dave re-signed with Atlanta, but, at twenty-nine, he played just one more year.

Heading toward the fall, I was feeling pretty good about my first full year in the business. With three new clients aboard, each giving back to his community—Hampton donated $1 for every yard he gained into research on curing sickle cell anemia—and a budding infrastructure, the future was bright.

There was one approach I changed, however, and that was how I recruited players. Simply meeting with those projected to be high picks, as other agents did, was not working for me.

Too often, I found I had nothing in common with these young men. Whenever I dared to mention contributing a small part of their bonus to a charity or aspiring to be a role model, I was greeted with a blank stare, as if I were speaking in Cantonese. I was not asking for much, just that they retrace their roots and establish programs that could make an impact. Worse yet, some of the players had the nerve to ask *me* for money as a condition for becoming my client, if not always in so many words.

"You know, man, I got bills," they would say, or something to that effect.

I got their message, and I made sure they got mine, an emphatic no. I made a promise to myself when I entered the profession that I wouldn't act unethically, no matter how long it might take to become successful, and no doubt it was related to the French exam at Berkeley.

Some players were more direct about asking for money than others.

Years later, I was walking down the street one night with an outstanding running-back prospect. We stopped in front of a jewelry store, and he fixed his eyes on an expensive watch in the window.

"If you guys buy me that watch," he said, "it will give you a better chance of signing me."

"We don't buy watches for players," I said. Ultimately, we passed on him.

It never ceased to amaze me, early on and throughout my career, how easy it was for players to lie right to my face.

"I haven't signed with anyone," they promised. "I have not taken any money."

I later found out a number of them had, in fact, signed with multiple agents, and been compensated by each one. One quarterback was rumored to have signed with *six* different agents. I once observed two agents, both fairly prominent, arguing in the hotel lobby at the Senior Bowl in Mobile, Alabama, over which one owned the rights to a top receiver coming out of college.

"He's mine," one agent said.

"No, he's not," the other said. "I signed him first."

I never did learn how their dispute was resolved.

Most players who accept money from agents finish their careers with no one discovering the truth. Makes perfect sense, doesn't it? The agent, afraid to damage if not destroy his reputation, won't say a word. Nor will the client, who loves the perks and attention he is receiving before he even turns professional.

The rare circumstance in which we find out, as we did in 2006 with USC running back Reggie Bush, is when a player signs with multiple agents and does not return all of the money. Bush would still have his Heisman Trophy and the Trojans would not have been put on probation if he had paid back the second agent.

Why, then, if I was offended by the rampant corruption in my profession, didn't I speak out more against this practice and turn in the guilty agents? I estimated 20 percent handed money to players when I began in the business, perhaps a lot more. They supplied them with drugs and prostitutes. At the same Senior Bowl where the agents argued over rights to a client, I saw prostitutes in the lobby, with no one attempting to hide their presence. I suppose this soliciting of players was not too far removed from the college recruitment trips some prospects took where they were flown first class, picked up in a chauffeur-driven limo, put up at a luxury hotel, and taken to a hot club where they could, to put it delicately, sample the local talent.

I did speak out, but I was careful not to name names. On one occasion when I did, it proved disastrous and it was my fault.

It started when I went to the dorm to meet with a highly rated player I was eager to represent. I opened the door and saw cocaine everywhere. After entering the room to talk to the player, I also made another, unrelated, discovery. I spotted a check made out to the individual by an agent I recognized. I was furious, and when the opportunity arose, without letting him use my name, I shared my observations with a writer who came with a photographer to my house claiming he was working on an article for *People* magazine about agents. I knew I was doing the right thing to clean up our business.

Only one problem: He was an imposter, sent by the agent in question, who threatened to take legal action. He was so outraged, he challenged me to a duel in the ring. We met at a gym in Los Angeles, put on boxing gloves, and threw a few punches. No one was hurt, thank goodness.

After our altercation, I was unable to furnish any proof and asked the agent for forgiveness, vowing never to speak about my suspicions again. The entire ordeal was humiliating but taught me to be extremely careful with unproven information that could harm another's reputation.

I continued, however, to speak about the problems in college football. The system is dysfunctional. No wonder players take money from agents and boosters. We expect these young men, a large percentage of them from disadvantaged homes, to be satisfied with an athletic scholarship, which barely allows them to meet their most essential needs, while their more privileged classmates drive nice cars, receive allowances from their parents, and apply for any jobs they desire. Meanwhile, these same institutions, who preach the integrity of the "student-athlete," earn millions by filling stadiums and selling team merchandise on campus and on the Internet. The athletes themselves perceive that they're being exploited and don't see accepting money as a moral issue.

The solution is simple: Provide players with a monthly stipend depending on need. We are talking $500, maybe $1,000. They won't live like the Sultan of Brunei, but they'll receive enough to eat and dress reasonably well and take a girl on a date once a week and have access to a car and visit their folks during the holidays. I don't quite see how offering these opportunities would destroy the integrity of the student-athlete, and it would certainly reduce the incentive to seek money in other, less overt ways.

Speaking of financial problems, I experienced my own in late 1976 and early 1977.

As fulfilled as I was in my new career, little money was coming in, and a lot was going out. In the first year or so, I probably spent roughly $25,000, much of it to pay expenses for friends to represent me at college All-Star games, including one in Tokyo. I needed to keep assembling an infrastructure no matter how much it required, and I was still making regular trips to Atlanta to check in on Bart.

Another complication was that I could not receive any income from the clients I picked up in those first two years till they came to terms with the franchises that drafted them, and that could take months. I once called George Young, the New York Giants general manager, about a week or two after the draft in April.

"George, we're ready to be the first to sign," I said. "No need to wait. We'll know when it's fair."

"Call me back in July," George said, and he hung up.

Why the delay? Some of it is economic. Teams prefer to hold off on paying out a lucrative signing bonus as long as possible so they can earn the interest on it. They also schedule vacations for their executives and coaches for much of June. Not until early July, with training camp approaching and the possibility of a holdout increasing, does everything begin to happen, and fast. On most matters, teams move rapidly and efficiently only under pressure of a deadline.

In the meantime, I kept my expenses as low as possible, sleeping on friends' couches at Cal. Later on, I even slept in my car, a '62 blue station wagon with a red hood, for a few nights during the week of the East-West Shrine Game in Palo Alto. It seemed like a lifetime had gone by since I made headlines with Bart's record deal, but it was less than two years.

As frugal as I was, with Hertz and PSA Airlines pulling my credit for unpaid bills, I could do the math. So could Dad.

"Look, you know I'm an educator," he said, "and I have done everything I can to help you, but you have now maxed out my credit cards."

I felt awful. My father was not exaggerating one bit. He *had* done all he could to help me, and so had my mother, and not just financially. Both gave their blessing when I spurned a more conventional, and profitable, legal career to become a sports agent. They would have supported me if I had decided to use my law degree to dig ditches. This is how I was repaying them? By putting them in debt? Great son I was.

Enter Bart to the rescue. During that pivotal year of 1977, he showed me the value of a true friend. Without Bart's help, I'm not sure I could have remained in the business, at least on my own.

Bart sent me a plane ticket to Atlanta, paid for a rental car, and offered his condo to use as a base while I headed into the Deep South to meet Joel "Cowboy" Parrish, a guard from the University of Georgia.

I've always carried a special fondness for offensive lineman. They receive too little credit when the play goes right and too much blame when the play goes wrong, so they bond with each other like no other players. Never pampered in high school or college, as their teammates in the skill positions are, they learn to be satisfied without needing constant praise. Landing Cowboy could provide me with the income I sorely needed until revenue from other clients came through. No doubt my representing Steve Bartkowski, the most popular player in the state, was a key factor for Cowboy and his parents.

I drove roughly two hundred miles to the small town of Douglas, Georgia, which was, conveniently enough, holding Cowboy Parrish Day, featuring a parade and other festivities. Cowboy, whose neck was twice the size of mine, took me for a tour of the region, which felt like another planet compared to Atlanta. At one point, Cowboy made a sharp turn, causing a cup of tobacco juice on the dashboard to spill all over my trousers. They were the only pants I had, and now I had to meet his parents.

As for where he would continue his career, there was heavy interest from the Canadian Football League, which in the prehistoric days when NFL franchises earned only $2 million apiece in television revenue, could compete for players. In this case, the Toronto Argonauts, based in one of Canada's largest cities, were ready to pay a premium over what the NFL would pay even for high first-rounders.

I soon received a call from my buddy Mike Brown.

"Don't sign up there," Mike said.

"Mike," I said, "are you willing to guarantee that the Bengals will draft Joel?"

"No, no, but there is a very good chance," he said.

That wasn't anything close to a promise.

By signing with the Argonauts, Cowboy removed any uncertainty over how he might fare in the NFL Draft. He could always go to the league after his CFL contract expired. Cowboy and I traveled to Toronto, where he then signed, and wrote me a check, and my practice went on. His teammate, tackle Mike "Moonpie" Wilson, also signed with the Argonauts. The two were known as "the Georgia Connection."

After deciding to profile the players I would recruit, the next question was: What precise qualities would I look for? The answer was easy.

I would look for athletes who would embrace being a role model by offering their time and money to the communities welcoming them and give back to the high schools and colleges that made their dreams of a life in pro sports come true in the first place. I put my reputation on the line, along with a piece of my soul, every time I took on a new client. I could not imagine putting forth that type of effort unless I believed in the young man's character as much as his talent. I was especially drawn to those with a history of being involved in charities.

Another sign of whether the player fit the profile was how he conducted himself in interviews. Back then, the information could be rather scarce, but today, with the Internet, there is no shortage of material, dating back to when the player was in high school. If in talking to the press he kept referring to himself in the third person, it raised questions. Another was whether he accepted praise or deferred to his teammates after a game. This applied to quarterbacks more than anyone else, as it was critical to be a team leader in that position. I shied away from anyone who had a habit of blaming the officials or his own players or insulting the opponent.

As for any prior troubles with the law or substance-issue problems, the question was whether it was a onetime experience or an unbreakable pattern. We all make mistakes in our youth, and I was more interested to see if they learned anything from their indiscretions. My feeling was that every player was allowed one—one DUI or one open container of alcohol in a car or one altercation in a bar. If there was a second incident, he clearly had a serious problem. What I could not afford, from a practical standpoint, was to take on examples of recidivism, in which the athlete repeated the illegal behavior even after he recognized the consequences.

Another warning sign was when I met parents who lived vicariously through their athletically gifted sons at the expense of their other children. I saw this often in families where the father hated his job, wasn't earning much money, or was dealing with his own sense of mortality. I felt awful for the sisters and brothers left behind, each trying desperately to be noticed in his or her unique way. Many of these parents were certain their son was the best player on the planet and couldn't accept it when others didn't feel the same.

On plenty of occasions, the player would handle a precarious situation in a cool, mature manner—until the father showed up.

"We have to get you out of here," one especially perturbed dad said after his son's squad lost a tough game at Candlestick Park in San Francisco. "Your offensive line is horrible and the coaches are terrible and you are wasting your life here."

I didn't dare interrupt the father's tirade even as I watched his son, a talented quarterback, grow more and more angry. I wasn't sure if my client was genuinely upset or merely accustomed to a lifetime of appeasing his overbearing father.

Either way, what could I do? A father is going to say what a father is going to say. He needs an opportunity to vent just as much as the player does. I learned that long ago with Peppy Blount. The parents are a critical part of the package, certainly during the recruitment process, and in the days leading to the draft and the signing of the first contract, I made a special effort to keep them regularly informed and engaged. Later, like any person in his twenties search-ing for his own identity, the player will gradually become more independent.

In person, I got a much clearer impression of a player's charac-ter, positive or negative.

Once, for example, a highly rated quarterback I thought about taking on told me he was offended I was recruiting anyone else at his position and proceeded to tear the other draftees apart, one by one. Needless to say, we didn't meet again, and I was not surprised he didn't last long in the league. On another occasion, when I brought up the concept of giving back to one's community, the player said, "My own charity is me," and ran a fast forty out of the office. He, too, did not become a star.

During the first meeting with any potential clients, I asked them to rank the values that were most important to them as they pre-pared to embark on their new career, before the challenges of com-peting in the National Football League became so complicated they couldn't think about anything except making it to practice on time and mastering the playbook.

The list of values included short-term economic gain, long-term economic security, geographic location, the importance of family, spiritual and religious considerations, potential endorsements, options in retirement, the type of system a team plays, the type of playing surface, the quality of coaching, becoming a starter, and being on a winning squad. I needed to hear what *they* thought, not what their parents or friends or girlfriends or coaches thought, or what they thought the world expected of them. Only by knowing the full extent of *their* deepest anxieties and fears and *their* greatest hopes and dreams could I be aware of how they really felt at their core.

Men share less easily than women. It is necessary to create trust and faith to make them comfortable to open up, which is why I made the request in my office, hoping the stillness of the moment might make them feel relaxed enough to peel back the layers of the onion, as it's referred to in psychological terms.

A number of them opened up immediately, surprising themselves, I think, with their answers. With others, the breakthroughs occurred while I spent time with them on their own turf, whether it was watching Greg Anthony, the UNLV basketball star, get a haircut, or going with Warrick Dunn, the Florida State running back, to visit his high school principal and coach in Baton Rouge and see the hills where he ran each day to develop his strength and stamina. I ate Creole food with Warrick and met his large family of brothers, sisters, and cousins. Warrick took on many of the duties of a parent after his mother, a police officer, was shot and killed during a robbery while he was in his teens. Watching Warrick interact with his family and friends told me more about his character than any words could ever reveal. He was later the NFL's Man of the Year based on a program we set up, Homes for the Holidays, in which Warrick made the down payment for single mothers on the first home they'd ever own. He was a special individual.

People assume recruiting is more of a science than an art, but so much of it is simply about appearing in an athlete's environment, allowing him to develop a sense of comfort with me. It takes time. The most significant skill is listening: asking the right probing questions and truly focusing on the text and subtext of the answers.

The order of their priorities, much as the players themselves, differed quite a bit from one to the next. Unless they were as arrogant as the QB who ripped his peers or the running back whose charity was himself, I was prepared to assist them on their journey. I was not even deterred by the athletes who placed the size of the signing bonus as their No. 1 concern. Economic security is everyone's key anxiety. What mattered most was that I could now truly understand each player uniquely on a deep level to try to fulfill his hopes and dreams.

Who *I* was, meanwhile, was also significant, especially to their parents. For years, since putting their kids into Pop Warner, they had been there each step of the way, and now, with everyone's dreams about to be realized, and with the amount of money on the line, they needed to trust their son's future with the right person.

Right person or wrong person, I could only be myself.

I certainly was not what they expected. They expected a middle-aged man in a pin-striped suit promising, like a fast-talking character out of the movies, to "make your kid a star." I wore a tennis shirt, jeans, and sneakers, and because I was only a few years older than their son and looked even younger, I needed to convey substance and authority. Other agents drove fancy cars. I drove a '72 Pinto. Other agents spent years grooming themselves for the corporate world. I came directly from Berkeley. I didn't have any time—or desire—to go corporate. The players, coaches, and most executives dressed casually. I fit right in. I never emulated agents who attempted to bond with players by giving them the elaborate soul shakes that were popular at the time. Yet that was the stereotype most parents had of people in my profession. One glance at me and they asked themselves: Is this fellow really an agent?

Once they realized that I was, and that I was sincerely interested in their son as a human being, and not just as a source of revenue, any defensive feelings they might have harbored disappeared. They started to regard me as a member of the family. I will never forget how shocking it seemed in 1990 when I was introduced to the mother of Andre Ware, the Heisman Trophy–winning QB from the University of Houston. I was older than Mrs. Ware. That had never happened with a client's parent.

Yet no matter how wonderful the rapport was with parents or anyone else in the player's extensive support network—girlfriend, brother, sister, best friend, high school coach, teammates, neighbors—most of whom I met during the recruitment process, I could never be sure I'd closed the deal. Whenever a prospective client began referring to "our future together" or "we," I knew it looked hopeful.

When they made it official, the deciding factor, more often than not, was that we bonded as human beings, not just two people cementing a business relationship. I truly understood their fears, as well as their dreams, and could help them become the best they could be, as a football player and a role model in whatever career they chose once the applause died, when they could no longer throw passes or make tackles. That day would come, sooner than any of them ever imagined.

By early 1977, my new approach in recruiting had produced the exact results I was aiming for, on and off the field, in Ted Albrecht, an offensive tackle from that explosive Cal unit, and Rolf Benirschke, a kicker from the University of California at Davis.

Ted, like Pat McInally, was a client made in heaven. He was smart and witty and could work a room like a master politician twice his age. His parents and I became very close. Ted was selected in the first round at No. 15 overall by the Bears.

Shortly after he signed, he launched the Teddy Bear Club, a program, in cooperation with the Shriners Hospital, to aid handicapped children in the Chicago area.

Rolf was more low-key but handsome, intelligent, and charismatic. At UC-Davis, he played for Jim Sochor, who, next to the staff at Berkeley, was the first coach I bonded with. His squads captured eighteen consecutive conference titles in Division II between 1971 and 1988, but, more importantly, the game was not the entire world to Jim. He dedicated himself to developing character and resiliency in his players, from the first-string quarterback to the third-string punter. At the time, I thought, *If I had a son, I would want him to play for Jim Sochor.*

Resiliency was never an issue with Rolf. After being the second-to-last player (No. 334) selected in the draft by the Raiders, he was cut in camp. Discouraged? Not Rolf. He hooked up in a hurry with the San Diego Chargers, where he converted 17 of 23 field goal attempts his rookie year, and nailed the game-winning 29-yarder in a classic 1982 playoff matchup against the Dolphins. Except for Dan Fouts, the All-Pro quarterback, no Charger was more revered than Rolf, and that's saying a lot for a kicker.

Rolf really made an impact as a role model. I helped him establish Kicks for Critters, in which he donated $50 for every field goal to the Department of Conservation and Research for Endangered Species at the San Diego Zoo, one of the finest in the United States. We also launched a poster pledge card campaign to enable people to contribute at their own level. It featured a picture of Rolf kicking a field goal from the pad of a baby elephant. A business could pledge $1,000 per field goal; a child or a fan, $1. Posters and pledge cards were distributed to businesses throughout the San Diego area.

The cause meant a lot to Rolf, whose dad, Dr. Kurt Benirschke, founded the department a few years earlier. Because of Rolf, an entire city became sensitized to the fate of these animals, and the money raised actually saved species. We assembled an advisory board of leading political, business, and community leaders, including Mayor Pete Wilson, to provide resources. The program became a model that has spawned hundreds of similar campaigns across the nation over the last thirty-five years. Rolf also raised awareness of Crohn's disease and ulcerative colitis, which nearly killed him in the late '70s. No client of mine has given back more than Rolf Benirschke.

I can't stress enough how 1977 set the tone for the rest of my career. Because of Bart's generosity and Cowboy Parrish's interest in the CFL, I paid my bills and stayed in the game. There were more than a few anxious moments when I wasn't sure that was possible.

Also, because of clients such as Ted Albrecht and Rolf Benirschke, I realized I did not require a star quarterback to make a difference. I just had to pick the right players and determine their top priorities, and there was no limit to what we could accomplish together.

I couldn't wait for 1978 to begin.

5
REACHING FOR THE MOON

As strong as my connections were at Cal, I needed to branch out.

I didn't branch too far, about forty miles, to Palo Alto, where, under the brilliant Coach Bill Walsh, Stanford was assembling an offensive unit every bit as powerful as Cal's. I would still root for my Bears in the Big Game—the annual contest between the two rivals—but the quality of individual that Stanford recruited, bright with high character, was perfect for me. The list included quarterback Guy Benjamin, offensive tackle Gordon King, and wideout Bill Kellar. I didn't go after one of the other gems, receiver James Lofton, a future Hall of Famer. There was such a thing as recruiting too many players from one school at one time. It would become harder to sincerely tell each player that he was uniquely important to me.

I felt a bond with all three. In Guy, a rebel, I saw a vision of myself eight years earlier. Bill was also counterculture, and so was Gordon. Going out on campus with them was a blast. The conversation was as likely to turn to politics or rock music as it was to the state of the Cardinal offense. To limit expenses, I often stayed in Gordon's room at the Delta house, or Guy's room, while they spent the night with girlfriends, who later became their wives. I didn't mind sleeping on other people's couches. I preferred having company to living on my own.

Of the three, Gordon was chosen first, by the New York Giants, at No. 10 overall. The Giants struggled in those days. Their savior, Bill Parcells, would not take over as head coach until 1983.

In negotiating Gordon's contract, I opted to try a novel approach people had been suggesting to me for years, which was to establish him as a corporation instead of an individual. Gordon would thus be able to take advantage of much lower tax rates for any potential endorsement income. In the past, teams had objected to the idea, as players might be less likely to defer money, and teams would thus not exert as much control over them. However, the Giants agreed to it. Gordon, with a deal reached in principle, left for training camp at Pace University in Pleasantville, New York. I went, as well, to oversee the signing.

The NFL, however, was concerned about the precedent it would set and didn't approve the deal. That's when things got complicated for me.

One unforgettable afternoon, I witnessed for the first time, though definitely not the last, how the pressures of being a general manager can make one go, well, ballistic.

The GM in this case was Andy Robustelli, the tough Hall of Fame defensive end for the Giants and Rams. Now in his early fifties, Robustelli had not mellowed one bit.

"We need to redo the contract," he told me while we were sitting in his office on the first day of camp. "Gordon needs to sign it as an individual."

"Andy, there has been an official offer and acceptance," I responded. "We've had this deal for several weeks."

I noticed the veins in his neck distend, and his face turned red.

"Where the hell is Gordon King?" he barked.

Once informed that King was on the practice field participating in sprints, Robustelli let loose.

"He can't be running, because if he is, the league will see we have an unsigned player in camp," he shouted. "It will cause a big scandal and we will be fined."

Robustelli indicated the only solution was to simply amend the contract to treat King as an individual, not a corporation.

"Leigh, you have to get Gordon to sign this contract right now!" he said.

"It's not what we agreed to. It's a totally different contract, Andy," I told him. "All the calculations were made on the basis it would mean hundreds of thousands of dollars in tax savings. We are going to have to go through the whole contract again."

That pushed him over the edge. His eyes bugged out. He screamed, "You motherf——er" and took his desk and flung it as far as he could in my direction, folders and coins scattering all over the floor. He then ran out of the office to find King as if he were chasing Johnny U back in the '60s. Thank goodness Wellington Mara, the Giants wise owner and one of the league's most influential figures, quickly intervened to get King signed within a few hours.

I learned another valuable lesson that afternoon. While I had every right to complain about Robustelli's less than professional behavior to Mr. Mara or perhaps the league, I did not say a word. We were in a tight fraternity whose members needed to look after each other. I knew early on that if I had a serious problem with male anger, I was in the wrong business. Everybody—owners, general managers, players—in the NFL has moments when they express themselves loudly. This was not croquet. I normally dealt with it by waiting patiently for the outburst to run its course.

Besides, the King contract was likely not going to be the last Robustelli and I ever did together. The point is, pressing your advantage may give you satisfaction in the short term, but at what cost? I spotted a significant mistake years later in reviewing a contract we'd reached in principle, and had even made official during a press conference, which would have benefited my client financially but also would have gotten the team's general manager in trouble with his owner. My office sent the paperwork back, and the contract was amended. Had my client signed the original contract, it would have broken the trust that both sides put in each other. In this business, our word is our bond.

Speaking of my peers, some of them did not have particularly nice things to say about me, either, dating back to the Bartkowski breakthrough in 1975.

Their attitude can be summed up in one word: jealousy.

Out of nowhere, my name appeared in papers and magazines everywhere. A *Los Angeles Times* headline referred to me as "the Agent in the White Hat." I could not have generated more flattering press coverage if I had dictated the stories word for word. I always separated public recognition from who I really was, my day-to-day life, and real relationships. I knew it was ephemeral, like sand castles on the beach washing away with the next wave. Nonetheless, these other agents called me a publicity hound, which was outrageous. The reporters called me. I didn't call them. What was I supposed to do? Hang up on them? Not return calls? Be unquotable?

The agents were shortsighted, at the very least. Instead of berating me, they should've thanked me for lifting the image of a profession that, let's face it, wasn't exactly known for its integrity. I was trying to make it easier and more respectable for every agent.

I learned early in my career, while I was in a hotel lobby shortly before the Senior Bowl, exactly how much integrity some of them lacked.

A stranger approached.

"Hey, aren't you Leigh Steinberg?" he asked. "I'm the uncle of [a well-known tight end], who is sure to go in the first round. Can you tell me about your program and how you do it?" The man was enormous. I could see the family genes.

I was happy to oblige. I gave him enough information in five minutes to make his head spin. Confident I now had the inside track to sign the player, I left for the game. Not long afterward, I spotted the gentleman again in the stadium and pointed him out to a friend next to me.

"That's [the tight end's] uncle," I said.

"No, it's not," my friend said.

He told me it was another agent, Harold "Doc" Daniels.

I was floored. This was not a world I was familiar with.

There was another explanation for their conduct. They were not, after all, the best and brightest coming out of law school. The best and brightest went to large corporate firms.

The lack of collegiality in the business stunned me, at least in the beginning. If another agent negotiated a successful contract or landed a high-level recruit, instead of praise or admiration, a standard response would be "Anybody could have done that," or "I would have gotten a much better deal." They seemed almost pathologically unable to acknowledge the slightest talent or ingenuity in their colleagues. I expected to be surrounded by my own band of brothers. That not being true was one of the biggest disappointments of my career, and it was to the detriment of each one of us. If we'd shared information, we could have negotiated better contracts for *all* of our clients. Out of thirty players, I represented no more than four in the first round of any draft. That left plenty for everyone else, and no reason for resentment.

I don't mean to indict everyone. There were many talented and ethical agents I deeply respected, such as Bob Woolf, Jack Mills, Howard Slusher, Tony Agnone, and Marv Demoff. There was a lot I could learn from them.

As for my other two Stanford players, Guy Benjamin went to the Dolphins in round two, while Bill Kellar was selected by the Chiefs in the seventh. I watched the impact a college coach could have on the draft as Bill Walsh lobbied Miami coach Don Shula on Guy's behalf. Guy played six NFL seasons. Bill, plagued by shoulder difficulties, played just one year but went on to be a top executive at Nike. Gordon fared the best, playing for a decade.

The client of mine from the Class of 1978 to become the biggest star was a player few experts were talking about before the season began in September. He wasn't even popular, at first, on his own campus; the fans in Seattle still missed Sonny Sixkiller, who had led the nation in passing as a sophomore in 1970. It didn't help that Warren Moon was black and from Los Angeles. That was three strikes against him. For me, however, he had one major plus in his favor, besides his talent. He was a fellow graduate of Hamilton High. I saw Warren in action when the Huskies visited Berkeley in early November, which said a lot. I rarely attended regular-season college games. The best way I can explain my reasoning is through a chat a few years later with Kenny Easley, the gifted Bruins safety who was upset I did not try to recruit him until late in his senior year while other agents had started to court him when he was a sophomore.

"You weren't interested until I was projected to be near the top of the draft," Easley complained.

"Kenny," I said, "would you rather that next fall I be at your football game in the NFL and have dinner with you on the night before, or that I attend a college game to recruit players for the following draft?"

Kenny didn't say another word.

As the season progressed, more and more people paid attention to Warren, especially after his MVP performance at the Rose Bowl when he ran for two scores and threw for another against heavily favored Michigan. It became obvious he was something special.

I wrote Warren a letter after the Rose Bowl, pointing out our Hamilton ties. We soon met in person at one of the college All-Star games. It took two seconds to know I wanted to represent him.

The questions he asked were unlike any I ever heard from a potential client. He was already thinking about his second career, as well as his first, which few players in Warren's position did at the age of twenty-one. Some did not think ahead at thirty-one. Seeing him interact with his friends and girlfriend, I was overwhelmed by his dignity, maturity, wisdom, and attention to detail. He was the father figure to six sisters, the one person in his family everyone relied on. If not for football, Warren could have been a movie star or a United States senator.

He also proved more difficult to sign than any other player in my whole career. Warren must have called me fifty times between January and March without giving any indication of where his decision was heading, except that he kept calling. He surrounded himself with the right people, including Bob Oates, the longtime NFL beat writer for the *Los Angeles Times*. Relying on experts such as Oates told me Warren knew how to network. Warren conducted a more extensive background search than the CIA does for its new recruits.

What finally got me the job? Seriously, I'm not certain. Maybe his phone bill was getting too high. The two of us had fun with the long courtship later on, appearing in a TV commercial together for Pacific Bell, the West Coast–based phone company, which ran for well over a year.

Selling myself to Warren was actually easier than selling Warren to the NFL. One of the reasons was simple and sad: racism.

Sure, there was more diversity than there used to be, with blacks in key positions on every roster, but here was a sport, lest we forget, that, in its modern era, waited until the 1940s to integrate black players. It was *1962* before the franchise in our nation's capital, the Red-skins, signed an African American.

The racism, in Warren's case, was less overt, although just as discriminatory. The unspoken theory was that blacks, with their diminished brain power, couldn't thrive in football's so-called thinking positions—safety, middle linebacker, center, and, of course, quarterback. Also unspoken was the reluctance of owners in the late 1970s to have a black quarterback as the face of the franchise. At that time, to allow a black man in the huddle was one thing; to bring him to the country club for a meet-and-greet was quite another.

Another obstacle he faced was that general managers preferred to groom the more traditional drop-back quarterbacks, while most blacks who played the position in college, including Warren, executed a wishbone or rollout run-oriented offense. I knew Warren would make the necessary adjustments, as every rookie does. All that mattered was whether he possessed the tools, physically and mentally, to master the toughest assignment in sports. To me, and those who played with or against him, there was no doubt.

There was, however, plenty of doubt in the minds of the GMs, and they were the ones who counted. Yet due to the respect they had for Warren as a pure athlete, they wanted to know if he would consider switching to wide receiver, running back, or defensive back. If he were open to that idea, they assured me, he would go much higher in the draft than as a quarterback.

I told him what the personnel people asked, and he responded defiantly as I thought he would. Warren was one of the most resolute individuals I have ever met. He would have been drafted as a quarterback in a lower round, but that would've meant long, uncertain years sitting on the bench. So he chose another path, signing with the Edmonton Eskimos in the Canadian Football League prior to the draft.

Some players might have sulked or been bitter about having to start their careers in distant posts such as Saskatchewan or Winnipeg. Not Warren. Sulking was not in his nature. He cared only about becoming the best quarterback he could be. He knew he would prove himself one day to the NFL general managers who did not believe in him, just as he won over the fans who had booed him mercilessly in Seattle.

His signing bonus in Edmonton and first-year salary were each $35,000. It was a better deal financially than what we projected he would have received in the NFL, and the team was a perfect spot to hone his QB skills.

Edmonton was coached by Hugh Campbell, who was a wonderful, caring human being and gifted coach. I added Hugh to the list of coaches I would have my son play for. One astute move Hugh made right away was to tell Warren there was no guarantee he'd start. Warren appreciated candor from a coach.

Campbell also believed in prolific amounts of offense. A former receiver at Washington State, Campbell installed a wide-open passing game, exactly the kind of system ideal for Warren's maturation, no matter how many snaps he took with the first unit. He was able to absorb a lot of knowledge by closely watching the team's other QB, thirty-five-year-old Tom Wilkinson, a fixture in the CFL since 1967.

It wasn't long before Warren took the helm and became a leader himself. In his rookie season, he threw 5 touchdowns as the Eskimos won their first of five straight Grey Cups. From 1979 through 1983, Warren threw for over 20,000 yards and was the MVP of the Grey Cup in 1980 and 1982.

Yet from our first meeting with Norm Kimball, the Eskimos general manager, in the spring of 1978, I never lost sight of the ultimate goal, and neither did Warren.

It was never a question of *if* he would try again to play in the NFL, only *when*.

• • •

Warren was not the only future star to come aboard in 1978. Another was John Anderson, a linebacker from the University of Michigan. I knew I could not make it limiting myself to one side of the ball, and John was my first defensive gem. He also was my first player from the Midwest. John, drafted in the first round by the Green Bay Packers at No. 26, finished as their all-time leader in tackles, and that's no small accomplishment for a franchise that featured Ray Nitschke and Willie Davis and other defensive legends in the Lombardi era. I was amazed at the iconic stature of the Packers in that region. The facility was always crowded with people taking photos of the trophies.

I was introduced to John by a reporter I knew, and although I certainly never asked writers to do my recruiting, I thoroughly enjoyed their company. Having been an editor in high school and still writing book and music reviews and columns, I felt a strong kinship with writers. I admired their work and recognized the obvious benefits of making their job easier. They knew they would receive the truth from me, whether we spoke about the details of a particular contract or broader league issues.

The time I spent with them also helped my clients because it gave me a chance to enhance their profile or gather information on how they were viewed within their own franchise and around the league. Such information would prove invaluable in future negotiations or trade discussions. No one has sources like the working press.

I had to be careful, of course. Sometimes it was better to say nothing. One ill-advised comment in the newspapers might aggravate a general manager or owner so badly it could set negotiations back weeks, or blow them up entirely.

I avoided that trap every time. Well, almost every time.

In 1979, I represented Theotis Brown, a handsome and hilarious UCLA running back chosen in the second round by the St. Louis Cardinals. Theotis was strong, fast—he ran the forty in

4.5—and elusive. He was certain to go in the first round, but there were rumors that Bruins coach Terry Donahue had complained to scouts that Theotis had a "heart the size of a pea."

I'm not sure Donahue, who was an outstanding coach, would disparage one of his own. Nonetheless, it reinforced how vital it is for players in college to make peace with their coaches or else they might pay a steep price in the draft.

Representing Theotis, as well as his backfield mate, James Owens, who went earlier in the second round to the 49ers, was rewarding for me. It meant I'd broken through in Westwood, bound to be fertile ground for years to come, and there was someone even happier than I was: UCLA's No. 1 fan, Warren Steinberg. Whenever I signed one of *his* Bruins, the thrill it gave him was worth signing five players from any other school.

As for Theotis, dropping to the second round meant he would not command the same bonus and salary as the first-rounders. That didn't mean I wouldn't lay out the strongest possible case for him, and that's how I fell into the trap.

The Cardinals were run by Bill Bidwill, who, to put it kindly, wasn't the best-paying owner in the league. He was like a lot of the owners from the '40s and '50s, long before pro football became what it is today, a multibillion-dollar industry. Back then, to pay players a decent wage was a luxury precious few teams could afford. Even while the league began to grow, Bidwill, like Mike Brown, operated a team in a small market, so his financial limitations were greater than franchises in larger metropolitan areas. If he were to spend too much he could find himself out of business in no time. To his credit, when the Cardinals moved to Arizona, he adapted to the league's new economics, paying competitive salaries and bonuses.

Too bad I didn't consider his unique challenges at the time. That could have saved me a lot of trouble. Instead, I assumed the role of agent-turned-populist who would force Bidwill to recognize the error of his ways. Talk about foolishness. Talk about a way to pressure an owner into becoming an enemy.

In interviews with the St. Louis papers, I argued that as the Cardinals had a record of not properly compensating their players and were repeating the pattern with Theotis, fans should rise up and demand Bidwill put a stop to his stinginess. I suggested it would be one thing if the owner would apply the difference in the two sides to a charity designated by Theotis, but instead he was planning on keeping it for profits. To top it off, I had Theotis show up at the entrance to training camp and stand with his fingers reaching through a wire fence, sending the message of a hardworking man denied a chance to earn a living. The photo appeared the next morning on the front page. Mission accomplished.

Of course, in my end-around to the fans, I forgot one small detail: A negotiation is not an election, and winning a debate in public doesn't get a player paid. Only the owner can do that, and the more I painted Bill Bidwill as Scrooge, the more stubborn he became.

Bidwill surprised us by pledging to donate the difference to a charity of *his* choice instead of a foundation for disadvantaged black youth, the one selected by Theotis. It really hit me how I'd miscalculated when, on the day after we finally made a deal, I saw a picture in the newspaper of Bidwill handing a check to a white kid in youth soccer. From then on, I never called out an owner in public again, not even Mike Brown. I would, in fact, go out of my way to praise an owner, even if he or she did not warrant it. My comments, if negotiations became tense, would be akin to "Bill Bidwill is a reasonable man. I'm sure we'll work something out."

There was, thankfully, one amusing moment in the Theotis Brown talks, which relieved a lot of the tension.

Theotis and I were in a motel room with Joe Sullivan, the St. Louis GM. Sullivan hated agents as much as Mike Brown did. I wasn't too thrilled about having Theotis sit in on the actual negotiations, but we were getting nowhere, and the last thing I wanted was for Theotis to miss camp. Running backs don't require the same tutelage quarterbacks do, and the extra pounding in the early stages of training camp can take a toll, but he was still a rookie who needed to adjust to life in the NFL.

Theotis didn't seem too bothered by the situation as Sullivan and I argued over what he was worth. He sat there flicking matches into the trash can, which was a habit of his. Sullivan was also under control—until he wasn't.

"You guys are despicable," he growled. "You may not even play for our team this year. I'll see you in hell before I will ever give you—"

Sure enough, our room did turn into hell as one of Theotis's matches hit the curtains and ignited a fire. I thought it was hysterical, though I don't recall Sullivan having a similar reaction. I don't recall Joe Sullivan ever smiling.

Theotis, as it turned out, rushed for just over 2,000 yards during six seasons in the league. His impact off the field was more lasting. He hosted a radio show with another running back, Otis Anderson, on KMOX, *The Otis and Theotis Show,* and developed a program for inner-city youngsters in St. Louis, and then in Kansas City after he was dealt to the Chiefs. He was a true role model.

So were Warren Moon and Gordon King. They were also true friends, who, like Bart, were there for me when I needed them most.

In the spring of 1979, I turned thirty. Growing tired of sleeping on friends' couches in Berkeley, I began to search for a place of my own.

I could not believe my good fortune when I found a four-level redwood house with floor-to-ceiling glass, massive decks, and a hot tub near the hills and just a few blocks from California Memorial Stadium, where the Golden Bears played.

From every vantage point, the panoramic views of Alcatraz, the Golden Gate Bridge, and the city itself were spectacular. Built in the natural Berkeley style—deer and raccoons patrolled the grounds—this was my dream house.

That was the problem. Maybe I was dreaming.

The house cost $168,000, and I didn't have $168,000. With new recruits in California and beyond, I was doing well but not *that* well. Warren and Gordon came through, loaning me enough to make up what I was lacking in the down payment. This was before the NFLPA outlawed players loaning money to agents. I moved into the house of my dreams, and it became my office. Friends were mesmerized by the view and could hardly speak. It's a miracle we got any work done.

Life was good. So what if I didn't have the cash to make the entire down payment? Making money was never a goal, only a necessity. Just as I felt growing up on Corinth Avenue, there were countless other riches to savor. I sat on the Board of Governors of the Commonwealth Club, the most influential public affairs forum in the country, headed by former actress and U.S. ambassador Shirley Temple Black. I served as quarterly chair, introducing speakers such as Donald Rumsfeld and T. Boone Pickens. I also served as president of the Coro Fellows Program, which supported training young people for public service.

Meanwhile, my social life in San Francisco was active. *Cosmopolitan* named me one of the nation's most eligible bachelors. I was also a contestant on the popular daytime show *The Dating Game*, in which a single attractive woman, after a series of somewhat risqué questions, selected one of three bachelors she wasn't allowed to see to accompany her on an exotic free trip. I was not the lucky one chosen, and I wonder if perhaps it had something to do with my answer to the question of how I'd handle an "aggressive" woman.

"As much as possible," I said.

All kidding aside, I had experience with aggressive women, and it was not pleasant.

After the article in *Cosmopolitan* came out, I received about ten thousand letters. Women also sent me their underwear and nude photos. One day, I returned home to find a naked girl in my hot tub. I kicked her out, in case you are wondering. My home was a refuge, and I was not too thrilled about people barging in on me.

6
CLIENT MAINTENANCE

Securing for my clients the best deals possible and working with them to give back to their communities, new or old, was just a start. There was much more to do, such as preparing them for their lives after football. All it would take was one wrong hit in the wrong place, during a game or a practice, and in that horrifying instant, everything they and their families sacrificed for could suddenly end. What then?

I hoped to set them up well enough in their first contract so they would be taken care of no matter how fate treated them, but it was not possible with every player, especially those drafted in the later rounds, who, in the late 1970s, might make less than $20,000 per season. Even if they earned several hundred thousand over three or four years, they paid a huge amount of taxes. They needed to look out for their futures, too. The situation changed years later when the money that could be made in the game exploded and players became set for life.

To prepare players meant dealing with their own worst enemy— self-absorption. Only then could they be aware of their opportunities away from the field.

Being self-absorbed was not the fault of the players. From the day they began in Pop Warner through high school, they were enabled by everyone—families, friends, coaches, etc.—who urged them to keep their focus on the field and not be concerned with anything else. Once they arrived in college, residing in football dorms, they became even more sheltered. Others performed for them the same basic tasks nonathletes in their age group performed for themselves. They weren't given the opportunity to seize control of their own lives. My goal was to empower them. As professionals, it made sense for them to consult with experts in law and financial planning. I just wanted to be sure they understood they had the responsibility to make the final call.

I taught them Networking 101.

"Whenever we walk out of a room together at a banquet or meeting," I said, "I want you to be able to tell me who everyone in the room was. I want you to shake their hands and ask for their cards, and when you get back to your room, I want you to write on the back of that card some way to remember that individual. Because, after a while, you will forget, and this way we will start to build your Rolodex. You are your own best salesman, but you need to focus on who the other person is, ask questions, and be a good listener."

Athletes have every quality and skill needed to succeed after their playing days end. They have an impeccable work ethic and extraordinary self-discipline, display great courage and judgment under extreme pressure, grasp a complex playbook in a relatively short period of time, and fully understand the importance of teamwork.

They also benefit from the fact that many of the most passionate fans in sports are successful businessmen who enjoy being in their company. These middle-aged men, as crazy as it may seem, pay $1,000 for an autograph scribbled on a piece of cardboard. Tapping into that group, the players can establish invaluable contacts lasting decades.

For example, I urged my clients on the 49ers to meet business-men in Silicon Valley, the center of the high-tech and venture capital community. Steve Young and Brent Jones took advantage, creating their own businesses in the Internet or hedge fund sectors.

In Kansas City, Deron Cherry, a safety for the Chiefs, through his Cherry Foundation, established friendships which led to him being awarded an Anheuser-Busch distributorship. I introduced him to Wayne Weaver, the incoming owner of the Jacksonville Jag-uars, and he became the first modern former player to own a piece of an NFL franchise. In Houston, Ray Childress, a Pro Bowl defen-sive lineman with the Oilers, established the Childress Foundation to help steer kids away from a life on the streets. He owned a car dealership, and Bob McNair invited him to become a minority owner of the Houston Texans. Bruce Smith became an executive in a prosperous Virginia construction company and a minority owner in a luxury hotel in Washington, D.C.

It is important to initiate those contacts as early as possible. During our first meeting when I had them rank their priorities for me, I asked, "If you were injured tomorrow and never played foot-ball again, what other interests do you have? What would you want to do?"

Some mentioned business, others coaching, broadcasting, and motion pictures.

For Troy Aikman, the opportunity came in broadcasting when Fox executive Ed Goren approached us about him doing commen-tary on NFL games. Ed proposed Troy start as one of two color analysts in a three-man booth, meaning he wouldn't have to chime in quite as often, leaving him more time to prepare his next point. It was an excellent idea.

Troy turned out to be as serious about broadcasting as he was about playing quarterback. When Matt Millen left, it created an opening for Troy to be on Fox's No. 2 team. A year later, when John Madden switched to ABC, Troy joined Joe Buck on the network's

No. 1 team. He's been the lead analyst ever since and no one in the game is better. Some doubted he had the personality to be successful on TV, but I always knew he was witty and opinionated.

I wanted players to begin thinking about their postfootball life in a serious manner. Even if they were lucky enough to escape any career-ending injuries, in their midthirties at the absolute latest, they would have to make the transition to the next phase. They might live as long as fifty years *after* they leave the game.

Quite a few players were not ready to plan that far ahead.

"Shouldn't I be focusing all of my attention on football?" they would ask. "That's what I'm getting paid to do, isn't it?"

No doubt they were right. Football *was* their No. 1 priority, and if they didn't dedicate themselves completely to the game, well, that second career would come a lot sooner than later. That was why, unlike other agents, I was not in favor of any of my clients, and that includes Troy Aikman and Steve Young, doing endorsements in their rookie season.

For one thing, the players Madison Avenue courted already had more money than they could possibly spend. For another, they ran the risk of alienating the very groups—ownership, other players, fans—they needed to appease starting with the first day of training camp. After paying out millions to a twenty-one- or twenty-two-year-old who had yet to play a single down in the National Football League, the last image the owner wanted to see was the player in a commercial when he should be spending every minute studying the playbook or working out with his teammates. Adjusting to the league was trying enough—there was no limit to the amount of rookie mistakes, from missing block assignments to throwing interceptions to committing stupid penalties—without any unnecessary distractions. The key was building a fundamentally sound career.

As for those teammates, they scrutinized a rookie's every move.

Does he carry himself with the proper humility? Does he have sufficient respect for the veterans? Does he fit in as one of the guys?

No wonder the older players were vigilant. They resented that many first-year players made more money than they did. They had proven themselves. The rookies had not. They conveniently ignored the fact that they, too, earned generous bonuses when they entered the league. What mattered was what they made now compared to these untested newcomers.

The fans would not be very forgiving, either, if a player was overexposed and then failed to live up to the hype. Who could blame them?

As for those who contend a player might not have the same opportunity in a year or two, all the more reason he should keep his focus on the field. Besides, if he truly has confidence in his skills and performs at a high level, he will generate more and better opportunities down the road. With Aikman and Young, we turned down countless proposals until each won his first Super Bowl. By then, the size and scope of the deals we signed far eclipsed the previous offers *combined*.

Helping them get acclimated in camp was only the first of many steps in client maintenance, a part of my job as important as any other. Too often, other agents overlook this particular duty because they are too busy trying to lock in their next blue-chip recruit. I never could figure out what they were thinking. Want to recruit more players? Make the players you *have* happy. Make Steve Young happy, and you'll wind up with his roommate, tight end Brent Jones. Don't make him happy, and you will lose Steve *and* the next player.

Client maintenance required checking in with them as regularly as possible and returning their phone calls by the end of the day regardless of how trivial their concerns might appear. When clients of mine ran into each other and one asked, "Have you talked to Leigh lately?" I wanted to be certain the answer was always yes.

At times, my office was their concierge, making hotel or flight arrangements. More often, they'd complain about one problem or another—working conditions, coaches, teammates, you name it. I listened politely and validated their viewpoint, and that's usually all it took for them to drop the subject.

My job was to give them a safe place to vent, knowing I'd never break their trust. It used to frustrate me to no end when I would hear "experts" make pronouncements about certain personalities that were blatantly false, yet, bound by confidentiality, I didn't dare correct them. Someone once spread a rumor about a client being gay. I had stayed with the player on numerous occasions when one breathtaking woman or another spent the night. Believe me, this man was not gay.

The key was to distinguish between more traditional griping and complaints that warranted direct action. The most common request I heard from players was "I want to be traded!" With rare exceptions, I didn't take it seriously. Half of the players in any sport want to retire the day after the season. They're physically and mentally drained and can't imagine playing again, but by training camp, they miss the game and can't wait to get back on the field.

Another important element of client maintenance was to meet with them on the evening before a game or right afterward. Speaking over the phone was useful, but nothing could match the intimacy we reached in person, in a relaxed setting, with no subject off-limits. With our busy schedules, these meetings were not easy to arrange.

Since it was more convenient and saved expenses, I planned the visits around any trips they made to Oakland, San Francisco, Los Angeles, or San Diego, the cities within a short drive from Berkeley or my parents' home. It required some juggling if I represented two or more players on the same team; I'd usually treat one to dinner and relax with the others in their hotel rooms. I would receive an itinerary a day or two ahead of time so I'd know exactly what their schedules were from Saturday afternoon till the bus left for the stadium on Sunday morning.

I cannot count how many times I waited for hours with no one showing up, and even after I was told by a clerk or bellboy the player had entered through a side or back door, it did me little good. There were no cell phones back then, and the hotel clerk would not give me the room number. The player would not know the number till he arrived, so we couldn't work that out ahead of time. As the night went on, the player might recall we were supposed to get together, but he would not know where or when, or how to make it happen, and before long, it was time for lights out. Years later, after I'd made strong connections with each team's coaches and PR guys, they would kindly pass word to the player I was waiting for him.

Once we got together, I discovered a great deal about my client and his team. That was the reason I didn't take part in fantasy leagues or gamble on any games. I went to Steve Young's room the evening before a playoff game and knew, when no other outsiders did, he was not quite himself because he was still recovering from a hit he received in practice from linebacker Charles Haley. Another time, I walked into Troy Aikman's room and couldn't believe how swollen his thumb was. He had problems gripping the ball. I could usually develop a sense of how focused the players were—or weren't—for the battle less than twenty-four hours away, leading directly to the level of performance they would give on Sunday afternoon. It is nearly impossible to maintain the same high degree of intensity week after week.

Trying to sneak in quality time with my players after the game was another challenge.

In the early years, before I received an all-access pass for the field and locker room, I waited with family members, wives, friends, and fans by the stadium tunnel. The scene could be chaotic, with everyone jockeying for position.

The art of timing and correct positioning in the parking lot was not a course offered in law school. I got to the point where I knew precisely which players stopped in the parking lot, where, and for how long, and which did not, and how many minutes they each took to reach the bus or their cars. All I needed was a minute or so, enough to establish contact. Whatever we talked about, if they were hurt or dissatisfied with their roles or having trouble with a coach or teammate, it was not as important as the fact that I got a moment to check in.

On occasion, prior to receiving the all-access pass, I was able to talk my way into the locker room, but there were numerous other times when I was stopped by a typically imposing security guard. I always reminded myself that the guard, whom I knew nothing about, might not receive much money or recognition in his work, but at that door he held the power, and the last thing I wanted was to create a scene in which I said something to the effect of *Do you know who I am?*

Once I received the pass, it was extremely helpful. For the first three and a half quarters, I'd either visit with the writers in the press box or sit in the owner's box or in a box paid for by the player. Either way, I was careful not to root for one team or the other. In the press box, it was not permitted. In the others, I was never quite certain who was sitting near me. If I criticized a particular offensive lineman for failing to protect my quarterback client, the lineman's folks might be a few seats away.

With about two or three minutes left in the game, I headed down to the field, which was often a special moment for me.

I was on the sidelines in San Francisco for the playoff duel in 1999 against the Packers when Steve Young connected with Terrell Owens for the winning 25-yard touchdown pass with 3 seconds left. To say hello to Steve as he dashed off the field in jubilation fixed me forever, in his memory, as a part of that experience. Another time, I watched Jim Harbaugh lead the Bears to a comeback victory against the Jets on a Monday night at Soldier Field. It was so cold I could barely speak, but I loved every minute. Being that close to the players, I was blown away by the force in every collision. It is unimaginable how massive the bodies are and the speed at which they move.

Even with the pass, I still needed to decide which clients I would approach in the locker room, and when, and what to say. My opportunity would normally come after the player listened to postgame reflections from his coach and took a shower. I might get ten minutes, if I was lucky. I needed to use each one of them wisely.

As for which clients to approach first, that was easy: the ones on the losing team. The winners didn't need to see me. They would be busy celebrating; any grievances they might have would be put on hold for at least twenty-four hours. The losers, however, did need to see me, and it was my job to stay positive, reminding them this was just one game. That simply wasn't possible, obviously, when the one game was a playoff game, as was the case in 1993 when Dallas beat San Francisco 38–21 to win the NFC title. I went to console Steve Young before congratulating Troy Aikman.

"You had a fabulous season," I told Steve. "You came so close. You'll do it next year."

I faced a much tougher assignment after the Tennessee Titans rallied in 2000 to defeat the Bills 22–16 in the Wild Card playoff contest known as "the Music City Miracle."

My three clients on the Bills—Thurman Thomas, Bruce Smith, and Rob Johnson—were devastated, and with good reason. With only 16 seconds left, after taking a 1-point lead, Buffalo was the apparent winner—till, during the ensuing kick return, Titans tight end Frank Wycheck threw a lateral across the field to Kevin Dyson, who went 75 yards for a stunning touchdown. For Thomas and

Smith, the team's premier players on offense and defense, respectively, their despair went much deeper than this one loss. Both were approaching the end of their Hall of Fame careers—Thomas was thirty-three, Smith thirty-six—and had been stymied again in an attempt to capture the ultimate prize, which had eluded them during the four straight years (1991–94) the Bills came up short in the Super Bowl.

Saying something as cliché as "there's always next year" to them would not offer any consolation.

"That was an absurd play," I told them. "There was nothing you could have done about it."

One year after the miracle was the mismatch, when the Baltimore Ravens crushed the New York Giants 34–7 in Super Bowl XXXV. Afterward, I went to comfort Kerry Collins, the Giants QB. Much of what I relayed to him wasn't exactly breaking news, but it is easy to overlook the obvious.

"You played your heart out," I told Kerry, "but you can't block and you can't play defense. If not for you, your team would not have been here." Referring to the Ravens, I added, "You went against a team with the most ferocious defense in the league. They embarrassed everybody."

I then got more personal with Kerry, and that's why it was essential for me to be aware of who these men were away from the game, and any traumas they might have endured. They were human beings first, football players second. In Kerry's case, the crisis centered around alcohol. In 1999, he checked into a rehab clinic in Kansas, addressing his addiction in a serious way for the first time. He is an inspiring example of recovery.

"Look where you have been," I said, "and look where you are now. You have so much to be proud of."

Another reason to visit members of the losing team was to make sure they didn't say anything derogatory to the press in the intensity of the moment about the opposition or their own teammates and coaches that they would regret when they read the next day's head-lines. I used to hear comments by a player's locker such as "the pocket really sucked today" or "we didn't have the right plays in our playbook" or "he dropped far too many passes." There was no harm in them venting a little, as long as their complaints weren't heard by teammates or the press. That would've really created problems. The players I was most impressed with were the ones who bravely shouldered the blame themselves, even when they were blameless.

These days, with the never-ending news cycle and influence of social media, players need to be even more circumspect. Fortu-nately, teams hold a brief cooling-off period before reporters swoop in looking to stir up the latest controversy. Just a few minutes for a player to comport himself before he speaks to the reporters can put a stop to any controversy before it starts. Once they have got-ten any anger out of their system and shifted their focus toward the next week's game, you almost can't tell if they won or lost by how they greet their loved ones afterward. Fans like to think the players carry the sting of defeat for as long as they do, but, except for playoff games, that simply isn't the case.

As for my clients on the winning team, the celebration, espe-cially during the postseason, lasted a long time. It was not uncom-mon for ninety minutes or more to pass between the final gun and when they would get on the bus.

It was not sufficient to just meet players at a road game in California. I needed to watch them in action in front of their home crowds. Only then could I accurately assess the effect they were having on the fans and community and decide if I had to assume a more vigorous role in elevating their profile. I spoke to the ush-ers and vendors about which players were popular among the fans and which were not. I surveyed the memorabilia stands to see what was available. I looked to see how many fans were wear-ing my players' jerseys and who was wearing them. Kids? Old folks?

Sometimes in these trips I discovered that the public perceived an action or statement from a player as being offensive. I tried to tell the truth to clients when it was critical for them to see the negative consequences of their behavior. That was my responsibility. As for those times I held my tongue, it was a matter of choosing the right battles. If a client felt I wasn't being supportive, it could break a bond I might never be able to repair. They needed to know I was totally on their side, no matter what anyone else thought. I was no different than anybody else in the workplace. Who among us states exactly what we are thinking most of the time?

The only people who confront them on a regular basis are their coaches. It used to make me laugh to watch 5'8" coaches scream at 6'5" defensive linemen, and the funniest part is how obedient they were. They would never accept that treatment so willingly from anyone else. Due to the profiling I did, the majority of my players were open to changing their perspective, as long as I offered my opinion without being confrontational.

Regarding those I didn't see play in person, I made it a priority to catch the highlights of as many of their games as possible.

In my first few years as an agent, long before the new cable network ESPN changed football forever and reshaped how people watched sports in America, that wasn't as easy.

Years later, watching the highlights, often from the press box, was the best way I could get an accurate read of how my clients performed. The statistics never revealed the complete story, especially on the defensive side of the ball. I sent mailgrams to players who excelled and consoled those who struggled. I made a lot of calls on Tuesday, the players' day off, knowing they would be home, nursing their wounds.

Of course, no matter how often I stayed in touch, there were always players who complained I wasn't spending enough time with them. One player told a magazine reporter he left my agency because I did not return his calls. He received as much attention as Troy did and still wasn't satisfied. As I became more successful, other agents used such criticism in an attempt to dissuade potential clients from signing with me.

"You will just be another name in the Rolodex to Leigh," they cautioned. "If Troy Aikman calls and you call, who do you think Leigh is going to talk to?"

I asked Troy about it once.

He assured me, "Leigh, that's ridiculous. I hope if the other player is having an emergency and I call just to chitchat, you accept their call, and conversely, if I am having an emergency you will talk to me."

As the years wore on, some players grew overly dependent on me, which had never been my intention. It was difficult for them when, for whatever reason, our business relationship came to an end, as many do. Professional athletes crave structure, whether in shoulder pads or a three-piece suit. They build their lives around it from their first days in Pop Warner and Little League, knowing exactly what time practice begins, when the bus leaves, and what their roles are on the field. That's why retirement is so disorienting, no matter how well they prepare. For the first time in their lives, nobody is waiting for them to show up.

As for my career, I could not have asked for much more as the new decade began to unfold. In 1980, I represented Brad Budde, an All-American guard from USC, taken in the first round by the Chiefs at No. 11 overall. Brad was my first highly drafted Trojan, and it meant I was involved in the two premier college football programs in Los Angeles, guaranteed to turn out one first-round pick after another. Brad was another ideal client. He and his wife, Nicolette, formed Brad's Buddies to help abused children in Kansas City.

In 1981, I met with UCLA's Kenny Easley. Once I had explained to him why I hadn't pursued him earlier like the other agents, we got along famously. Among my clients who played defense, he, Derrick Thomas, and Bruce Smith were on a whole other level. A three-time All American, Kenny finished with a school-record 19 picks and was ninth in the 1980 Heisman Trophy race. His range was unbelievable. He shut down half the field.

The Seattle Seahawks, picking fourth, seemed the most likely destination—until I received a call from Bill Walsh, the ex-Stanford coach now at the helm of the 49ers, slotted to pick at No. 8.

"I really want Kenny to come here," Walsh told me. "If you tell Seattle he is not going to go there, I will pay the same money in the eighth spot that you would have gotten in the fourth."

Kenny loved the idea. San Francisco was much closer to Westwood, and the Niners, with Joe Montana running the show, were clearly a team on the rise.

The Seahawks, however, did not love the idea and told me an emphatic no when I suggested a trade. Kenny was who they wanted, and they were the ones with the power.

We negotiated a nice deal, although I recall how we celebrated more than the specifics of the contract. Every restaurant we drove by in Seattle was closed, so we ended up at Chuck E. Cheese's. There I was, attempting to explain the nuts and bolts of the deal while dozens of kids ran around screaming with the deafening noise of video games in the background. Welcome to the big time, Kenny.

Meeting potential clients in California, Arizona, or other nearby states, made sense on several levels. At little cost, I could visit with players on campus without too much advance notice, and there was a strong likelihood their families, friends, and others in their support network lived nearby, as well. Then, if they were to become clients, they could stop by my offices in Berkeley or Los Angeles, and we could bond further.

The advantages became more obvious in the late '80s as my staff grew and we opened a lavish office in Newport Beach. Players in the vicinity visited almost every day, learning how to use the whole firm, the secretaries, interns, everyone.

In the Class of 1981, I also represented two other outstanding NFL prospects, Curt Marsh, an offensive tackle from the University of Washington, who went at No. 23 overall to the Raiders, and Portland State quarterback Neil Lomax, chosen in the second round by the Cardinals.

By all appearances, Easley, Marsh, and Lomax had little in common, other than the profession they chose. They played different positions and possessed different temperaments. Yet they'd be linked forever in a way I could have never anticipated, and when I think about it, my heart breaks all over again.

Back in the summer of 1981, when they were young and invincible and ready to live their dreams, their future could not have been brighter.

7

THE FRANCHISE QUARTERBACKS

Even now, thirty-one years later, no single NFL Draft stands out as much as the one that occurred on April 26 and 27 of 1983 in New York, at least when it comes to quarterbacks, the most glamorous position in sports.

That wasn't always the case. For many years, the heavyweight champion of the world held that prestigious spot. One could also argue nothing could surpass being the starting center fielder for the New York Yankees; Joe DiMaggio and Mickey Mantle were icons of their respective generations. Then pro football took over America, and legends such as Unitas, Starr, Namath, Bradshaw, and Montana stood above the rest.

No other player in football—in any sport—could enhance the fortunes of his team as profoundly, and rapidly, as the QB.

Yet for many years, the term "franchise quarterback," was not widely used in referring to quarterbacks teams aim to build around for at least the next decade. Teams were always aware that QB was important, but the critical nature of the position has dramatically increased due to rule revisions, which opened up the offense and altered the ratio in total plays from scrimmage from about 55–45 percent rushing to 55–45 percent passing. A quarterback has been the top overall choice in twelve of the last sixteen drafts. Teams do not succeed in today's NFL without an exceptional quarterback.

Of the twenty-one most recent Super Bowl champs, only the 2001 Baltimore Ravens (Trent Dilfer) and 2003 Tampa Bay Buccaneers (Brad Johnson) did not feature a franchise QB. On rare occasions, he can emerge from obscurity—Tom Brady was New England's sixth-round pick, and Kurt Warner had starred in the Arena Football League—but normally selections in the first or second rounds, if teams choose the right individual, will lead to greater success in the near future.

I had first seen the impact a player can make, on a franchise and a city, when Bart signed in 1975. Fans in Atlanta, disillusioned with the Falcons struggling year after year, embraced Bart as the savior they prayed he'd be, and for the most part was, from ticket sales to TV ratings to the win-and-loss record. From 1977 through 1980, the Falcons, who had registered just two winning seasons *ever*, went 34-28, securing their first two playoff berths. Factoring in the opportunity to be a strong role model, and the player's potential for endorsement income, it occurred to me I should build my practice around these difference makers. I would recruit players I believed fit that description and then, in the actual negotiations, make the argument to the team that chose the player in the draft. I almost felt as if I were copywriting the term "franchise quarterback," which to me meant someone whose franchise would win *because of* rather than *with* him, and who would elevate his play in the most critical situations to lead his team to the Super Bowl.

The first client I pictured in that role after Bart was Neil Lomax, who would have gone in the first round if not for Portland State being such a small school. I was certain Neil, after playing for coach Mouse Davis, a pioneer in the run-and-shoot offense, would excel in the more sophisticated NFL. I became fast friends with Mouse, who was diminutive in size but had an expansive personality. Neil was big and strong, had a shotgun arm, and was fun to be around.

Two years later, with the 1983 class, in which six quarterbacks were among the twenty-eight first-rounders, I seized an opportunity to make the case again.

Of those six, the No. 1 pick was John Elway, the first quarterback to receive that honor since Bart eight years earlier. If ever a player fit my profile perfectly, it was Elway, coming from Stanford, where I achieved success in 1978 and which was part of the California infrastructure I worked hard to assemble. However, he already had an agent, who also represented John's dad, Jack Elway, the head coach at San Jose State. Another Hall of Fame quarterback from that remarkable 1983 class was the University of Pittsburgh's Dan Marino, who was picked at No. 27 by the Dolphins.

Two other highly regarded QBs were Tony Eason and Ken O'Brien, each with ties to California. I represented both and I could not have been more satisfied.

Tony, amiable and low-key, grew up near the Bay Area, in the suburb of Walnut Grove, and played for the University of Illinois, where in 1982 he broke a series of passing records and led the Illini to their first bowl game in nearly twenty years. Tony, who had also been coveted by the USFL and CFL, went at No. 15 to the Patriots, who were concerned about their injury-prone starter Steve Grogan.

Kenny, meanwhile, attended UC-Davis, coached by the man I held in such high regard, Jim Sochor. The son of a physician, and from a large and close Irish Catholic family, Kenny was also a tremendous fit for me. The Jets chose him with the twenty-fourth pick, three spots before Marino.

Representing two quarterbacks for the first time in the same draft, one may assume, could become a little complicated. How do you tell one he is special when he suspects you might be giving the same speech to the other? Isn't there an inherent conflict of interest, and, with the effort necessary to nurture the young men and go through the normal channels to see which franchises might favor them, aren't you doing a disservice to one, or perhaps both? Not really. I could advocate for my clients until the end of time, but I never claimed the ability to persuade someone such as Bill Parcells to choose one player over another.

With Tony and Kenny, there was never a problem. In fact, representing both was a distinct advantage. Teams could not make the same promise to either one—we will take you with our pick—without the other finding out. They had been good friends since high school, rooting for each other to wind up in the best possible situation. Then, when it came to the contracts, Kenny was happier to have me work out the details first for Tony, since he was drafted higher, than have another agent set a lower bar.

Ultimately, both fared quite well over the ensuing decade. Tony would lead his team to the AFC championship, and Kenny would be named to two Pro Bowl squads (1985, 1991). Unfortunately for Tony, at the 1986 Super Bowl in New Orleans, the Patriots ran up against the memorable Chicago Bears unit that featured the likes of Jim McMahon and Walter Payton and a superb defense. The game was a rout, and Tony was pulled for Grogan.

Once the outcome was clear, I began collecting my thoughts for what I might say to Tony afterward.

With members of his family outside the locker room, I waited and waited . . . and waited. Player after player emerged, but there was no sign of Tony. By the time he came out, every vehicle associated with the Patriots had left the scene, meaning, in a fitting conclusion to the whole miserable night, I walked with Tony's family and friends sixteen blocks back to the hotel in what felt like a funeral march. Nothing I said got through to him. That's how it is sometimes.

•   •   •

I represented one quarterback preparing to enter the NFL who was not eligible for the 1983 draft. He did not even play in the United States. He played in Canada. I'm referring to Warren Moon.

That fall, Warren played in his sixth and final season for the Eskimos. He was more productive than ever, throwing for a CFL-record 5,648 yards and winning the Most Outstanding Player Award. He was ready, at last, for the next level.

A year earlier, anticipating the arrival of the United States Football League (USFL), I crafted a new two-year deal for Warren that would make him a free agent for the 1984 season, putting him in position to entertain offers from three different leagues. I called it the setup contract, and it was sometimes the most important contract I negotiated for a player because it set him up to have leverage for the one afterward, which would presumably last longer and earn him more rewards. The strategy was to provide the player with the maximum contractual freedom for the time I anticipated he would be most valuable as a performer. I depended on the player's feedback and my growing network of scouts, coaches, and reporters to make the right projection.

No player of his stature had ever been a free agent, and at twenty-seven, he was entering the prime of his career. Free agents wouldn't become commonplace till a full decade later. Teams could only acquire players of Warren's caliber through the draft or in a trade. In this case, they could sign Warren without surrendering picks or players.

What *was* Warren worth on the open market? It was impossible to predict. All I knew was that the rules of free enterprise would apply and he would be worth whatever the market would pay him. The sum was guaranteed to be record-breaking, as long as we could line up at least two serious bidders. At one point, I threw out the idea of $1 million plus per year, which I repeated over and over, because it would be more than John Elway was making, and I wanted Warren to become the highest-paid player in NFL history. In a more conventional negotiation, I would look at the comparables—the players at his position a client should be compared to in experience, productivity, and how much they earned—but with Warren, the only relevant issue was the amount any bidders were willing to pay.

He had everything going for him. He was handsome, articulate, and charming, qualities I first noticed when we met in '78, which were even more evident as he matured, and he would not have to be tutored as thoroughly as the quarterbacks coming directly from college. If there was any potential pitfall, it was the perception by some GMs that for everything Warren accomplished north of the border, he had yet to prove himself in the big leagues, the NFL. I wasn't concerned. The numbers didn't lie. Nor did the film. The challenge was not whether enough teams would display interest. The challenge was which team to choose. I knew Warren would go through the pros and cons of each possible destination as meticulously as any athlete I ever worked with. Look how long he took to settle on me.

Many teams already had their franchise quarterbacks or players with the potential to be one, such as the 49ers (Montana), Chargers (Fouts), Broncos (Elway), and Dolphins (Marino). Others, including Dallas (Danny White) and the Bears (Jim McMahon), also felt no urgency to make a change.

Looking at who needed a QB, we cut the list to five serious options: the New York Giants, Tampa Bay Buccaneers, New Orleans Saints, Houston Oilers, and Seattle Seahawks. We also spoke to officials from the New Orleans Breakers of the USFL, as well as from the Montreal and Toronto franchises in the CFL. I suspected Warren, like Bart nine years before, would go to the NFL—he had already been through his USFL-type experience in Edmonton and was anxious to see how he might stack up against the sport's finest—but it was my responsibility to provide Warren with the maximum amount of possibilities. As with Bart, it served us well for the GMs in the NFL to realize there was a reasonable chance Warren would sign with either of the other leagues.

The Warren Moon national tour kicked off in late 1983. The story received substantial press coverage wherever we went. Nothing like the Moon sweepstakes had ever been seen before. *Sports Illustrated* assigned reporter Jill Lieber to follow us.

The first stop was Houston, Texas, which Warren would visit twice. During one of those trips, Bud Adams, the owner, took him to an oil well.

"This could be yours," Adams said.

Warren was impressed, but the possibility of owning an oil well was not what would make Houston such an attractive destination. The coach was. He was Hugh Campbell, his former mentor in Edmonton, whom the Oilers hired after he spent one year with the USFL's Los Angeles Express. Under Campbell, whom I also represented, Warren knew he could run a wide-open offense that would take full advantage of his skill set. He trusted Hugh.

From Houston, we traveled to New Orleans.

"See that skyline?" Saints owner John Mecom Jr. said. "You could own this town!"

Our next stop was New York City, where the allure was obvious. So were the drawbacks.

This was Warren's first visit to the Big Apple. It didn't take him very long to get acquainted. About six in the morning, we exited the terminal at JFK. The wind was blowing trash and papers everywhere. While waiting for a ride to the Giants facility, we saw two taxis collide. The drivers jumped from the cabs and started a brawl.

I turned to Warren and said, "Welcome to New York."

Our first meeting was with George Young, the Giants general manager. George was rather distinctive looking, with his small, oval eyeglasses perched on a figure resembling Pavarotti. I trusted George so much I asked him for advice whenever I ran into a chal-

lenging situation. He could speak about a wide range of nonfoot-
ball topics, from the history of Jews in Miami to the works of
Shakespeare. George did not make promises like the others in Houston and New Orleans. He didn't have to. To be the starting quarterback for the New York Giants, one of the most celebrated franchises
in pro football history, was special enough.

George didn't have the money, though. The Giants were out.

One person we thought might have the necessary funds was
Donald Trump, the flashy owner of the USFL's New Jersey Gener-
als. We figured we might as well see what Trump, then in his late
thirties, had to say. First, we watched "The Trump Experience," a
video presentation of his various holdings. Donald was cordial and
no doubt serious about investing in Warren, but he had already
committed a fortune to the team.

Then it was on to Tampa, where Bucs owner Hugh Culverhouse
brought Warren to the city's state-of-the-art high-rise.

"How would you like to have a floor or two of this building?"
Culverhouse asked. He told Warren he could live next to the water
and own a boat.

Last, we met with Chuck Knox, the Seattle coach, on the beach
in Hawaii during the week of the Pro Bowl. Chuck wore black and
red checkered slacks and a knit shirt and was sweating profusely
as he made his presentation.

Seattle, where he went to school, made the most sense as a location for Warren. He was a hero in the Pacific Northwest, and he
lived in nearby Redmond in the offseason. I stayed with him every
winter while recruiting players, calling it my Northwest office. The
Nordstrom family, who operated the luxury department stores,
owned the team. I had liked Knox since he took over the Rams in
the early '70s, and I had a great relationship with the Nordstroms
dating back to the Kenny Easley pick in '81.

The tour concluded, we soon eliminated New Orleans and
Tampa. The choice was between Houston and Seattle.

I had no idea which way Warren would go. It would come down, as usual, to the priorities I asked players to list on the first day we met: short-term economic gain, long-term economic security, geographic location, etc. The amount of money each franchise offered was exactly the same, $5.5 million over five years. The only discrepancy, and it was a significant one, was that the Oilers guaranteed a $4.5 million bonus with $200,000 a year in salary, while the Seahawks proposed a $1.2 million bonus and the rest in salaries, which were not guaranteed. Either way, each offer averaged $1.1 million a year, the largest in the NFL, exceeding the $1 million-plus benchmark I set based on the Elway contract.

On February 3, Warren decided on Houston. His heart was in Seattle, but, as practical a man as I ever met, he could not turn down the $3.3 million difference in the signing bonuses. Bonus dollars are guaranteed whether a player is cut or gets injured. Beneath their bravado, these amazingly gifted athletes know how fragile the human body can be, especially when it's pounded over and over, week after week, year after year, by opponents stronger and faster than ever. Warren had already played six seasons.

That evening, Warren broke the news to the press and fans camped out on the lawn of his home. He handled a terribly awkward moment with the poise he displayed his entire life, in and out of the huddle.

Little did we know Warren would wind up playing seventeen years in the NFL, more than making up for the six he missed when he was in Canada. He accomplished this remarkable feat by remaining in shape the whole year round, not merely playing his way into it during training camp, and by his ability to escape the pocket. He was not a scrambler in the mode of an RG III or a Steve Young, but he was mobile enough to avoid being a sitting duck the way Bart was. Although Warren is in the Hall of Fame, he's often omitted in considerations of the top QBs of all time, and that is only because he never took his team to a Super Bowl. Yet, as somebody who made his team a consistent winner and flourished in any situation he was thrown into, Warren was a true franchise quarterback.

So was Steve Young, who became a client around the same time the Moon talks began to heat up. I was quite busy, to say the least. Fortunately, two years earlier, I had hired Mike Sullivan, a bright young lawyer, which meant I had someone to back me up for the first time. I also brought on board my first secretary.

Meeting Steve took a while.

Because of the rather ambiguous rules regarding the solicitation of recruits, I waited a long time for him to make the first contact. His father, LeGrande, a corporate attorney, eventually made the call, and I flew to Greenwich, Connecticut, to meet with the family. An extremely blunt man, LeGrande asked a series of probing questions. I wouldn't have wanted it any other way. His nickname became "Grit" when he played fullback for BYU in the late 1950s. I stayed at their home, in Steve's bedroom, and LeGrande and his wife, Sherry, treated me like another son. LeGrande, stern on the outside, was incredibly warm once you got to know him. So was Sherry.

Then, on the day Steve and I were set to meet, at the airport in Salt Lake City—the closest to BYU, where he, too, went to school—we wandered around the terminal, neither knowing, in the pre-Google world, what the other looked like. I had seen him play on TV, but his helmet was always on, and he didn't stick out in a crowd the way Steve Bartkowski did. He expected somebody much older who dressed like a traditional agent, while I expected somebody who resembled a football player. The only reason we found each other was because Steve finally paged me. We found a restaurant in the airport and talked presidential politics. He supported Reagan's reelection bid; I didn't. I asked whether he would embrace the idea of being a role model. "Without a doubt," he said.

As with Warren, I knew right away Steve was my type of client.

A direct descendant of Brigham Young himself, Steve, with aspirations to be a lawyer, was as intelligent as anyone I ever represented and passionate about his Mormon faith. Yet he never took himself too seriously and had a self-deprecating wit.

On the field, he was very serious. Steve was the most gifted quarterback available in the 1984 draft, almost guaranteed to go No. 1 overall to the Cincinnati Bengals and my good buddy Mike Brown.

Enter stage right Don Klosterman, the general manager of the USFL's L.A. Express. Preparing for the team's second season that spring, Klosterman had his eyes on Steve before I did, and when he was that focused on a goal, he didn't let up, not for a second. This was a man who, after a horrible ski accident in his late twenties, was told he would never walk again. He walked within a year. He was an elegant dresser and former GM of the Rams and Colts, with connections to everyone in entertainment and politics. He later brought Jane Fonda and Ethel Kennedy to my house and then escorted a group of us to the closing ceremonies of the 1984 Summer Olympics in Los Angeles. Five minutes with him and he made you feel like you had known him forever; he reminded me of my grandfather.

Understanding L.A. as well as anyone, Klosterman knew that its fans, more than those in other towns, longed for larger-than-life stars, whether on the silver screen or the playing field. High profile attractions were especially critical in rallying support for a new team in a city that already had the Rams, and the Raiders, the Super Bowl champs, who fled Oakland in 1982. Starting in February, the Express would also have to compete for entertainment dollars against the Magic Johnson–led Lakers of the Showtime era. What better way to generate excitement than by snatching the presumptive

No. 1 pick in the NFL Draft? It was critical to the future of the USFL to have a popular franchise in the country's second-largest market and secure a bigger TV contract.

Klosterman flew to Connecticut to meet with LeGrande Young. He realized there was a large hurdle to clear before any serious talks could take place, and that was the notion of Steve considering playing anywhere other than the NFL. The NFL is every youngster's dream when he first puts on pads, and Steve was no exception. He grew up with a poster of Cowboys quarterback Roger Staubach above his bed.

Klosterman's presentation to LeGrande must have been the same as it was to me. "We have John Hadl, who just worked with John Elway during his rookie year in Denver. He will bring your son along. We also have, as a consultant, Sid Gillman, the architect of the modern passing game. We'll turn Steve into a drop-back passer. We have signed offensive linemen as good as any Steve would have in the NFL (including future Hall of Famer Gary Zimmerman). One more thing: We have signed your tight end from BYU, Gordon Hudson."

Klosterman, an ex-quarterback himself—he was a member of the Rams and Browns in the '50s—wasn't done quite yet. That was merely the football part of his presentation. He understood every aspect of Steve's psyche, and I thought I was the expert in profiling.

"Steve will be in Los Angeles, which has a massive Mormon temple and a large Mormon population," he went on. "I have connections to the city's law schools, and I assure you your son will go to law school. He can go every fall semester, and we will set up a scholarship fund for him at BYU."

Backing Klosterman up the whole way was William J. Oldenburg, the owner of the Express, a larger-than-life personality in his own right. He was head of Investment Mortgage International, a corporation that linked buyers and lenders for large-scale construction projects. With his private jets, Daimler limousines, and a gong that rang in his office each time a million-dollar deal was consummated, he was Gordon Gekko, the corporate raider later portrayed by Michael Douglas in *Wall Street*. To Oldenburg, money was no object when it came to acquiring what he wanted, in this case, Steve Young.

Even after Klosterman's compelling presentation, the NFL remained Steve's priority, though Cincinnati, where he was likely headed, was far from ideal. The Bengals had a quarterback, Ken Anderson, who at thirty-five was still effective, which meant Steve would probably sit on the bench for a season or two. He was the type of competitor who didn't like to ride the bench for two *minutes*.

In March, I met with Klosterman one morning at the team's offices in El Segundo, near the Los Angeles airport. I had no sense of how our talks would turn out, but going in, as I had with Warren, I adopted a benchmark of exceeding Elway's $1 million per year. Little did I know we would demolish it. Steve was a perfect match for Los Angeles—gifted, athletic, handsome, charismatic—and the Express was anxious to get its man.

How anxious became clearer by the hour, as each time I said no, Klosterman kept upping the dollar amount, from the signing bonus, which easily eclipsed what we expected, to the annual salaries to a special annuity. In midafternoon, we moved our discussions to his house in the Hollywood Hills, with its breathtaking 180-degree view of the City of Angels.

It was easy to keep saying no, but I couldn't believe the numbers.

Steve, if he took the offer, would start right away, be tutored by experts, and be financially secure for life.

Through the night, I woke up Steve, who was in Provo, Utah, and his father in Greenwich. I must have called four or five times.

I also checked in with Mike Brown, who confirmed Cincinnati would definitely use its No. 1 pick on Steve. Klosterman and I broke for dinner, resumed, and stopped again around two in the morning to take a dip in his swimming pool—only in Hollywood.

At 3:00 A.M., we went back to work. Staying up at night was part of my lifestyle, and I was blessed with seemingly endless stamina. Finally, about 7:00 A.M., nearly twenty-four hours after we started, we finished negotiating, and what an offer it was: $5 million in bonus and salary and $37 million—yes, $37 million—in an annuity for a total of $42 million, undoubtedly the richest contract in the history of sports. The annuity was critical because it offered lifetime security that couldn't be taxed till it was received, and any higher bonus and salary would have gone in large portions to the government.

As a courtesy, I reached out to Mike Brown. Steve and his dad did not want to close the door on the NFL just yet.

I relayed to him details of the Express offer. I did not expect Mike to match the offer for a second, but I felt there was a slight chance he might propose a serious enough counter for us to at least consider. Mike once told me he was a "whore for quarterbacks," and here was his chance to prove it.

Instead, he answered as only he could.

"The only way I would match that offer," he said, "is if we found an oil well below Spinney Field." That was the Bengals' practice facility.

So much for the NFL. I called Steve and his dad. They agreed to the deal.

Several days later, Steve and I flew to San Francisco to meet with Oldenburg and Klosterman to make it official. As usual, I expected to review some of the more complicated language in the documents to make certain everything was in order. I knew Steve, as bright as he was, would grasp the fine print.

That was not the case with every client, no matter how careful I was to go over every key point in the contract. It never ceased to amaze me when a veteran player would be confused about the terms later on.

Some misunderstandings were more amusing than others.

One example involves Ki-Jana Carter, the Penn State running back selected No. 1 overall by the Bengals in 1995. After we reached a $19.2 million deal, which included a $7.1 million signing bonus, Ki-Jana and I drove from his home near Columbus to training camp, where a press conference would be held to make the official announcement. It seemed as good a time as any to prepare him for his first comments as a Bengal.

"Ki-Jana," I said, "can I explain the contract to you now?"

"Fine," he said.

He then cranked the music as if we were at a rock concert. The lyrics "Make the music with your mouth, bitch" blared out of the speaker. For some reason, I wasn't very confident he would catch every nuance of the contract. Players routinely cranked up the stereo systems in their cars so loud my ears would ring when I stepped out. They used to have a competition to see which player could be the first to rattle the license plate off the back of his car from the vibrations.

When we arrived at the press conference, Ki-Jana took a glance at the check and was appalled.

"Leigh, someone stole my money," he said. "You told me I got a $7 million bonus, but this check is for only $5 million."

"Ki-Jana," I said, "that someone is the Internal Revenue Service, and they can do anything they want."

By the time Steve and I arrived at Oldenburg's office in late afternoon, word of the impending record-breaking contract had begun to leak.

Oldenburg could not wait to celebrate, especially as it was also his birthday, which no one bothered to tell us. After several minutes of small talk, he went to his office while his attorneys and I pored over a pile of documents in the conference room. Steve, studying for a college exam, waited in another room.

This stage of the process can be a bit tedious, yet we were careful not to go too fast. After coming this far, against overwhelming odds, the last thing we or the Express could afford was any sloppy clerical mistakes.

If only Bill Oldenburg had felt the same. He popped in three or four times to check how we were proceeding, more agitated with every visit. Apparently, no one on his staff warned him this might take a while. He was used to making real-estate deals in a manner of minutes, then ringing the gong.

"Why aren't you guys signing the contract?" he asked. "Are you having second thoughts?"

Of course not, we assured him, before he left us alone again.

Around nine o'clock, running out of time to enjoy a celebration on the town, he returned once more. He had evidently been relieving his anxiety by consuming a few adult beverages.

"What's the problem now?" Oldenburg asked.

"Guarantees," one of us said.

That did it. Unable to contain himself any longer, he pulled a giant wad of $100 bills from his wallet and threw them across the room.

"Here are all the [bleepin'] guarantees you'll ever need," he said.

I kept my cool just as I did when Andy Robustelli dumped his desk on me in 1978—I learned long ago not to take such outbursts personally—and so did the owner's attorneys. They had seen their boss lose his temper on more than a few occasions.

Oldenburg was just getting started. A few hours later, his plans for the night ruined, he barged in for the last time.

"Steve, Leigh, I want you both in my office right now," he said.

He let me have it first.

"Why are you doing this?" he asked. "I made you an incredibly generous offer, the best in the history of sports, and you accepted it."

Steve was next. Now I was really worried. Until this moment, Steve had been kept out of it.

"Do you want to be my quarterback or don't you?" Oldenburg continued.

Steve didn't blink, affirming his confidence in the process.

That wasn't convincing enough for Oldenburg. He flung out his arm and knocked a row of glasses off a table a few feet away. The glasses scattered, sending shards of broken glass everywhere.

"I don't know if you are man enough to be my quarterback," he said.

He jabbed a finger into Steve's stomach and punched him in the chest. I was too startled to make any attempt to stop him. It didn't matter. Steve didn't need my help.

"You do that one more time," he said, "and I'm going to deck you."

Oldenburg stopped hitting Steve, thank goodness, but he was not quite done. He picked up a chair and got ready to throw it out the window. Steve grabbed his arm to stop him. Oldenburg then notified security and ordered armed guards to escort us out of the office. It was 3:30 A.M. Steve and I were deposited unceremoniously on an empty—and I mean empty—street in downtown San Francisco, in pitch-blackness.

Good thing Klosterman showed up a few minutes later to offer us a ride to Berkeley, although it looked like the trip he should take was to the hospital. He was pale as a ghost and shaking. I thought he might be having a heart attack or a stroke. He had spared no effort in recruiting and signing Steve, and suddenly, the entire $42 million deal was in jeopardy. As much as the signing would be a major coup for the USFL, it would mean even more to the Express.

During the ride, the color returned to Klosterman's face as he clued us in about Oldenburg's birthday plans and how he had believed an official deal was only a few hours away. In returning to my Berkeley tree house, we were very fortunate to have a safe haven after such an unsettling experience. If Steve had flown directly to Utah, stewing over what occurred in Oldenburg's office, and me to Los Angeles, the eventual outcome could have been much different. Being together, Steve and I would be able to address his concerns as we continued to debate the pros and cons.

I only wished I had been aware of Oldenburg's expectations when the day began. It was my job to work around the idiosyncrasies of wealthy businessmen, and I respected them for believing any deal worth doing should get done relatively quickly.

"The player is here and I'm here," I would have told him, "and we are totally committed to this offer and we will not leave the building until we go through every last piece of paper. So go out and enjoy your birthday, and we'll sign tomorrow."

At the same time, shouldn't we have immediately backed out of the deal after Steve was subjected to such shocking behavior?

I tried to apply perspective.

For one thing, imagining myself in Oldenburg's position, I could understand his frustration. He offered an untested rookie the richest contract in sports history, and the player accepted. So why the holdup?

Second, whatever quirks he had in his personality, they were not relevant. The real relationships that mattered for a player in the NFL were with his teammates and coaches, not the owner. Besides, as far as Steve knew, maybe every owner in professional sports lost control when he didn't get his way. Steve grew up around a lot of influential people in Connecticut, but he went to BYU, as removed as you can get. Without the experience of going through the NFL Draft, where a lot of young men first observe how the business world works, he was being thrust into an unfamiliar, high-stakes environment. It was a lot to process in a very short period of time.

Later that day, after we slept for a few hours, Oldenburg called to apologize. It was the first of dozens of calls we received, many from the most prominent names in the sport, including Commissioner Pete Rozelle, Howard Cosell, Roger Staubach, and Joe Namath. I don't know how Rozelle and Staubach learned Steve was in my house, but I would not be surprised if Klosterman got word to Cosell and Namath in hopes of sealing the deal. The man was the most gifted salesman I knew.

"You can be a star in this league," Cosell told Steve, "and be a pioneer in an enterprise as impactful as the old American Football League."

Cosell needed Steve, as his network, ABC, was the USFL's main television partner. The theory was, the more stars, the better, especially in the two largest markets, New York and Los Angeles. New York had Herschel Walker. Now it was critical Los Angeles land someone of similar stature.

Namath could certainly relate to the decision Steve faced.

"I started in a different league," Namath said, "and people thought it was controversial, and I ended up winning a Super Bowl."

Rozelle and Staubach, meanwhile, interpreted the absence of a formal announcement as an opening to change Steve's mind.

"The league needs you," the commissioner said. "You are exactly the type of player we want."

It was Steve's childhood hero, Staubach, who presented the most compelling case.

"The NFL is the way to go," he told him. "You will be a great quarterback, and that is where you want your legacy."

Still, in the end, the opportunity for Steve to join the Express was impossible to resist, and it was not because of the money.

Steve, who used to joke he grew up in the poor part of Greenwich, one of America's wealthiest cities, didn't make any decisions based on money. At BYU, he drove an old car and wore inexpensive clothes. Once he was playing for the Express, he would leave game checks uncashed in his sock drawer. His mother told me the team would call her constantly to ask why Steve hadn't made any deposits.

If anything, the money embarrassed him, especially as the story attracted an unprecedented amount of coverage in newspapers in the United States and around the world and over the airwaves; Dan Rather led off the *CBS Evening News* with the signing. The sheer scope of the deal was a symbol to many of how far out of control pro sports was threatening to become in our society. With modern economics, we are long past being shocked by how well any player is compensated. Back then, though, no one had heard of these kinds of numbers. We *were* shocked. Steve, through no fault of his own, had become the poster boy for those outraged by the excessive salaries. It was unfair to him, to say the least.

For Steve, the Express offer was irresistible because of how he might develop as a quarterback under John Hadl and Sid Gillman, as opposed to sitting on the bench in Cincinnati, and the opportunity to give back to his alma mater and support other causes that meant a lot to him.

We held a press conference at the Beverly Wilshire Hotel in Beverly Hills to make the formal announcement. I had attended a number of similar gatherings before; usually a dozen or so local newspaper beat guys and TV reporters showed up. This was at an entirely new level, with writers and cameras everywhere—and I thought the Bart signing in Atlanta was a big deal. Steve, still sensitive about the money issue, was hesitant to come out.

"Leigh, can you do the press conference without me?" he asked.

That was Steve.

He had nothing to worry about. He handled the press with skill and maturity.

•   •   •

If only his experience in the USFL could have been as successful.

He was the same Steve, all right, driving his beat-up car, wearing his old clothes, but, despite his best efforts and ownership's, the Express did not become a hit in L.A. Steve used to look up in the stands in the Coliseum, which seated more than 90,000, and literally count the number of spectators. The situation became so dire that in 1985, the team played its last home game of the season, believe it or not, at a *junior* college (Pierce College) in the San Fernando Valley.

Even that was not the lowest point. The lowest point was when the team bus driver, his check having bounced, pulled off to the side of the road on his way to the college, refusing to go farther unless he was paid in cash immediately. The players took up a collection, though some may have wondered if it was worth the effort. To top it off, the Express lost the game 21–10 to the Arizona Outlaws, and a week later, Steve lined up as a running back for a few series. The regular running backs were hurt.

Good thing we didn't need to take up a collection for Steve.

He received the rest of what he was owed, including the then-market value of his annuity, from the league when the Express suspended operations in 1985. It was not too long before the USFL itself folded, though I have always believed its demise, despite the serious financial challenges, was a bit premature. If the owners had just hung on a little longer, given how popular pro football was becoming, and how sports on cable TV, led by ESPN, was on the verge of exploding, five or six of the USFL franchises, at the very least, would've been absorbed into the NFL and skyrocketed in value. The owners felt they had lost too much money. What they lost was their will.

Perhaps the worst casualty of all was Bill Oldenburg. In addition to the money he lost with the Express in 1984, Oldenburg's empire also crumbled.

For Steve, however, those two years in Los Angeles, just like the six Warren spent in Canada, helped him mature greatly as a quarterback and as a man. As it had for Warren, his chance to compete on the stage that mattered most, against the best players on the planet, would come soon enough.

8
TRIUMPHS AND TRIALS

The lives of Warren Moon and Steve Young were not the only ones to change in 1984.

So did mine, dramatically, with dozens of journalists from major magazines, newspapers, television networks, and radio talk shows seeking to determine how I'd been able to rise so rapidly in the profession. I was featured in the *Los Angeles Times* and *San Francisco Chronicle,* interviewed by *Playboy,* and appeared regularly on CNN. ABC also did a piece on me for its Summer Olympics coverage.

What had been maybe thirty phone calls a day turned into three hundred.

Just as in the wake of the Bart success, I was glad to oblige, capitalizing on a golden opportunity to spread the message of athletes being role models for their cities and schools. At Berkeley, when we were not trying to build parks or stop wars, we wondered which of us would be the ones to retain our values under the pressures of the real world. More than a decade after graduation, I could safely say I hadn't lost mine.

In early 1985, I took another important step, though I certainly didn't realize it at the time. It began when the Super Bowl between the 49ers and Dolphins, billed as Joe Montana versus Dan Marino, took place at Stanford Stadium in Palo Alto. I was not on the list for the commissioner's party, the week's premier social event for the sport's movers and shakers. Why not, I thought, hold my own? I loved to throw parties. In law school, I hosted '50s-themed parties, games of charades, all kinds of creative events. In this case, I knew just the place, my house in Berkeley.

Barely an hour away, it fit roughly four hundred, with balconies on four decks and the roof. I invited writers, friends of both teams, and almost anybody not attending the commissioner's affair. The next morning, gazing at guests sleeping on couches, and recognizing how the Super Bowl had evolved from a football game to a convention of Americana, with big business, big politics, and big media converging for a week of fun and networking, I decided to make the party an annual event. Year after year, we chose venues that reflected the city or region where the game was held, such as the *Hello, Dolly!* set on the back lot of 20th Century Fox in Los Angeles, Jazzland in New Orleans, or the San Diego Zoo. The music, food, and decorations were all evocative of the area. We had caricaturists, magicians, ventriloquists, and African dancers.

The first three were given at night, until I realized the benefits of getting together on Saturday afternoons while no other major parties were scheduled. I wanted a gathering that, unlike the others, wasn't noisy and filled with alcohol, where my clients and their families could mingle without worrying about being smothered, and where people could meet and network with others. As many as seventeen U.S. senators, Republicans and Democrats alike, came to one party, including Ted Kennedy, Patty Murray, and Harry Reid, along with their wealthy donors. Ted became a good friend, phoning me, as Al Davis did, for late-night chats to discuss political races and the pennant race. He loved his Red Sox. I also became friendly over the years with Rush Limbaugh, whom I met in the press box during an Oilers-Steelers game. Rush regularly mentioned me on his radio show.

"Rush," I once told him, "you are going to get me kicked out of the Berkeley Alumni Association!"

We had celebrities from every walk of life, including Adam Sandler, Jennifer Hudson, and LL Cool J, as well as players and owners from just about every major sport. I invited whoever was hot in American culture at the time. When the reality show *Joe Millionaire* was a hit on Fox about a decade ago, Joe Millionaire himself came, as did Ruben Studdard when he won the second season of *American Idol*. Another time, I hired the popular hip-hop duo OutKast to perform.

Humor was also an important part of the festivities. Jay Leno sent comedian Rob Schneider to one party dressed like the fitness guru Richard Simmons. Only Schneider was the anti–Richard Simmons. He ate Twinkies and kept trying to persuade Steve Young and other players to smoke cigarettes. Leno showed the tape on *The Tonight Show* to the real Simmons, who couldn't stop laughing. Another year, Leno did sports trivia interviews for his show. Our party became *the* daytime party. Tickets were so valuable they sold one year on eBay for $3,500.

I felt it was important, as well, to have a charitable aspect to each gathering. In New Orleans, we honored first responders after September 11. In Tampa, Gabby Giffords, the congresswoman, helped us host a live telecast on a big screen where celebrities, owners, and athletes talked to troops in Iraq for ninety minutes. The troops later sent me the flag that had flown over their base. We also set up a phone bank for people to contact wounded soldiers in military hospitals around the world. In Arizona, at a party centered around the environment, Governor Janet Napolitano and I released a hawk into the wild. During another affair, Jenny McCarthy and Jim Carrey auctioned off a Jaguar to raise money for Autism Speaks, the largest organization in the country that fights the disorder.

●　　　●　　　●

For me, the festivities every year kicked off on Thursday of Super Bowl week. That's when I shuttled from one corporate event to another, meeting with sponsors and those in other sports-related businesses. I also made sure to spend time with each client. For several years, between Pittsburgh, Dallas, New England, and San Francisco, we represented large numbers of players in the big game. Their focus, of course, was on the contest ahead, the one they would be remembered for, win or lose, and they could not be certain they would ever be back.

Yet, with numerous friends and family members eager to interact with them, many seeking extra tickets, players could easily get overwhelmed. Early in the week, there was no harm in going out to dinner or walking the streets, even if that meant being recognized. In that environment, I signed autographs and posed for pictures. Someone would say, "Hey, there's Bruce Smith," and soon there'd be ten, twenty, or maybe more fans circling him. One night he lifted me on his shoulders so we could escape the frenzy.

By Thursday, players realized it was time to shut it down. It wasn't as if they went to bed at nine o'clock, but at least they were away from the chaos. The lone exception was Ben Roethlisberger. Ben went to our party the day before the game in 2006. Ben had a remarkable ability to multitask. When game time came, he was hyperfocused and led his team to victory.

On Fridays, I turned my attention to the future, to college players I would be representing in the draft a few months later. I felt it was important they caught a glimpse of the world they were about to enter.

We took them to an area in each convention center known as Radio Row, where hundreds of stations from across the country broadcast their daily sports talk shows for most of the week. By getting these young men on the air, and introducing them to the coaches, owners, and team executives in town, along with the print and electronic press, I was able to elevate their profile. They also witnessed, for the first time, the business side of sports, a side they needed to understand.

I sat in Radio Row for six or seven hours, doing one interview after another on a wide variety of topics, with stations from Boston to Seattle. One year, I did thirty-three shows nonstop from 7:00 A.M. to 10:00 P.M.

I met, as well, with star veterans looking to switch agents. That always made me uncomfortable. It felt like dating a divorcee: Was the first relationship simply a case of two poorly matched people, or was the woman unable to sustain *any* relationship? The last thing I wanted was to inflict unnecessary pain on another agent if there was a chance to save their relationship.

On Friday nights, I attended the commissioner's party—I was now on the list—where I worked the room, speaking with general managers and owners and other front-office personnel. The one night I didn't make it, I was watching Bruce Smith being interviewed when he fainted on the air. I rushed to the hospital. I couldn't let my friend be there alone. Luckily, he was suffering only dehydration.

On Saturday mornings, I would do an interview with Brian Kilmeade of Fox News. One year, we did the show from an aircraft carrier. In Tampa, on the set of CNN, the cannons from the Gasparilla Pirate Festival behind us blasted so loudly that another interviewer and I couldn't hear each other.

Then it was on to the four most frenetic hours of my year, even more than day one of the draft. At the draft, there wasn't much for me or my players to do except wait. At the party, there was *too* much to do. The hardest part was keeping track of hundreds of names and remembering the business I'd conducted with each of them in the past, and how we might work together again in the future. As host, I also made the introductions; the challenge was not to slight anyone and to connect those with mutual interests. With a line of people constantly waiting to talk and take a picture with me, there wasn't a moment to relax. By Saturday evening, I barely had enough energy to converse with my own staff. Nothing I did as an agent stimulated or drained me as much as Super Bowl week.

Not long after our first party ended, back in '85, we began to concentrate on the draft three short months away. We had the potential to have four high picks for the first time.

By June, more than a month after the draft, I was feeling confident enough about the firm, and the athletes we secured—they went fifth, seventh, eighth, and twelfth in the first round—to take a week off for a trip to Hawaii. I went with a woman I'd known from college. We met at the Cal football game on Homecoming Day. That woman became my wife.

Lucy and I had kept in a touch a bit during the late '70s, but it was not till she moved to Southern California in 1983 that we started to see each other again. Our wedding, half Jewish, half non-Jewish, was chronicled by Robin Leach's *Lifestyles of the Rich and Famous*. Warren Moon, Steve Young, Neil Lomax, and Kenny Easley were among the groomsmen and Steve Bartkowski was best man.

Also in the wedding party were clients who, though not as widely known as football players, meant just as much to me: the television news and sports anchors and radio personalities I'd represented for years in the Bay Area. In getting to know their world, I became an expert in hair, makeup, and lighting, along with learning production values and how to properly evaluate résumé tapes. These outstanding professionals included Jan Hutchins, Dave McElhatton, Wendy Tokuda, Wayne Walker, Suzanne Saunders, Pete Wilson, Dennis Richmond, Elaine Corral, Colleen Williams, Stu Nahan, Ross McGowan, Ann Fraser, and Jan Yanehiro.

The ceremony, staged in a Spanish-style building with a giant courtyard in Newport Beach, with the wedding party descending from a balcony, went off just as we planned—well, except for one tiny detail: The priest who was to marry us did not show up. We called everybody not at the wedding who might know how to find him. No one had a clue. The guests were beginning to wonder what was causing the delay. The priest, we found out much later, had gotten drunk. Fortunately, among the guests was William B. Keene, a good friend of Lucy's parents. Keene, a retired judge who also played the judge on TV's *Divorce Court,* conducted the ceremony. Lucy and I were off to Maui.

Staring at the waves. Reading novels. Eating delicious food. A honeymoon in Maui would be just the serenity I needed before another summer of dealing with NFL owners and general managers.

Some serenity. On the second day, the phone rang. It wasn't room service. It was Peter Boermeester, a friend and former client—he was a kicker at UCLA—who had been at the wedding. I wondered whether this could wait. It couldn't.

"Leigh, Mike Sullivan is leaving the practice," Peter said. That was upsetting enough. Then came the bombshell.

"He was soliciting clients at your wedding!"

To suggest I was shocked would be a massive understatement. Anger, confusion, disappointment—name a reaction, and I am sure I experienced it. I would have to spend the rest of the honeymoon, with apologies to Lucy, on the phone to limit the damage to my business. Thank goodness Peter called when he did. If he had not, I would not have been able to act quickly, and that was the key to holding on to our clients.

One of the first calls was to Sullivan. I had tried to ascertain his motivation on my own, but for a more accurate read of the threat, I needed to talk to the man himself. I was not surprised when he didn't call back.

The next call was to Jeff Moorad, an attorney who had joined our practice in March. Splitting our roster of forty clients, Jeff and I went to work. Soliciting support from those who had been with me for years was simpler than from players such as Tony Eason and

Ken O'Brien, who started when Sullivan was already on board and enjoyed a good relationship with him. The last thing any of them expected was to be caught in the middle of a divorce between dueling agents. Even if they selected me over Sullivan, the relationships I'd carefully nurtured were bound to be weakened. We didn't have the type of clients who enjoyed that type of conflict.

Once back in Los Angles, I reached out again to Sullivan. How could I make peace, one might wonder, with someone who had just stabbed me in the back?

Easy. The practice needed him. My first obligation was to the incoming rookies who had put their faith in me. They did not care about my future or Mike Sullivan's future. They cared only about their own.

We met in a park at the end of Overland Avenue near my parents' house.

"Mike, why would you want to do this?" I asked. "We have such a good thing going here."

"I just want to run my own shop," he said, "and I need to do it my way."

It became clear there was nothing I could say to change his mind.

The Warren Moon contract with Houston was a major source of contention. Because he completed the paperwork, Sullivan told clients he handled the contract, not me. Nonsense. I set up the timing for the three leagues to compete against each other, accompanied Warren across the United States, and negotiated the primary terms with the Oilers and Seahawks. I also managed the press. The paperwork was the least important part of the process.

Either way, without Sullivan, Jeff and I, once we kept our clients from bolting, now had to get them signed with the franchises that drafted them. It would not be easy. Jeff, just four years out of law school, had never been through an experience like this and would not have much time to adjust. Good thing Sullivan only took a few of the forty, and they were less accomplished veterans.

As it turned out, hiring Jeff Moorad was one of the best decisions I ever made. Even better was later making him a full partner.
He had a shrewd analytical mind and a wonderful way with people. Together, we built an unbreakable bond. Since I wasn't motivated by money, I was fortunate Jeff knew how to control costs,
collect fees, and keep us hugely profitable. In key negotiating situations in football that required a team, he was always my first
choice.

Our skills complemented each other's perfectly. I would frame
the overriding concept and create leverage, while he was the most
relentless nuts-and-bolts negotiator imaginable. At some point, he
would say to the other side, "Let's forget about the arguments and
focus on the numbers." We could communicate without saying a
word.

Once the USFL started to unravel, NFL owners, still seething over
being pushed around for three years by an inferior enterprise, were
eager to regain full control. To them, the leverage that had been
used against them was another word for blackmail. It would not be
sufficient to merely freeze the advances in salaries from those three
miserable years. They wanted to roll salaries back to when rookies
had no power, and with the opening of training camp fast approaching, time was definitely on their side.

In mid-July, with almost no movement to report, I saw only
one solution: Hit the road. I reached my share of agreements over
the phone, but there was nothing quite like negotiating with the
other person face-to-face, seeing the look in his eyes and the body
language that could not tell a lie. I headed to San Diego to meet
with the Chargers about Jim Lachey, a hard-nosed Ohio State offensive tackle who went at No. 12 overall.

I got a kick out of Jim. While I was recruiting him, on a typical
winter day in Columbus, the snow piled as high as my waist, the

temperature about 20 degrees, we went out drinking on High Street. Appropriate name, isn't it?

We had a wonderful time. I felt pretty confident he'd ask me to be his agent.

Perhaps too confident.

"I'm almost ready to sign with you," he said, "but if you do what I ask, you'll never have to prove your courage in any other way. We are going to walk all these blocks through the snow and up to the stadium."

We are going to do *what*?

I had no choice. I was a thin-blooded Californian wearing just a sweater, and it took about three seconds before I began to shiver and my feet turned into blocks of ice. Yet somehow I made it in one piece to Ohio Stadium—and back.

"Okay," Jim said, "I'm ready to sign."

The next stop was Tampa to work out a deal for defensive end Ron Holmes, the eighth pick out of the University of Washington.

Ron was like many of my clients. He did a lot of deep thinking, and that wasn't necessarily a good thing. Other agents had a problem with players who didn't want to accept an offer because the money was not right. My problem was players who weren't sure their choice of profession was right. A very successful quarterback I represented once asked me, "Is football really this important? Isn't this the time of my life when I should be traveling or saving the environment?"

With Ron, everything appeared in order—until he called from his home in Seattle hours before he was to take a red-eye to Tampa for the signing and press conference.

"Leigh," he said, "I'm having second thoughts."

I wasn't surprised. I represented plenty of clients who had second thoughts, and they didn't always relate to signing contracts.

Bart was a perfect example. Months ahead of time, I'd secure his commitment to appear at a public event, but when the day arrived, he would invariably ask, "Can you get me out of this?" Once he showed up, though, he had a good time. Others shared similar reservations about making appearances in the community, yet in almost every case they told me afterward how much the experience meant to them.

It wasn't always clear whether a player was suddenly ambivalent about a career in pro football, or the team that drafted him, or the city he would live in, or if he was merely going through separation anxiety. I tried to prevent any last-minute hesitation by guiding clients through the signing process as carefully as possible, but with Ron, it made little difference. I brought up a number of reasons, but he still could not identify the source of his discontent.

"Just get on the plane, Ron," I told him, "and we'll talk about it when you get here."

The next morning, the plane arrived, but without Ron on it, which brought up another problem: How do I explain his absence to Bucs owner Hugh Culverhouse and general manager Phil Krueger? Culverhouse would have every right to ask, Am I investing in the right person? Does this guy have behavioral problems? Is he simply unreliable?

I didn't know exactly what I would tell them but I knew one thing: I would not lie. One lie could easily lead to another, and the trust between us and the Buccaneers would be lost.

"He had problems catching the plane," I said.

Ron did have "problems" catching the plane. He didn't make the next flight or the one after that.

Yet I assured Culverhouse and Krueger he would be in town the following day. "In a month or so, you won't remember this happened at all," I said.

Now if only I could assure myself.

"You have to take the first thing out or it's going to get real uncomfortable," I told him around 4:00 A.M. Seattle time. "I'll think about it," he said. I tried to reach him several times over the next few hours without any luck. For all I knew, Ron went fishing in the Yukon, anything to escape the pressure.

As it turned out, he was on the flight. I can't imagine what I would have told Culverhouse and Krueger if he hadn't been.

"Hopefully, you'll have an entertaining story," I said when I greeted him that evening at Bucs headquarters. "I've had to convince these people that you're not flaky."

"I just needed more time to think," he said.

Don't we all?

Ron signed that day and went on to play eight years in the league for the Bucs and Broncos.

With Jim and Ron under contract, I was halfway home. The other two rookies were both from Southern Cal: linebacker Duane Bickett, who went at No. 5 to the Indianapolis Colts, and offensive tackle Ken Ruettgers, taken two picks later by the Packers. I had grown up in a UCLA family, but these two very intelligent men were tremendous role models who made me excited to be associated with USC.

Since it did not matter to me which team I met with first, I asked Culverhouse for his suggestion. As head of the NFL Management Council, he wielded more power than just about any other owner and stayed in close contact with every franchise. He sat with his back to Tampa Bay. Tendrils of lightning framed his leonine head behind him. He looked like Moses in *The Ten Commandments*.

"Hang on a second," he said. "I'll be right back."

Why Culverhouse couldn't answer right away made little sense, and then it made all the sense in the world. To keep salaries as low as possible with the USFL on the verge of falling apart, in my mind the NFL owners acted in a manner that suggested they were colluding, though I could not prove it, nor could anybody else.

The only proof I'd ever need came several minutes later when Culverhouse returned. He had gone to make a phone call. To the owners, it seemed to matter which team I visited first.

"If I were you, son," he said, "I'd go to Indianapolis."

On to Indy it was, where I met general manager Jim Irsay, son of owner Robert Irsay, at, of all places, a junior high school, our legs folded into desks meant for twelve-year-olds.

Jim loved rock 'n' roll, and the fact that I'd met Jim Morrison and Jimi Hendrix and had gone to Berkeley in the late 1960s. This helped to forge a bond between us that would endure for decades. It didn't take long to reach a deal for Bickett, although whenever I think of Duane and the Colts, I can't help but reflect on what transpired several years later during talks over a contract extension. Duane was an All-Pro by this stage, and Jim and I again reached a speedy agreement.

Less than twenty-four hours later, Jim called to say the deal was off.

"I don't know how to tell you this," Jim said, "but my father won't do it."

"What do you mean?" I asked. "We agreed. I told Duane and he accepted it."

No matter. Mr. Irsay had made up his mind, which was what I explained to Duane on our way to the airport the next day. He was not pleased. When he pulled up at the terminal, he got out of the car and threw my bag to the ground.

"Nice f——in' job, Steinberg," he said and drove away. That was not a restful plane flight, but I later reached a deal with the Colts nearly as favorable as the one the elder Irsay rejected.

Bob Irsay was not afraid to say or do anything when he felt it was in the best interests of his franchise. This is the man who moved the Colts from Baltimore, their longtime beloved home, to Indianapolis in the middle of the night. The painful image of a fleet of Mayflower trucks hauling off team property was etched in the memory of fans who would despise him forever.

My most memorable encounter with Irsay Sr. took place when we discussed contract terms for quarterback Jack Trudeau. After failing to make much progress, Irsay said, "The only way we're going to get this done is to bring Jack Trudeau himself here." He was referring to his ranch in town.

I was leery of the idea, recalling how Peppy Blount tried to strangle Al LoCasale, but Irsay insisted. He would soon wish he hadn't. We sat across from him at the bar in his den.

"Mr. Irsay," Jack said, "I would give anything for this team. I just want to take you to the Super Bowl."

"Take me to the Super Bowl?" Irsay echoed. "You will never take us to the Super Bowl. You don't have the balls to take me anywhere. You're nothing but a mediocre quarterback."

I had heard owners criticize players to their face before, but this established a new low. Trudeau obviously felt the same way. He cocked his arm to throw a punch, and I stopped him just in time. Irsay was petrified. The talks were done for the day.

Only Ken Ruettgers remained, and what a relief. I was burned out, sleeping sporadically, living on Diet Coke, having long since run out of clean clothes. Life on the road, before the invention of laptops, cell phones, e-mails, and texting, was not like it is today. It was grueling, which may explain why I was a bit drained when, due to mechanical problems with the plane, we were forced to land in Appleton, Wisconsin, and take an hour-long bus ride to Green Bay. If that weren't discomforting enough, the welcome I received from Packers head coach Forrest Gregg, a local hero since he starred for Lombardi, was, one might say, less than hospitable.

"Oh, another agent's in town," Gregg told reporters. "We'll have him over for dinner. My wife will cook rat poison."

How Gregg felt was not much different than how a lot of coaches felt about men in my line of work. Even as esteemed a figure in the league as Redskins coach Joe Gibbs didn't hesitate to criticize me, telling the press in 1992 I was "sitting behind a desk in Los Angeles or someplace with [my] feet cocked up" while Heisman Trophy winner Desmond Howard, the team's first-round pick, was in the seventeenth day of his holdout.

In any case, without too much difficulty, Packers GM Chuck Hutchison and I were able to reach an agreement for my client, and we celebrated with a bottle of Chardonnay till one in the morning. It was sure better than rat poison.

I called Lucy to give her the good news. "I just finished Ken Ruettgers," I told her. "I'm on my way home."

Lucy did not jump for joy, and after the honeymoon in Hawaii that never was, and the road trip which seemed as if it would never end, she certainly had a point.

"Next time, marry Chuck Hutchison," she said. "I won't be here when you get back." She promptly hung up.

Nonetheless, I was in good spirits flying back to California. Overcoming the bitterness of NFL owners, I negotiated solid contracts for our four first-round picks, and they all arrived at training camp in plenty of time to get in the work they needed to perform at the game's highest level.

With Jeff Moorad aboard, we also expanded our baseball practice. Baseball was both of our first loves.

I had already represented baseball players for a number of years. My first client was Carney Lansford, a gritty third baseman who had a fifteen-year career with the Angels, Red Sox, and A's. His whole family was gifted, and I ended up representing his two brothers, Jody, a first-round pick of the Padres, and Phil, a first-round pick of the Indians. I also represented first-round picks Ron DeLucchi (Pirates) and John Bohnet (Indians).

After Carney led the American League in batting one year for the Red Sox with a .336 average, we ended up in arbitration, a very uncomfortable process, as he would have to sit in a New York office building and listen to owner Haywood Sullivan denigrate his talents. Directly across from our hotel was a building with enormous red numerals that read "666." Carney, who was religious, said, "That's the devil's sign. We have no chance tomorrow." He was right.

I also represented reliever Tom Niedenfuer, whose nickname was "Buffalo Head," since his head was so large. Representing a closer is nerve-racking because the outcome of the game is usually in his hands, but for me it was a dream come true. Tom pitched for my beloved Dodgers.

When Jeff Moorad came to our firm in 1985, he was sitting in an apartment on Balboa Island, which was his office, with a series of names scrolled on a chalkboard. He had signed Matt Williams, a third baseman for the Giants, Will Clark, a first baseman for the Giants, and Cory Snyder, an outfielder for the Indians. Jeff took the lead from then on in baseball, first building our practice through the draft. We secured a long string of first-round picks. Matt and Will were soon major stars as we became competitive with the two top firms representing baseball players.

In December of 2000, Jeff got free agent Manny Ramirez, the ex-Indians outfielder, to sign with the Red Sox for $160 million, which would have been considered one of the game's all-time best contracts if Alex Rodriguez hadn't received $252 million at the same time. We added All-Stars such as first baseman Adam Dunn, catcher Pudge Rodriguez, and pitcher CC Sabathia. Jeff hosted the first All-Star parties, patterned after our Super Bowl parties. I was thrilled when he signed Dodgers outfielder Shawn Green, which gave us a Jewish role model in Southern California. We also represented Giants manager Dusty Baker. Jeff negotiated superbly for every one of them.

There was one occasion, however, when he ran into somebody

just as strong-willed as he was: Bill Polian, the former Buffalo Bills GM, who had taken on a similar role with the Carolina Panthers. We were in talks with Polian over Kerry Collins, the No. 5 pick in the 1995 draft. Jeff asked to take the lead, and I was happy to let him. Polian, another to easily lose his temper, was a better fit for Jeff. That was not my style of negotiating. Bill and Jeff also bonded over their love of baseball.

In preparing for the meeting, Jeff told me he planned to ask Polian to hold off on any objections until he finished his entire presentation. I told him he was in for a shock.

"Jeff, Bill Polian built the Buffalo Bills team that went to four straight Super Bowls," I said. "He's a master of talent assessment, and he believes agents who don't have any football background have no business talking about it. You're never going to get through the part where you talk about how superb Kerry Collins is. The odds of you presenting an unchallenged five minutes with Bill Polian without his head twisting around like the little girl in *The Exorcist* are about 10 percent."

Not believing me, Jeff began his pitch. "Kerry has the ability to read defenses and—"

Polian jumped out of his chair and cut him off. Jeff barely made it past five *seconds*.

"I'm not going to stand here and let you try to tell me about talent," Polian said. "When did you own a team? When did you scout? When did you play?"

"That went well," I told Jeff afterward.

Was I taken aback by Sullivan's attempted coup? Absolutely. Did it, for even a moment, lessen my commitment to the business I had chosen? Absolutely not.

I had been raised with resiliency and the ability to regroup. Whenever I suffered a setback, I put my life in perspective: I wasn't a starving peasant in Darfur. I didn't have cancer. Instead, I lived in the free, democratic, and prosperous United States in the most technologically advanced time in history. There is, therefore, no excuse but to keep trying to make a difference in the world. I still believed in the positive role athletes could play by giving back to their communities.

Take Steve Young, for instance. There was no more positive role model I knew.

During the visit to Tampa to work out a deal for Ron Holmes, I spoke to general manager Phil Krueger about Steve, who had been the No. 1 overall pick by the Bucs in the 1984 NFL Supplemental Draft, in which teams secured the rights to players from the USFL and CFL for whenever they'd become free agents. Steve was chosen ahead of Mike Rozier, Gary Zimmerman, and Reggie White. In the summer of '85, with the USFL running the Express, a clear breach of his contract because he had signed with a franchise and not the league, he was now free to join Tampa.

It was not, however, clear to USFL Commissioner Harry Usher. The league, planning to move to a fall schedule in 1986, still believed Steve had to abide by his agreement. Yet Usher, like any astute businessman, was prepared to let Steve go—for a price, of course, a most exorbitant one: $2 million. Steve might not have made earning money a high priority, but that did not mean he was willing to give it away. Yet refusing to pay could mean another season, or longer, in the USFL, if the league somehow stayed in business. After a lot of soul-searching, Steve decided we should negotiate with Usher. Two seasons in the USFL was long enough.

In the end, we reached a compromise settlement with Usher for $1.2 million and agreed in September to a six-year, $5 million package with the Bucs. Steve Young would finally fulfill his dream of playing in the National Football League.

Or would he? On the flight to Tampa, Steve agonized over his decision. His teammates on the Express had told him he was making a mistake in buying his way out of his contract, because the league would soon fall apart on its own. They also questioned his agreeing to play again in the fall, just a few months after the Express finished its grueling, and humiliating, eighteen-game season.

I wasn't surprised to hear his teammates weigh in. Players are always willing to offer each other advice they'd never take themselves.

Some of the most familiar comments I heard over the years included "You should have gotten more money," "You could have been a free agent," and "If you had a better agent you would pay no taxes."

Steve was no different than most of the quarterbacks I represented. On the field, they are incredibly courageous, but off the field, because they are brighter, they are more introspective than other players. Steve's second thoughts didn't go away. After arriving in Tampa, he wouldn't leave the hotel to sign the contract. He was beginning to make Ron Holmes appear decisive.

Finally, Steve signed.

The Bucs, however, were the least successful franchise in the NFL. Even Heisman Trophy winner Bo Jackson, the No. 1 overall pick by the Bucs in the 1986 draft, rejected them. The team flew him into town to have dinner with several players so they could encourage him to sign. The players instead advised him against joining the team. He signed instead with baseball's Kansas City Royals. Bo didn't want to know losing.

The year was soon over, and what a year it was.

I lost a business partner and gained a wife. I secured contracts for 4 of the top 12 first-round draft picks in the most adversarial environment I'd encountered since becoming an agent. I guided one of my most prized clients to the league where he belonged. I helped athletes establish dozens of new community and charity foundations. I started a Super Bowl party that would become a fixture for the next twenty-five years.

Jerry Jones (Dallas Cowboys Owner) and Leigh at Super Bowl XL in Detroit in 2006. *(Personal Photo)*

Leigh's fiftieth birthday party with Robert Kraft on a boat in Newport Beach, CA. *(Personal Photo)*

Leigh and Steve Young at Super Bowl XXXVIII Party in 2004, held in Houston, TX. *(Internal Office Photo)*

Then presidential candidate Barack Obama and Leigh at Balboa Bay Club Campaign Fundraiser in 2008. *(Courtesy of Obama for President Campaign)*

Art Rooney, Ben Roethlisberger, and Leigh, July 2004 at his signing with the Steelers. *(Personal Photo)*

Leigh, with Georgia Frontiere (then owner of the Los Angeles Rams) in June 1992, at ADL Man of the Year Awards. *(Internal Office Photo)*

Kenny and Gail Easley with Leigh at his thirty-fifth birthday party, at his home in Berkley, CA. *(Personal Photo)*

Leigh, with Desmond Howard, announcing Howard's signing with the Oakland Raiders in 1997. *(Personal Photo)*

Leigh on the beach in Venice, CA, circa 1950. *(Personal Photo)*

Warren Moon and Leigh at Super Bowl XL in Detroit, 2006. *(Super Bowl Party Photographer)*

Robert Wuhl *(Arli$$)*, Ted Kennedy, and Leigh at Super Bowl XXXIII Party held at the SeAquarium, Miami, FL, 1999. *(Internal Office Photo)*

Cameron Crowe and Leigh at Super Bowl XXVIII in Atlanta, GA, 1994. *(Personal Photo)*

Cuba Gooding Jr., Leigh, and Tom Cruise on the set of *Jerry Maguire*. *(TriStar Pictures Set Photo)*

Leigh with Oliver Stone at Super Bowl XXXIII Party held at the SeAquarium, Miami, FL, 1999. *(Internal Office Photo)*

Leigh and Lennox Lewis. *(Personal Photo)*

Steinberg *(far left)* with Warren Moon, Jerry Jones, and Troy Aikman in 2006. *(Seth Browarnik/WireImage)*

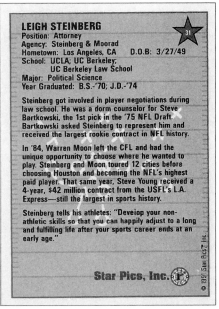

Star Pics Trading Card Front.
(1991 StarPics, Inc.)

Star Pics Trading Card Back.
(1991 StarPics, Inc.)

Leigh at Hamilton High School
(Los Angeles, CA) graduation,
1966. *(Personal Photo)*

Jay Leno with Leigh
at Super Bowl XXXV,
Tampa, FL, 2001.
(Internal Office Photo)

Leigh, as Berkeley student body
president, 1970. *(Personal Photo)*

At family home in Los Angeles in 1968, *(L-R)* Dad, Leigh, and brothers Don and Jim. *(Personal Photo)*

Grandfather, John Steinberg, holding Leigh in 1950. *(Personal Photo)*

Family photo from 1952, *(L-R)* Dad, Leigh, Jim, and Mom. *(Personal Photo)*

Leigh and only daughter, Katie, 1999. *(Personal Photo)*

Filming commercial for Pac Bell, Leigh with Warren Moon in 1985. *(Personal Photo)*

This is *(from left to right),* Jon, Katie, and Matt Steinberg in December 1999 for the holiday card that year. *(Personal Photo)*

Leigh and Warren Moon on stage of Hall of Fame Ceremony after Leigh presented Warren, August 2006, Canton, Ohio. *(Internal Office Photo)*

Yet I was just in my midthirties. There was so much more to accomplish.

Steve Young did not have much fun in Tampa. His experience was symbolized in one loss to the Packers at Lambeau Field; an unforgettable picture appeared in *Sports Illustrated* of Steve's helmet covered with ice. In 1986, his first season as the main starter, the Bucs went 2-14, dropping their last seven in a row while relinquishing 30 or more points in four of those contests. The only good news was that being so pathetic put the Bucs in line to draft first again, and this time, they wouldn't have to wonder whether the object of their desires might choose another sport.

The bad news was that Hugh Culverhouse, who had been in love with Steve two years earlier, was now in love with another quarterback, Vinny Testaverde, the 1986 Heisman Trophy winner from the University of Miami. Vinny was an icon in the state of Florida the way Montana was in the Bay Area. Vinny would sell tickets. In 1986, the Bucs drew fewer than 50,000 fans in six of their eight games at Tampa Stadium. The capacity was over 70,000. That's a lot of empty seats.

In my opinion, however, the Bucs had a franchise quarterback, and Steve was still only twenty-five.

I brought up my concerns with Culverhouse.

"Mr. Culverhouse, for Steve to come to you in the first place, he had to pay money to buy his way out of the USFL," I said. "He had a run-for-his-life experience the last two years and never complained. You told him Tampa would be the last place he'd ever have to be, but that turned out to be wrong. We accept that Vinny's your new savior, but you need to consider Steve's feelings about where he wants to go, because if we end up in a third situation like these last two, Steve may choose to retire."

Steve was not going to retire, but the promises Culverhouse

made—he said he'd set him up at Stetson Law School in Tampa—
were so significant, we felt justified in taking a hard stand.

Culverhouse, to his credit, listened carefully and vowed to treat
Steve fairly. I knew quite a few owners who wouldn't have been as
accommodating. So where *did* Steve want to go? Where was his
best opportunity to come in as the starter right away?

Among the early suitors were the St. Louis Cardinals and San
Diego Chargers, and while there were positives to both destina-
tions, another stood out from the rest: San Francisco. The 49ers
organization, with Super Bowl championships in 1982 and 1985,
was perhaps the best run in football, and no head coach was more
venerated than Bill Walsh, dubbed "the Genius" for his creative play
calling and establishment of what came to be known as the West
Coast offense, defined by short, horizontal throws designed to set
up longer passes downfield. The mid-1980s was the Walsh era in
professional football, just as today is the Bill Belichick era.

Walsh, with whom I had been close from his days at Stanford,
was intent on solving problems, on and off the field. In the early
'80s, when drugs were rampant in the league, he walked into my
office one day as determined as I ever saw him on the sidelines.

"Can you sort of walk me through the whole concept of marijuana and cocaine?" he asked. I spent the next hour or two giving
Bill an overview of the types of controlled substances that were
commonly used.

Bill was very interested in acquiring Steve. Listening to his
pitch, I realized he was a genius in more ways than one. "Joe Montana's back is so bad," he told me, "I don't think he is going to play
anymore."

That was certainly news to me, and I was as connected as anyone in the game. I'd figured Montana, who missed eight games in
the prior season with a ruptured disk, would make a full recovery.

"Bill," I said, "Joe Montana is the high priest of the Bay Area."

I lived in the area and *I* loved Montana, and I didn't even represent him. Jon, my four-year-old son, worshipped Joe. After he was traded, when Steve playfully asked Jon who his favorite quarterback was, my son didn't worry about hurting his feelings. Steve cracked up.

"There is no way," I added, "after the two experiences Steve had, we are going to have him play in San Francisco if Montana is there."

Bill acknowledged my point and went back to presenting his case. That was Bill Walsh. He never quit.

"I will turn him into the most productive quarterback in the NFL," Bill said. "He will make the Pro Bowl under me and learn to be a pocket passer with an escape dimension rather than being perceived as a pure running QB. In my system, he will throw for a high percentage and he will go to Super Bowls. He will end up in the Hall of Fame. Montana will be retired."

I almost felt like shouting, *Sold to the gentleman from San Francisco.*

Bill first held a secret workout for Steve in Provo. That sealed it. I approached Culverhouse again. "We want to go to San Francisco," I told him.

Culverhouse made it happen in late April of 1987, shipping Steve to the 49ers for a second-round and fourth-round choice and $1 million in cash. By settling for less than he could have received from another team, Culverhouse was true to his word. For the third time in four years, Steve was headed to a new start.

In 1986, I also represented UCLA wide receiver Mike Sherrard, the first-round pick (No. 18) of the Dallas Cowboys. The Cowboys in the pre–Jerry Jones era, to put it gently, weren't the most open-minded people to deal with. Their attitude was that a player should feel divinely blessed to suit up for the franchise with the blue star on the helmet and therefore accept whatever terms they offered. "America's Team" was not just a marketing tool. They believed it.

Mike held his own strong beliefs, and one of them was that he should be paid his fair market value. After Mike turned down the team's proposal, Cowboys vice president Joe Bailey asked to meet him in person. Bailey assumed, as management often does, that the reason the two sides failed to come to terms surely must be that the agent wasn't passing on accurate information. If the agent were, the theory goes, the player would recognize how generous the offer was. In 1981, when Ronnie Lott, the future Hall of Fame safety, was drafted by San Francisco, Bill Walsh asked his friend John Robinson, Lott's coach at USC, to tell him that the deal the 49ers were offering was strong and that his agent was unreasonable.

I was very reluctant to abide by Bailey's request, but, understanding Mike, I made an exception.

The son of a professor at Chico State, several hours north of San Francisco, Mike was extremely bright, if perhaps a bit aloof till he knew someone well. After that he was very affable. Early during the recruitment process, whenever I phoned to ask him a few questions, the silence seemed endless. His father was no more communicative. People have a tendency to become unnerved with silence at the other end of a conversation, but it is important to resist the temptation to fill it by saying the wrong thing. Sometimes, when you have said all you can to a recruit, or during contract negotiations, the best move is to wait and see what develops.

Mike wouldn't be intimidated by the aura of the Cowboys. Training camp in Thousand Oaks, California, would start without him.

"I don't think you accurately understand how good a deal we're doing for you," Bailey told Mike.

"I understand every detail, and I know exactly what people in my situation were getting paid last year," he responded.

I was proud of Mike. Do players feel tremendous pressure to sign a deal? Yes. Can the other side hold out much longer? For sure. Do you just cave in? No way.

Day after day went by with no progress. Meanwhile, Mike worked out in Westwood, about an hour south of Thousand Oaks.

Finally, with little hope of reaching a compromise, and the Cowboys about to embark on a trip to London for an exhibition game, Bailey called with a rather novel idea.

"Let's take the difference between your offer and our offer [about $300,000] and flip for it," he said. He suggested a good spot would be on the tarmac at the airport before the Cowboys' plane took off.

Flip for it? A man's livelihood was to be determined, not which team would receive the opening kickoff.

Nonetheless, I told him I would relay the offer to Mike. That is my duty as an agent, no matter how ridiculous I think an offer might be.

"Are they crazy?" Mike asked.

I decided to play devil's advocate. That's another part of my job.

"Well, let's give it some thought, because who knows if they will ever change their mind," I said.

No, Mike said, let's not, and he was right.

The agreement we eventually reached, worth about $1.5 million, was much closer to our proposal than the Cowboys' at the time Bailey mentioned the coin flip.

I was always regretful when my players held out, especially quarterbacks, because even if the player achieves his financial goals, he loses. Missing any camp may affect how quickly he is able to start the first year and how his career unfolds. In Mike's case, though, I felt no regrets. Mike deserved every dollar the Cowboys would give him.

A year later, it looked like I'd have another holdout, University of Michigan quarterback Jim Harbaugh, chosen in the first round by the Bears.

I met Jim in the winter when I traveled to Ann Arbor, although the day did not go as smoothly as I hoped. Throwing a bunch of quarters into a pay phone, I gave him a call when I landed at the airport in Detroit, roughly thirty minutes away. No answer.

I stopped at a café once I arrived in Ann Arbor. No answer. I went to his house and banged on the door. You guessed it, no answer.

Waiting for Jim was not that unusual. I waited for players constantly. Every agent does. I once waited for hours in the St. Louis airport for a lineman who never did show up, and that was back in the day when I had no money. With nowhere to go, I slept on the floor near one of the gates.

After fifteen minutes, I gave up on Jim and took a little tour of the campus. Once I was certain I had the right day, I headed back to his place and tried again. This time, I pounded on the door. Still no answer.

Finally, I detected a faint voice that sounded like it belonged to an old man. "I'll be there in a minute."

The door opened, very slowly, and it was Jim, all right, peeking his head out, dressed in a white sheet as if he had just returned from a toga party, sweat pouring off his forehead.

"I'm sorry, but I can't meet," he said. "I have the flu."

"Jim, I empathize with you, but I flew all the way from California just to see you," I told him. "Do you think you might be able to pull it together for a few minutes?"

He gave me the blank stare he's known for now as a head coach but agreed to meet. The two of us had a productive chat, and I became his agent.

Working out a deal for Jim proved to be just as challenging. Being selected by the Bears meant dealing with team executive Ted Phillips and coach Mike Ditka. I knew we'd better get Jim into camp on time or Ditka, famous for his temper and lack of tolerance for agents and holdouts, would have a fit.

We finally made some headway with Phillips. Taking turns, Jeff Moorad and I spent fourteen straight hours with him on the phone. At one point, I left the office and went home and slept, only to return the next morning to find Jeff still on the phone talking to Ted. We still did not close the deal, and the start of camp was just a few days away.

I could almost hear Ditka getting ready to erupt.

Jim and I headed to Dubuque, Iowa, about twenty miles from Platteville, Wisconsin, where the Bears trained. I called Phillips after we arrived. He reminded me unsigned players were not allowed to participate in camp.

"I know the rules," I said. "I just thought we should meet in person to get this deal done as quickly as possible." Phillips agreed.

On the way, Jim and I got into a conversation about Al Capone, of all people, probably because we were close to Chicago, where Capone and others in organized crime became legendary. It dawned on me: What if we purchased a few machine guns that squirted water, then stormed into Phillips's office pretending to be gangsters from the 1920s? I suspected Phillips, from our prior conversations, had a pretty good sense of humor—at least, I hoped so.

He sure did. Phillips cracked up when we sprayed him, and the prank broke the tension. (Given the outbreak of tragic shootings in recent years, I obviously would not be insensitive in that way today.) By the end of the day, we reached an agreement and Jim reported for duty. There would be no rant from Ditka.

In September, with my clients under contract, the 1987 season got under way. Two weeks later, the players went on strike.

No one was shocked. Five years had passed since a similar work stoppage, which went on for fifty-seven days and reduced the season to nine games. The NFL Players Association had sought the type of unrestricted free agency baseball players had enjoyed for over a decade. The NFL owners were willing to concede on some issues, but they were not willing to surrender the tight grip they'd had on player movement forever. In their view, playing in the NFL was a privilege, not a right. The concessions would come years later, and professional football would never be the same.

The strike in 1987 was much different than the strike in 1982 for one simple reason: The owners hired replacement players this time. The games would go on.

NFL players are paid their entire salary spread over the course of sixteen games plus a bye week. That means that if they were to miss four games, they would lose 25 percent of their yearly salary. Moreover, since they were paid only between September and January, and few budgeted their income very well throughout the remainder of the year, any missed payments caused a lot of stress.

The replacement games were played in NFL stadiums, with team uniforms, network broadcasts and graphics, and regular announcers. To many viewers, the games looked almost normal. Yet as valiantly as NFLPA leaders Gene Upshaw, Dick Berthelsen, and Doug Allen fought, the players started to cross the picket lines. No one would confuse them with the vanguard of the Bolshevik Revolution. They were sons of coaches, born-again Christians, brought up playing a disciplined sport. This was not baseball, with a history of winning strikes where older players reassured younger ones that they would win if they held the line. This was the sport with the the shortest career span, nonguaranteed contracts, and the ever-present specter of injury. The strike collapsed, and the players were once again under the sole control of the owners. What they could not win through striking, they would later win through the courts.

In '88, I represented two first-round picks, both, naturally, from California: USC offensive guard Dave Cadigan (No. 8, New York Jets) and UCLA running back Gaston Green (No. 14, Los Angeles Rams).

Their backgrounds couldn't have been more different. Dave was the son of a wealthy white businessman from Newport Beach; Gaston was the son of a black teacher from Watts. This epitomized what

I always wanted my practice to be: a place where the only qualifications that mattered were talent and character.

I worked hard, as usual, to recruit Gaston—as it turned out, harder than necessary. "Gaston," I said, "it would be really good for me to know which parts of the presentation worked and which parts didn't. That would help me a lot with future clients."

He looked at me in disbelief. "Leigh, I've been following your career since I was a little boy," he said. "I always knew that I wanted you to be my agent."

That draft day meant as much to me as any ever would. The two players and their proud families, numbering around fifty, gathered at my parents' house in West Los Angeles to await the official word. This was still during the days before the top picks assembled in New York to shake hands with the commissioner and put on their new caps before the TV cameras.

The front page of the following day's sports section in the *Los Angeles Times* featured two pictures in color: one of me with Dave and his family, the other of me celebrating with Gaston and his loved ones.

The *Times* was the paper I couldn't wait to read each day before I left for school. My brothers and I fought with Dad for the sports page. I was particularly inspired by the legendary Jim Murray, whose columns I put into a scrapbook. The pieces he wrote about me decades later meant more than any others.

"Well, son," Dad said, "I think you had a pretty fair morning."

I sure did, and having Dad share it with me was the best part.

9

TROY AND JERRY

They both came into my life at roughly the same time, both of them tenacious and ultracompetitive, driven to bring a franchise in decline back to prominence. They collided on occasion, as most people with strong wills do, but there is little doubt neither would have succeeded without the other.

I met Troy Aikman in the late winter of 1989 when he was living in an apartment about a half mile from my parents' house. After years of taking planes and renting cars, to travel by foot to visit a potential client was a refreshing change. In that initial meeting, I came away as impressed with Troy as I had been with Warren and Steve. Not only was he the premier quarterback prospect in America, he was, like the other two, brighter than a twenty-two-year-old had the right to be. He had a wry sense of humor and might have possessed the least tolerance for phoniness of any athlete I ever met.

He also surrounded himself with astute advisers. Many of my quarterbacks did. Playing the position with the highest profile, they constantly befriended alums on campus and in the community who, well connected in business, law, and other professions, adopted a keen interest in the players' futures. In Troy's case, these men, from the oil and gas industries, acted as a screening committee, and among their most critical tasks in the early days was to select the right agent. The wrong one could set Troy back for years.

I met with them in Oklahoma City and knew I had to be in top form. They would interview me as if I were applying for a job, which I was.

The questions kept coming. "How would you cope with the pressure in Dallas?"

"Have you ever been fired?"

"What is the size of your practice?"

"Do you handle endorsements?"

On and on the interview went, Troy sitting quietly, ignoring the barrage by reading a newspaper. I couldn't decide if that was a good sign or a bad sign. For all I knew, I could have been just one of four or five agents going through the process. Only later did I conclude Troy had already made up his mind. The job was mine as long as I cleared this one last hurdle, and I did.

In early 1989, it became increasingly clear that the Cowboys, after a disastrous 3-13 season, needed a franchise quarterback desperately. They had not had one since Roger Staubach left the game in 1980. That's a long drought for any team, let alone America's Team.

However, it would not be the triumvirate that had ruled Cowboy Nation forever making the final call—coach Tom Landry, president and general manager Tex Schramm, and vice president of player personnel Gil Brandt. Each of them had favored drafting Troy, creating something called "Aikmania" to rally Dallas fans after he completed 19 of 27 passes for 172 yards in leading the Bruins to a convincing 17–3 triumph over a very talented Arkansas squad in the Cotton Bowl.

Now there would be only one man in charge, Jerry Jones, and he would be in charge, all right. His famous line after taking over was that he would be involved in every aspect of the franchise from "socks to jocks," and no one has ever doubted that to be the case. One of his first moves was to hire his good friend Jimmy Johnson, who played with him on the University of Arkansas team that won the national championship in 1964. Jimmy, who coached Miami to an NCAA title in 1987, wasted little time. He set up a throwing session for Troy at UCLA. Any doubts that the new regime would pick him ended in those forty-five minutes. Short, deep, posts, outs, curls, whatever the route, Troy mastered each one.

I first got to know Jerry, who had just returned from visiting President George H. W. Bush, when Troy and I met with him, his son Steve, his business partner, Mike McCoy, and Jimmy at the team's offices in Texas.

Going in, I was aware of how dealing with an owner one-on-one was vastly different from speaking to a general manager or other top executive. These men became billionaires by reaching goals in the free market system they had been told were impossible. They can be convinced to make a decision that has been rationally demonstrated to advance their interests, or they can become intractable and intransigent in ways that impact players profoundly. When I arrived in Texas, I elected not to press Jerry regarding his comment to reporters that Troy and I needed to cut our "asking price" in half before any agreement was possible. We hadn't uttered a word about any asking price.

The discussion, at first, was harmless, revolving around three other passions in the Lone Star State besides football—fishing, hunting, and riding horses. I'd been reading six newspapers a day and a wide variety of magazines, so I was able to participate easily. I often tell aspiring agents to keep up on pop culture, politics, and business to develop more common ground with other people. Knowing the world of sports is not enough.

At 1:00 A.M., after a late dinner in a 1950s-style malt shop at our hotel, we finally began to talk the business of football. People soon left, one by one, until about four, when it was just Jerry and I lounging on two large chairs in the lobby. We did not stop until around seven, and we were not even negotiating. The carpet cleaners came by at one point, and Jerry, in his usual assertive manner, told them to go clean somewhere else.

I quickly realized I had found the kindred soul who could help take the NFL to its true potential. The NFL had surpassed baseball in popularity, but I felt it had the capacity to dominate entertainment in America. An owner such as Jerry, who was brilliant, creative, and open to new ideas, could be a wonderful partner.

The growth of football and player salaries had been kept back for too long by rigid, in-the-box thinking. The challenge in the NFL should never have been labor versus management in self-destructive public battles. The real challenge was to take on the NBA, Major League Baseball, Home Box Office, Walt Disney World, and every other form of discretionary entertainment spending. Sports does not provide fans with food on the table or transportation to work. Sports is entertainment the public can choose or reject. Our job, therefore, should be as stewards who build the brand. Any negative collective bargaining dispute pitting billionaires against millionaires evokes little sympathy, and any stoppage of games being played breaks the bond between the sport and the public. Players complaining they can't survive on $10 million alienate fans with a median family income of $50,000. Conversely, when there is labor stability in the NFL, the focus can be on driving television revenue, utilizing social media, monetizing stadiums, and coming up with other ideas to enhance the fan's total experience.

I told Jerry he had the best brand in football and it could become the most valuable entertainment franchise in the world if he could tap into all the ways to spread it. We talked about the changing world of the computer, fantasy sports, a potential NFL network, and naming rights. It was exhilarating. Having a marquee quarterback with movie-star looks and a name out of Central Casting—Troy Aikman—set the basis for a productive relationship and would make carving an expansive pie much less contentious.

Bob Kraft, who would become the owner of the New England Patriots a few years later, possessed the same pioneering spirit and vision. So did future owners Dan Snyder, a freewheeling entrepreneur (Redskins), imaginative Jeffrey Lurie (Eagles), and brilliant businessman Arthur Blank (Falcons). These men assembled information from every source they could find about what it took to build a winning organization. What is the key to a successful general manager or personnel evaluator? What are the most advanced training techniques? What are the critical qualities in a coach? They were secure and committed to excellence enough to listen. My job was to envision an owner's interests and offer helpful suggestions on how to best achieve them. We would certainly have differences on a player's compensation, but they paled in comparison to the common interest of building the revenue and popularity of the game. The fact that I represented the starting quarterbacks or key players on many teams gave me better entrée. I began to sit with the owners during the games, and they became close friends.

The key to expanding the NFL was the television contract. Owners such as Art Modell thought the $17 million per team per season they were receiving from television in the current contract was unbelievably inflated, which was why they wanted to extend the deal with the same terms before the networks pushed back hard for lower amounts. Teams had received only $2 million apiece in 1976, so I understood the owners' perspective.

I had, however, held a Super Bowl party on the back lot of 20th Century Fox Studios where Rupert Murdoch told me he would be interested in bidding on the NFL when it became available. Cable and satellite were turning three networks into hundreds. I knew they would bid more money on rights fees than they could recoup in advertising in order to have Sunday afternoon or night games promote their Monday through Friday programming. Such promotion would dramatically multiply the value of the network. No offense, but outside of *The Simpsons* and *Beverly Hills 90210,* who had any idea what shows were on Fox?

The extension was going to be raised at the NFL league meetings at the Biltmore Hotel in Phoenix in the early '90s. I went there with a set of potential revenue projections based on open bidding that showed the amazing wealth that could be achieved and how that revenue would substantially raise franchise values and salaries. Owners with a similar mindset were able to block the extension, and the process was opened up. Fox, TNT, and ESPN jumped into the bidding. The next contract was for about $35 million per team. It later jumped to $73 million. In 2012, each team earned well over $100 million from its share of the national media package.

Jerry was a hard-nosed businessman who could deal with any amount of criticism. There was universal mourning and condemnation following his abrupt dismissal of Coach Landry, the only head coach in franchise history, who brought the city two Super Bowl championships and the status of America's Team. As much as Jerry believed in Troy as a savior, he wasn't about to hand him a blank check. Jerry Jones did not hand a blank check to anyone.

In mid-April, shortly before the draft, Jerry attempted to leverage us. "We're not going into the first draft without signing our first pick," he said. "If you don't take what we're offering, we'll draft Tony Mandarich."

Tony was a very gifted 6'6" 315-pound offensive tackle from Michigan State. He would make any team better. He would not, however, lead the Cowboys back to the Super Bowl. There is no such thing as a franchise offensive tackle.

I don't recall what Jerry offered, but it was not enough.

"Jerry, if that is what you think is right, please go ahead and do it," I said, "and make sure to put Tony on the cover of your press guide and have him as the center of your season ticket program, because people are really inspired by your rebuilding of the team around an offensive lineman."

Jerry got the point. He always did.

Shortly afterward, two days before the draft, we reached an agreement: six years, $11.2 million, the most lucrative rookie contract ever, $3 million more than Vinny Testaverde received in 1987.

"This deal is going to make me look ridiculous," he said, "in comparison to past draft picks. I'm new. Other owners will think I'm crazy."

I couldn't have disagreed more. It was never in my interests to do a onetime deal that appeared so outrageous it would expose an owner to public ridicule or create financial problems. I would likely need to work with him over and over again. Even Steve Young's package would have made economic sense if the USFL owners had demonstrated more patience.

Troy and I were the ones at risk.

"In three or four years," I assured Jerry, "Troy will be underpaid. The whole world will think you got a steal."

I told him the combination of explosive growth in television revenue combined with eventual free agency would make all current salary numbers appear obsolete. Our outstanding staff, lead by attorney Scott Parker, had assembled projections, which would prove accurate.

With the deal completed and a press conference imminent—Jerry's first major one as the owner of the Dallas Cowboys—he asked me, "How should we characterize the contract?"

"A lot of owners," I said, "say 'terms not disclosed' when the question is asked by the media, but I have never understood that.

You have the opportunity here to show your commitment to the franchise and get the benefit from having spent the money."

What did Jerry do? He did what makes him Jerry Jones. He exhibited the type of showmanship that would define his long reign in Dallas. He understood he was not merely in the football business. He was in the entertainment business. Not for a moment did he try to conceal the specifics of the contract. Jerry made everything in life appear bigger than anyone else did.

"This is the largest rookie contract in the history of football," Jerry said, "and we're proud to pay it because we got the best player."

Troy and I flew to New York on the team plane with Steve Jones and his sister, Charlotte, for the formal announcement of the pick by Pete Rozelle. It was his last draft after nearly thirty years as commissioner.

We were still floating on air, even after the plane touched down at JFK. We went to see *Phantom of the Opera* with Charlotte and Steve, who were remarkably poised for being in their early twenties, but I was worried about Troy's response. I didn't need to be; he loved the show. Troy could not wait to follow in the footsteps of Roger Staubach, and I had my first No. 1 overall pick since Bart in 1975. This time, I would have a chance to be with the player on draft day, which made the occasion even sweeter.

Two months later we recieved a shock. The Cowboys used the first pick in the supplemental draft to select another potential franchise quarterback, and not just any quarterback. They chose Steve Walsh from the University of Miami, who led the Hurricanes to a 23-1 mark in two seasons as a starter, including a national title in 1987. Walsh became available after skipping his last year of eligibility. Most alarming was that Jimmy Johnson coached Walsh in college.

Troy and I thought back to all the wonderful conversations with Jimmy and Jerry and Steve Jones about their plans to build a team around him. How could we believe another word now? At least Hugh Culverhouse waited two years to select another quarterback in Tampa. Jerry Jones waited two months.

I called Jerry.

"You have to trust me we're doing the best we can, and that Troy is our guy," he said.

The Cowboys certainly had a strange way of showing it.

Jerry went on to assure me the team would end up trading Walsh. Perhaps. Nonetheless, drafting him, in my opinion, was destined to generate a quarterback controversy, one that could have easily been avoided, and Troy was facing enough pressure trying to be the savior for a franchise rebuilding from the bottom without Walsh breathing down his neck.

Camp started several weeks later, and Troy and Walsh engaged in a fierce battle for the starting job. I almost wished Jerry had taken Tony Mandarich.

Troy won the job and Dallas went 3-1 in the preseason. Fans thought perhaps the Cowboys would be the Cowboys of old sooner rather than later, but their heroes began the season 0-8 before knocking off the Redskins, 13–3, and then lost their last seven to finish 1-15. Troy threw 9 touchdowns and 18 interceptions. Until the Washington game, the joke was that if Jerry Jones purchased the 7-Eleven franchise, it would change its name to 0-and-11. So awful were the 'Boys that an exasperated Troy once told me, "I had more talent on my UCLA team."

I asked him if I there was anything I could do.

"Nothing," said Troy, showing the toughness that would later separate him from his peers. "I just want them to give me the ball. I will know what to do with it."

Months later, though, there was something he wanted me to do, and it was fairly drastic.

"You have to get me out of here," he said.

I didn't blame Troy. The team wasn't showing any signs of improvement, and—surprise, surprise—Steve Walsh had not been traded. Yet I was certain Dallas was still the best place for him and made my case.

"Do you believe Jimmy Johnson is a good coach?" I asked Troy.

"Yes."

"Do you believe Jerry Jones is very bright and creative?"

"Yes."

"They have a great computer," I continued. "What's missing is that they just don't have any intel yet. They don't know how to draft players and make trades, but don't you think they'll catch on? And for somebody who went to high school in Oklahoma and loves country music, is there a better place for you to fit into than Dallas, Texas?"

End of discussion.

Jerry and Jimmy caught on, all right, and quickly. The Cowboys, with Troy, running back Emmitt Smith, and wide receiver Michael Irvin, won the Super Bowl in 1993, 1994, and 1996.

Troy improved dramatically thanks to Cowboys offensive coordinator Norv Turner, who helped him refine his technique. More significantly, Norv became a close friend who made Troy feel it was no longer him against the world. No wonder Troy would pick him to be his presenter at the Hall of Fame.

Troy's growth as a leader was even more impressive. The Dallas team of the early 1990s featured more than its share of unpredictable characters, lead by Irvin and linebacker Charles Haley. Somebody had to keep the inmates under control. A head coach, even one as driven as Jimmy Johnson, can only do so much. Each team needs several players to take charge, especially its quarterback. Troy assumed the role with no hesitation.

People thought his public persona—he never provided bulletin board material for the opposition—was bland. They didn't know the real fire in Troy's personality, but his teammates did.

Troy was never in better form than at the Rose Bowl in Pasadena, when he won his first Super Bowl. I was stunned, and not just at his performance. What hit me the most was how, in the course of just three hours, a player's entire legacy can change so profoundly. He walked on the field against Buffalo on January 31, 1993, as Troy Aikman, the Dallas Cowboy quarterback. He walked off as TROY AIKMAN, MVP, SUPERSTAR. As I told him in the limo on the way back to the hotel in Santa Monica, his life would never be the same.

There were, as usual, drawbacks to success. A few days later, Troy flew to Hawaii for the Pro Bowl. He wasn't too thrilled about playing the game in the first place. Few players are. They cherish the honor of being selected for the squad and enjoy being in Hawaii, but to suit up with nothing at stake and risk a serious injury is not their idea of a good time. One day, during a break between his obligations as the Super Bowl MVP when he finally had a minute to himself, Troy was walking by a wading pool at the Hilton Hawaiian Village Hotel. A minute is about all he had. A crowd began to press against him. Troy stepped back and back until he was pushed fully dressed into the pool.

Jerry, on the other hand, has never shied away from the spotlight. He is a powerful draw. It serves his interest to bring awareness to the Cowboys brand whenever he can. I sat in his box in Dallas on a number of occasions during the '90s, and once at a playoff game in San Francisco, which didn't enthrall Eddie DeBartolo, the 49ers' owner, also a good friend. At one stage, the TV camera showed me sitting next to former president George H. W. Bush.

"What the hell were you doing sitting in Jerry Jones's box?" DeBartolo asked. "You've got Steve Young, Tim McDonald, Gary Plummer, Merton Hanks, Eric Davis, and Brent Jones as clients, and you're sitting with our archrivals?"

"Eddie, this is like the Civil War for me, and I love both teams," I assured him. "Besides, Jerry asked me first."

Jerry brought fresh ideas and a pioneering spirit back to the NFL, and his influence has been historic. He hasn't been back to the Super Bowl since '96, but from what I can tell, Jerry still runs the show in Cowboy Nation from "socks to jocks."

God bless him.

10

LEADING THE DRAFT

If I thought Troy performed well in his workout at UCLA with Jimmy Johnson, it paled in comparison to the demonstration put on one year later, in 1990, by the next can't-miss quarterback prospect, Jeff George.

Jeff, a high school hero in Indianapolis, started out at Purdue but transferred after his freshman season to the University of Illinois, where in 1989 he threw for 2,738 yards and 22 touchdowns in leading the Fighting Illini to a 10-2 mark and a win in the Citrus Bowl. He was still only a junior, but due to a new rule permitting players to leave for the pros three years after the graduation of their high school class, Jeff, who sat out a year when he transferred, was now eligible for the NFL.

Whether Jeff would come out was another matter. His coach, John Mackovic, did not think he should, and he supported his opinion with feedback from various NFL teams. He told Jeff he would likely be drafted no higher than the second round.

Jeff asked me what I thought. With respect to Coach Mackovic, who laid out a strong case, my take was a little different. "It is impossible, with your skill set and the need for franchise quarterbacks in the NFL, that you won't get drafted in the first round," I

said. "If I were John Mackovic and I had the choice between recruiting you to stay one more year or going out and recruiting a
brand-new quarterback, I'd use everything at my command to keep
you in college."

Mackovic felt no differently than other coaches who don't want
to let go of their precious talent until they have no choice. The new
rule created tension between colleges and the pros. Lou Holtz became so furious he banned scouts from practices in South Bend. I
never advised the parents of juniors that their sons should leave
early, telling them only how high I projected they would go *if* they
were to come out. I didn't want a player to look back at age fifty
and regret the loss of his senior year.

My view was that players should be able to turn pro at any
point during their collegiate careers. Of course, I wish every young
person in the United States would go to college and graduate, but
for a lot of these "student-athletes," there is nothing in the study of
Near Eastern religions or the Pythagorean theorem that is necessary to tackle a running back for a 5-yard loss. I think we should
focus instead on the students who want to be in school and ensure
their graduation rates are as close to 100 percent as possible. Keeping disinterested athletes trapped in college leads to discontent,
making them more susceptible to bribes from boosters or agents.
Over time, even if at first more students left school after their
freshman or sophomore year to play pro football, the new trend
would not last. The first wave of underclassmen to enter the pros
would realize their bodies were not mature enough to handle the
pounding. The first wave would most likely be the last wave.

Jeff chose to turn professional, and as his throwing session,
which is the most critical factor in evaluating quarterbacks, proved,
it was the right decision.

You can dissect a quarterback from here until doomsday, and
praise him for the so-called intangibles of character and resiliency,
but they don't mean a thing unless he has a strong arm and is

accurate. If he does not possess those qualities, he will not be rated highly by the scouts. In the past, a quarterback could get by with a below-average arm as long as he converted the short and intermediate routes. Today, he also has to be able to make the deep throw.

Andre Ware, another client of mine, the Heisman Trophy winner whom the Detroit Lions selected at No. 7 in that same 1990 draft, didn't last long in the league. I once asked a scout why Andre, a remarkably gifted and intelligent athlete, wasn't more successful.

"He wasn't accurate enough," the scout said.

If that was the case, I probed further, how did he compile numerous records in college?

"It was a different level of competition," he explained.

Jeff was uncannily accurate. In a fifty-minute workout for scouts on the University of Illinois campus, he made every route look simple. The football never touched the ground. The scouts walked off in awe, one after another proclaiming it the best throwing they had even seen from a quarterback. They later referred to it as the $15 million workout video, because that's what Jeff signed for.

In 1990, the No. 1 pick belonged to the Falcons. There were similarities to Bart from fifteen years earlier. Same city. Same team in shambles. Same skill set for a quarterback—powerful arm, quick release—at the top of the draft. There was only one problem with the comparison: Atlanta wanted Jeff, but Jeff didn't want Atlanta.

When I asked him to list his top priorities, he did not hesitate for a second.

"Number one, I'd like to be the first player picked in the first round," he said. "Number two, I'd like to be the highest-paid rookie ever, and number three, I know they don't have a first-round draft pick, but I'd like to play in Indianapolis." Anything else, Jeff?

Talk about a tough assignment. Besides having no pick of their own to use as trade bait, the Colts already had a promising quarterback, Chris Chandler, still only twenty-four, as well as Jack Trudeau, who took over when Chandler was hurt in 1989 and also hadn't yet entered his prime. On the plus side, in charge of the Colts was my friend Jim Irsay. Jim attended Jeff's famous throwing session. He was as blown away as anybody else and decided on the spot he was game for a deal. Now it was just a matter of persuading the Falcons to go along.

On April 19 the Colts and Falcons reached a tentative agreement. For the No. 1 pick, Indianapolis would send offensive tackle Chris Hinton, wide receiver Andre Rison, and two of its own choices, including a first-rounder in 1991, to Atlanta. The trade, a steep one for the Colts—Hinton was a six-time All-Pro, and Rison caught 52 passes in 1989, his rookie season—was contingent on Jim and I coming to terms on a contract for Jeff within roughly twenty-four hours. Deals of such magnitude often do not get completed in twenty-four *days*.

We went right to work, the hours drifting by, dawn fast approaching. Jim made a run to the local Steak 'n Shake. He might have broken an all-time record for the place, purchasing well over $100 worth of food and beverages.

Jim and I made plenty of progress, but there was one problem: He wasn't the only Irsay I needed to satisfy. On this occasion, with a lot more on the line for both the Colts and myself, the elder Irsay again proved to be obstinate. He called over and over to object to various elements of the deal after Jim and I had reached an agreement. After three or four interruptions, I started to seriously doubt we'd settle our differences before the deadline.

Somehow, we did, around 5:30 A.M. The terms for Jeff George— six years for $15 million, including a $3.5 million bonus—were even more attractive than the ones for Troy. Jeff, believe it or not, was also set to earn more than Marino, Montana, and Elway.

Only a few months later, though, his chances of making an

immediate impact in Indianapolis took a big hit, and it wasn't his fault.

The culprit was the team's star running back, Eric Dickerson, who had recently become a client. I thought he was the best runner in football and had rooted for him when he played for the Rams. After two full years in Indy, Eric hoped to be traded to, of all places, Atlanta. There was nothing wrong with that. Where Eric made a mistake, a substantial one, was to go public with his discontent and demand to be dealt. Bringing it up in the open is almost a guarantee *not* to be traded. The minute other teams discover a player is unhappy, they'll attempt to acquire him for a significantly lesser price, making it harder for any transaction to occur.

Nonetheless, with training camp about to open, I was close to getting Eric what he wanted. All he had to do was report like everyone else, but he wouldn't.

"If I report, they'll have me trapped," Eric said, "and then they'll never trade me."

"Eric," I said, "it's all been worked out. I have the word of the owner."

He didn't believe me. He stayed away from camp. Instead, Eric believed the word of people around him, his posse, another mistake too many athletes commit.

"You hired me to tell you the truth," I said. "The truth is you are surrounded by sycophants who will cheer and second anything you say no matter how irrational or self-destructive it might be. If you were standing on the ledge of the ninetieth floor of a building and were about to jump, they would say the law of gravity doesn't apply to you. Go ahead and show them they're wrong."

In late August, Eric was suspended by the Colts and lost a significant amount of his salary. He also lost me as his agent, which sent a clear message to people around the league about what our firm stood for: abiding by one's contract. I also felt his stance was a tremendous waste of time and money.

I failed as well to convince him to trust I was giving him the best advice. He was doing what he thought was in his best interest.

Jeff did not have the greatest time in Indianapolis, either. A major reason was that the Colts, in exchanging Hinton and Rison to acquire him, parted with the very two components he needed to thrive, someone to protect him in the pocket and someone to catch his passes.

It turned into a classic case of unintended consequences. He figured playing at home, where his friends and family lived, would be a refuge whenever times got tough, as they invariably do in the NFL. Instead, Jeff learned playing at home can be a burden. If you fail somewhere else, you can always return home to lead a normal life. In this case, there was no escape. Jeff *was* home, and the fans were highly critical. He could handle it himself, but he felt very protective when the attacks extended to his family. They couldn't go to a 7-Eleven without somebody bringing up the latest defeat.

In the summer of '93, Jeff failed to show up for camp while he was still under contract. The local Taco Bell proclaimed, "Jeff George has made a run for the border." An especially nasty T-shirt showed Jeff in a playpen sucking his thumb; the caption read MOMMY WON'T LET ME COME TO TRAINING CAMP.

In 1994, he was sent to the franchise he spurned before, the Falcons, where he matured as a quarterback and finally fulfilled his promise, throwing for 47 touchdowns his first two years. Jeff was ready to sign a long-term deal, but team president Taylor Smith didn't envision Jeff as the quarterback of the future. He was traded again, this time to the Raiders, where he played well once more. Only this time, Jon Gruden took over as coach, and he wanted a more mobile quarterback. Then, after Jeff made a strong showing with Minnesota in 1999, the Vikings switched to their top draft pick,

Daunte Culpepper. Once again, we needed a new team for Jeff. After running into Dan Snyder at the league meetings, I signed him to the Redskins, but coach Norv Turner didn't want him, either. Jeff never could quite find the right fit.

In the category of frustrated quarterbacks in the early 1990s, no one can match Steve Young. In Los Angeles, a member of the doomed Express, he played his last home game at a community college. In Tampa, he lasted for just two seasons before the Bucs drafted Vinny Testaverde. Now, in perhaps the most discouraging environment yet, he sat on the bench in San Francisco, the years passing, the chances of putting up numbers and victories like his idol, Roger Staubach, fading away.

It was never supposed to be that way. Bill Walsh said so back in 1987 when he recruited Steve, and the last thing he wanted was a quarterback controversy. Bill truly believed Montana was done, and I believed *him*. Otherwise, Steve and I would never have accepted the trade to San Francisco. Steve was a young, dynamic player. There were plenty of places where he could have been the starter, and succeeded—even, eventually, in Cincinnati!

Joe was done, all right. In 1987, he threw a career-high 31 touchdowns. Hardly the most physically gifted at his position, he was similar to Peyton Manning. Nobody worked harder or was more competitive. If Joe was anywhere near healthy, he'd fight like a junkyard dog to keep his job. That's just who he was, and the mere presence of Steve, ready to take his place, only motivated him further. Over the next three seasons, Joe started 41 of 48 regular-season games, leading the Niners to Super Bowl victories in 1989 and 1990. In that same stretch, Steve tossed 13 TDs of his own, but he remained the backup. What saved Steve was attending law school at BYU. He immersed himself in books instead of brooding.

Yet during the season, as supportive as he was, the despair was there, always.

"Leigh, I feel bad," Steve said while we were at a Chinese restaurant in Palo Alto. "I want you to know that you're not obligated to represent me anymore."

"What do you mean?" I asked.

"You expected me to be a big superstar," Steve said. "I'm just a backup. If you want out, I don't blame you."

Leaving Steve would never occur to me, no matter what happened—or did not happen—on the playing field. Our relationship was much deeper than agent to client. I loved him like a brother. Besides, I never lost faith. I was certain that once he got his chance, he would make the most of it.

In the fall of 1991, Steve did just that. With Joe recovering again, this time from a devastating elbow injury, Steve took over and led the NFL in passing with a rating of 101.8. He threw 17 touchdowns and averaged 14 yards per completion.

Many fans in the Bay Area, though, were not willing to accept Steve just yet as Joe's successor—certainly not while Joe still registered a pulse. The most rabid Joe fans behaved like Moonies. In their view, Joe Montana never missed a pass and never lost a game. Whenever Steve threw a pick, they would chime in, "Oh, Montana wouldn't do *that*." Steve didn't receive any help from Joe, either, except what he learned from watching Joe play well. Joe said Steve campaigned for the job. That was never the case.

I finally became so irritated that during an interview with the *San Francisco Chronicle,* I called for the 49ers to trade Steve, which was the only time I ever did that with any player I represented. One must understand how dominant pro football was in San Francisco during the '80s and '90s. If a third-string offensive lineman was injured, it was a front-page story. I felt I was doing my part to improve Steve's situation in a very unsettling atmosphere.

I discussed what I told the *Chronicle* with Steve afterward, and he was not exactly excited about it. Steve revered the entire 49ers organization, and with good reason.

From the gorgeous practice facilities to the first-class travel to the fact that Eddie DeBartolo truly liked his players—there were owners who didn't—the 49ers set the standard for class and winning in the NFL. For the 1989 Super Bowl in Miami against the Bengals, he chartered two jets, one for the families of the players, and then put the families up and provided them with a rental car to get around the city. Eddie was passionate about winning. He threw objects in his box when he was upset during a game, and he didn't speak to Bill Walsh for a few months after the Niners lost in the playoffs to the Vikings, but no owner treated his players better. The team also had a general manager in Carmen Policy, nicknamed "Charmin' Carmen," with a real gift for problem solving. He and I became very close.

"There are folks in the Bay Area who would rather lose with Montana than win with Young," I essentially told the paper. "Joe Montana might be the greatest quarterback who ever stepped onto a football field, and this is not disrespectful toward him, but to be in his shadow, and to not be acknowledged for one's own greatness, is not why anyone goes into sports."

My objective was simple: urge the people who favored Steve as the starter to come forward, and urge those who favored Joe to back off. If they felt Joe should start, then bring it up with the coach, who was now George Seifert, but stop blaming Steve. He wasn't doing anything wrong. He was, as a matter of fact, doing everything right.

Eventually, Joe, not Steve, was traded, in April of 1993, to the Kansas City Chiefs, where he finished his career.

Steve went on to prove the organization made the proper move, playing at an incredibly high level in 1992, 1993, and 1994. The moment I'll cherish forever came on January 29, 1995, at Joe Robbie Stadium in Miami. Steve had just tossed a record 6 TDs, leading his team to a 49–26 rout of the Chargers in Super Bowl XXIX. I saw him for a minute on the field immediately after the game.

We hugged. I was in tears. He was in heaven.

"The monkey is off my back," he shouted. "The monkey is off my back."

In 1991, for the third straight year, I represented the top overall pick in the draft, Russell Maryland, a warmhearted defensive tackle from the University of Miami, chosen by the Cowboys. He later established a foundation for underprivileged kids in Chicago, where he had been raised. Russell was brought up by one of the wisest and most compassionate couples (Jim and Rita) I had ever been around.

Russell did not set a record for rookie contracts, as Troy and Jeff did, but that was fine with him. He was just excited about playing for Dallas and being the No. 1 pick, thanks to "Rocket" Ismail, the game-changing Notre Dame runner/receiver/kick returner who signed with the Argonauts in the CFL. I also represented Eric Turner, the star defensive back from UCLA, taken second by the Browns. Having the two top picks for the first time was a real thrill. Russell and Eric got along very well, as my clients did within every draft class. They were embarking, together, on a new adventure.

On draft day, we rented a suite on the top floor of the Marriott on Fashion Island in Newport Beach, inviting dozens of family members, friends, coaches, and media who would not have been able to attend if Russell and Eric had gone to the ceremony in Manhattan. Watching these two young men share the day with the people who loved them, who sacrificed so much, made the occasion even more satisfying. It is their achievement as much as the player's.

There was plenty to celebrate.

Eric, in fact, received a better deal than Russell, though Russell still made more money than he would have if, as originally projected, he'd been chosen later in the draft.

With my success, there was a price, a significant one. It was a price I'd pay over and over, as other agents were more jealous than ever.

Just earlier, prior to the string of No. 1s, I was, believe it or not, among the more popular members of my profession. Sure, some resented me for the amount of press coverage I attracted in the late '70s, but by 1985 I was very active in ARPA (Association of Representatives of Professional Athletes). One year I was the president. When the USFL unraveled and NFL owners, seemingly acting in collusion, tried to roll back salaries, I convened a conference in Chicago, inviting every agent with a first-round pick. I stood in front with a chalkboard.

"Let's see who has the leverage here," I said. "Let's see what order makes the most sense to do these in, and we can help each other for all of our benefit."

Soon afterward, I advised an agent negotiating with the front office of the team I'd dealt with the year before. I thought we were colleagues. I was wrong. The agent, who worked for IMG, blasted me behind my back. IMG, I was told by people who had worked there, later put together a Nixonian enemies file on me. Representing elite athletes in just about every major sport, IMG resented the fact that I dominated the quarterback supply year after year with a staff of ten while they employed thousands.

Creating a file was one thing. Slandering my reputation was another. Yet that was what other agents did on a regular basis, and it happened long before I became an alcoholic. A prime example occurred when I recruited a player who stood an excellent chance of becoming the top pick in the draft, which would have, as it turned out, given me seven No. 1s in a row. After we hit it off, the player was ready to hire me. Even the paper in his college town reported the news. Well, weeks went by and I couldn't reach him. I'd never had a potential client vanish so mysteriously.

When I finally talked to him, I couldn't believe what he told me.

"I really wanted to sign with you," he said, "but another agent scared my dad. He told him he would be committing malpractice as a father if he let his son sign with Steinberg."

The player named the agent who had spread lies about me. I was not surprised. Ironically, that agent did not land the player, either.

The most vivid display of the animosity took place when one publication did a fairly extensive profile on me. The article itself did not bother me too much. It was filled with the familiar complaints: Steinberg craves publicity and does not care about his clients. I'd learned to ignore those unfounded attacks long ago. While almost half of the players in the league switched agents after their first deal expired, we lost very few, and the most prominent—Bartkowski, Aikman, Moon, Young, etc.—stuck with our firm for their entire careers.

What bothered me was when I discovered how the article came about in the first place. Another agency paid the writer a sizeable amount. How do I know? I know because a private eye I hired uncovered a check from the agency to the writer. It had seemed suspicious to me that a piece billed to be such a negative portrayal contained no substance. Something had to be wrong.

Did I confront the agency? No. I didn't consider it for a second. I remembered too well what transpired the last time, in the mid-'70s, when I played the role of crusader. I was not going to go through that humiliating experience again. I never confronted any of my enemies. Unable to imagine myself behaving in that manner, believing, as my parents taught me, that people were generally good, I would not have known what to say.

I could only control my own actions, which was why I was always extremely wary of taking on players represented by other firms. I knew how agonizing it felt to lose a client, and I didn't wish that fate on anybody, even my worst detractors. It was easy to lure in a dissatisfied player. Just stroke his ego. Tell him he's worth a lot more than what his current agent secured. Name one player who doesn't want to be flattered like that. Other agents play that game constantly. I represented one client who, on the plane to the Pro Bowl, was awakened by an agent to tell him how inadequate his contract was, and that he should fire me. He did not, and as a matter of fact, his contract was as favorable as it could be, given that he wasn't among the top 10 players in the draft. My hope is that a younger generation of agents with good values and ideals will change this pattern of behavior.

I was as cautious as ever when I received a call in the winter of 1990 from Derrick Thomas, the sensational Chiefs linebacker, who had recently finished his rookie season. Derrick said that after doing his own research in the library, he wanted me to represent him. That was a first. I was intrigued. I was also encouraged by how open he was to the idea of role modeling. Yet I told him what I would tell anybody, "Go back to your original agent and see if you can work it out. I don't want to be the guy who breaks up a happy marriage. If you are still interested next year, then call me back."

One year later, he did just that, and Derrick was a client for the rest of his eleven-year career.

He was unlike any other client I ever had. He had a troubled youth. Yet, with the support of a strong, loving mom—Derrick's father, an air force captain, was killed on a mission in Vietnam—he found something he loved, football, and it might have saved his life.

He made nine straight Pro Bowls for the Kansas City Chiefs, and in one game sacked quarterback Dave Krieg seven times. Derrick was larger than life with an effusive warmth that endeared him to hundreds of friends. Derrick committed his share of mistakes and would be the first to admit it, but he cared about having an impact, more off the field than on it. He testified before Congress on the plague of illiteracy, and at the Vietnam Veterans Memorial in D.C., standing next to President Clinton, he spoke passionately about his late father and the sacrifice he made for his country. Others who lost a parent in the war were deeply touched. He also established the Third and Long Foundation, which deals with children's dyslexia in Kansas City. In 1993, the NFL named Derrick its Man of the Year for his humanitarian work. I would not have been prouder of him if he had captured four MVP awards.

His death at the age of thirty-three in February of 2000 hurt more than I can ever describe. He had so much more to give. Derrick suffered spinal cord injuries in a car accident two weeks earlier, but when I visited him in the hospital, I saw glimpses of the man I loved: spirited, kindhearted, full of purpose. Then there was the blood clot no one saw coming and he was gone. I gave one of the eulogies at his funeral. I miss him terribly.

In the 1991 draft, I represented two very talented QBs: Dan McGwire (Mark's younger brother) from San Diego State, who went at No. 16 to the Seattle Seahawks, and Louisville's Browning Nagle, picked in the second round by the Jets. Another quarterback in that draft was USC's Todd Marinovich, chosen by the Raiders. I met with Marinovich and his family, but he signed with another agent.

For a while, it appeared I might have missed out in a big way. In the regular season finale versus the Chiefs, Marinovich threw 3 touchdowns. The *Los Angeles Times* headline proclaimed A STAR IS BORN. Only later, from my client, Kansas City's Deron Cherry, did I learn the performance was not as impressive as I first thought.

"Deron, you study more film than any human being I know," I said. "You have been to the Pro Bowl multiple times. How could you possibly let a rookie do that to your secondary?"

"We knew we had to play him in the next game, in the

playoffs," Deron said. "We didn't show him anything. We were just setting him up."

The next week, the Chiefs won, 10–6. Marinovich threw 4 interceptions.

A year later, I represented David Klingler—that's when I made the "Oh my God, it's Mike Brown" gaffe—as well as Michigan wide receiver Desmond Howard.

Desmond was the most socially conscious client I ever had. He wore a dashiki to his signing, and his smile lit up the room. He and I had long talks, and he was the most grateful recipient of the hard-cover books I sent to all of my clients, usually one for training camp, the other at Christmas. The training-camp books tended to be thrill-ers from authors such as Tom Clancy or James Patterson, while for Christmas I chose ones I felt would be more thought-provoking. Desmond especially loved Sidney Poitier's *The Measure of a Man*. One year, I sent Al Gore's *Earth in the Balance*, his warning about the environment. Many of my clients vehemently objected to Gore's thesis. A conservative athlete, I suppose, is a campus liberal who suddenly adjusts his politics after seeing the taxes withheld from his first bonus check.

Prior to each negotiation, my staff, especially Scott Parker, who was a genius at analyzing data, and I engaged in comprehensive research.

- We carefully evaluated the background and personality of every negotiator, judging whether he enjoyed total authority or needed to relay information to people higher up in the organization.
- We checked into the economic status of each team, determining how much it generally paid players, and how it preferred to structure its contracts.
- We had someone on our staff present the other side's most compelling arguments.

We were prepared for business as usual in the National Football League.

In 1993, however, business would not be usual. Business would never be usual again.

11

FREE AT LAST

Major changes often start in the courts, and changes in pro football were no exception. In a 1990–92 suit involving running back Freeman McNeil and several other players, a jury concluded the NFL's limited free agency system violated antitrust law. I testified around the same time in another case, presided over by Judge David Doty and revolving around All-Pro defensive lineman Reggie White, that led to a new collective bargaining agreement creating unrestricted free agency for players after four years of service.

Before, the only real leverage in negotiations came when GMs feared a player might sign with another league. That's why I was able to land such lucrative deals for Bart and Warren. Except for the AFL, though, those leagues faced enormous obstacles from the start and didn't last long. Besides, the WFL or USFL had not been their dream destination to begin with. The NFL was. It always will be. Once those leagues folded, the players were forced back to their previous state of well-paid bondage.

Now, starting in 1993, there'd be competition between teams in *one* league for their services, which meant, as with any business in the free enterprise system, higher compensation. No wonder, between this brave new world and the usual allotment of draft picks, 1993 was my busiest year ever as an agent. It made 1985 almost feel like a vacation. Almost.

Each negotiation in 1993 offered its own series of challenges. Take Tim McDonald, the All-Pro safety I'd represented since he was drafted in the second round by the Cardinals in 1987. He was a devastating hitter and team leader. After six years with the organization, enduring one losing season after another, Tim was excited to take advantage of the new rules and test the marketplace. Even though teams retained the right to take one player out of free agency by putting a franchise tag on him, Tim was exempt because of his involvement as a plaintiff in the McNeil lawsuit. He made trips to Philadelphia, Atlanta, and San Francisco, and met with Bill Bidwill and the Cardinals. Remaining in Phoenix, in spite of his frustrations, was still a viable option. There was a lot to be said for not having to adjust to a new city and system.

The challenge for Tim, as it was for every free agent, was to figure out which priorities mattered the most. With so many to consider, that can be very difficult, and that's when the player experiences a feeling known as cognitive dissonance. Swinging back and forth between the various priorities—this team pays more money, this one offers a better chance to start, this one employs a system ideally suited to my skills—the human psyche can withstand only so much anxiety. The player eventually will make a decision, *any* decision, simply to relieve the stress, and he will feel better right away. The problem is it very well might have been the *wrong* decision.

To avoid this pitfall required that players tap into their core values just as they did in our introductory meeting years before. Something in life has to be more important than something else, because if you have fifteen considerations, all of which have equal value, you are never going to come to a resolution. Prioritizing values and rating each option can provide clarity and make the strategy simple.

In Tim's case, above anything else, he wanted to live as close as possible to Fresno, where he grew up and still had a family. So much for Philadelphia, Atlanta, and Phoenix.

"Get me the best deal you can with San Francisco," Tim said, which we did—$2.55 million a year, a record for defensive backs. Tim helped the 49ers win a Super Bowl his second season in the Bay Area and played through 1999, earning more trips to the Pro Bowl.

The Pro Bowl was a familiar destination for another client of mine, Buffalo Bills running back Thurman Thomas, who received the distinction in 1989, 1990, 1991, and 1992. In each of those years, Thurman gained well over 1,000 yards, but because he was drafted in the second round in '88, he was never paid what he was worth. That happened to quite a few players coming out of college who exceeded expectations. It would take years before they could renegotiate their contracts to earn fair market value. Franchises that got a bargain were often not in a hurry to redo a deal. Later, though, when contracts were extended, the player received more than he would have gotten via free agency.

In Thurman's case, the Bills could have forced him to play the upcoming season at $1.45 million, the salary he signed for, and then designate him in 1994 as their franchise player, keeping him from becoming a free agent if they were to pay him an average of the salaries of the five best players at his position. That was a one-year figure, though, without the signing bonus he would earn in a long-term contract. Thurman would likely make a maximum of about $1.6 million in '94, and we felt he should receive a lot more.

The choice we faced was whether to try to work out a new contract with the Bills before or after Emmitt Smith, a restricted free agent, re-signed with Dallas. Emmitt and Barry Sanders were the only runners in Thurman's class. If Emmitt received a hefty raise, that would surely aid our cause.

Then again, what if he didn't? What if Jerry Jones signed Emmitt to a contract that wasn't as favorable as we hoped? That would surely harm our cause, and knowing how shrewd Jerry and his people could be at the bargaining table, I was not willing to take a chance. In these situations, I bet on our own negotiating ability over anyone else's. We would happily go before Emmitt.

The argument I made to the Bills was that Thurman was their key offensive tool and should be compensated like one. The top 5 quarterbacks averaged about $4.2 million a season, about three times more than what the top 5 running backs earned. I presented charts and graphs. To simply walk in and make a demand was insulting to the team. Free agency pricing was a function of competitive bidding: supply and demand, what the market would bear, unlike arbitration, which relies on a third party to make the decision. In a one-on-one negotiation, with the team holding rights to the player, the question was whose reality would prevail to form the basis for a deal. It was our job to construct, with research and logic, a packet that could appeal to general managers, who would then show it to their owners.

Days, then weeks, went by with little progress, and suddenly it was time for training camp to begin.

Thurman showed up in upstate New York and worked as hard as ever. He believed as firmly as I did in honoring a contract, no matter how disillusioned one might be.

I went, too, and spoke at great length with Ralph Wilson, the owner of the Bills since they began play in the old AFL in 1960. Hanging out together in the relaxed atmosphere of Fredonia State College, where the team practiced, helped Ralph and me better understand each other. I've always believed a little small talk—about films, restaurants, anything—can go a long way toward breaking down potential barriers during what can be an extremely intense process.

Ralph was worried about finances, but he was smart enough

to know how much Thurman meant to his team and the city of Buffalo. It also helped that John Butler, the Bills GM, valued his players. Not every general manager does.

We soon had a deal: four years at $13.5 million, a record for a running back. The Bills more than made up for the inadequacy of Thurman's earlier salaries. Wilson never regretted paying that much. Thurman, meanwhile, went over the 1,000-yard mark four more times, leading the Bills to another Super Bowl. Ralph and I became good friends. Every year he sent me a solid chocolate football, and we watched many games in his box. He still mails me postcards from around the world. The league has been very lucky to have him.

The only person who wasn't happy was Jerry Jones. He had to negotiate with Emmitt Smith, a holdout. Emmitt wouldn't be satisfied unless he received at least $1 more than Thurman.

"I thought we were friends," Jerry teased me.

Emmitt was no different from many other players in the league. Demanding a larger bonus and salary isn't important because it would allow them to buy the Winnebago they've been admiring or a nicer house in the suburbs. It's important because athletes are competitive and one measuring stick is how much they are paid. Earning a salary less than a player they feel superior to drives them crazy.

Lo and behold, Emmitt, after a sixty-four-day holdout, signed a four-year contract for $13.6 million. He edged Thurman by $100,000. Emmitt deserved every penny, but he had Thurman to thank.

During the same hectic year of 1993, I also negotiated new contracts for Steve Young, Troy Aikman, and Derrick Thomas. Even so, as usual, I spent a lot of time with the potential stars of the future. In this draft, two newcomers stood out, both QBs, Rick Mirer from Notre Dame and Washington State's Drew Bledsoe. At first, I assumed I would be representing Mirer. His dad, Ken, had approached me in 1992 when Rick considered turning pro after his junior year.

I tried to be neutral but told him, "If, for any reason, your son wants to go back to school because he feels he has unfinished business or wants to make sure he graduates, or thinks these years are special and doesn't want to look back, at age fifty, thinking, *I could have had one more year of college,* then he should remain in school." On the other hand, if there were urgent financial reasons for him to come out early, I said I could project, based on his past performances and how he might fare in the All-Star games and at the scouting combine, where he would likely go in the draft, and whether he would probably make out better if he waited a year.

Sounds like an enormous amount of work, doesn't it, for somebody who was not even a client? I didn't look at it that way. I looked at it as an opportunity to help a young man reach a very critical decision. In the end, Rick elected to stay in college, a wise choice. Still, Ken Mirer and I kept in touch, and we established a genuine connection. The core values I cared most about—role modeling, donating time and money to one's community, integrity—were common throughout the Midwest, and Goshen, Indiana, where the Mirers lived, was no exception. I was hopeful Ken Mirer and I would make it official in the spring after his son's senior season in South Bend.

Before then, though, I met another proud father. I met Mac Bledsoe. It was by far the strangest first encounter I ever had with the father of a prospective client.

I waited forever for him in front of a hotel in Yakima, Washington, looking for a middle-aged man with short hair, perhaps wearing a coat and tie. After no one fit that description, I called his home. His wife insisted he was there. I looked again. Seeing a man with bushy hair and a mustache sitting on a motorcycle, I figured I had nothing to lose.

"You Mac Bledsoe?" I asked.

"Yes, I am," he said.

Before I knew it, Mac and I were going for a ride—yes, on the Harley—back to his house.

I felt totally at ease right away with Mac. He and his wife, Barbara, had done a remarkable job with Drew. After Drew's last game as a Cougar, I became his agent, which meant I wouldn't work with Rick Mirer.

As the draft approached, with the New England Patriots on the clock, everybody wanted to know: Who would the Pats pick, Bledsoe or Mirer? Making the final call, no doubt, would be Bill Parcells, their new coach, hired only a few months earlier. With Seattle picking second, Drew would wind up there if the Patriots took Mirer, and, being so close to the town of Walla Walla, Washington, where he grew up, he would be thrilled.

Two words made me advise Drew playing for the Seahawks might not be such a good idea: Jeff George. Thomas Wolfe was right. You can't go home again.

There is also a special honor in being the top pick in the NFL Draft, which a player carries with him for the rest of his life, no matter how his pro career may turn out. After the first pick, however, there is no longer the dramatic drop in bonuses that existed before the more restrictive 2011 salary cap was instituted. That's why I find it strange to see guys ecstatic to be chosen third or fourth. Teams pick that high for a reason. They tend to be among the weakest organizations, unless they traded up to get in that position. Wouldn't it be preferable to be a lower pick, as Ben Roethlisberger was, and be on a contender from the start? The money can be made up quickly, and the player's experience in the NFL will usually be better.

Drew and I flew to Boston to meet with Parcells. In these situations, I was used to a warm welcome from a coach or general manager, even if they were not willing to tip their hand. Gil Brandt, the former Cowboys vice president, and the leading authority in the NFL on a college player's draft potential, was careful to praise everyone.

I once represented a player who met with Brandt at the East-West Shrine Game.

"He told me they are very serious about me being their first pick," the player said, unable to contain his excitement. His roommate blurted out, "That's the same thing he said to me." Then yet another player, standing a few feet away, said, "Both of you guys are crazy. That's what he said to *me*."

Bill Parcells, believe me, was no Gil Brandt. Praise? Quite the contrary.

"We looked at the films," he said, "and we're not sure you can move around quickly enough."

By the time he was done with us, the way Parcells kept putting him down, I almost felt Drew would be fortunate to be drafted anywhere.

"What was that all about?" he asked me.

I wish I knew. Perhaps Parcells was testing Drew to see how he might respond to adversity. I certainly hoped there was a logical reason for his behavior.

"I don't think that has much to do with whether he drafts you or not," I told Drew.

True enough, the Pats chose Drew over Rick. The next question was, How much were they willing to pay him?

That year, for the first time, we faced another obstacle, a rookie salary cap. The point of having a cap was for teams to spend more money on veterans and less for signing bonuses on untested rookies. I put my three children through school based on what I earned from rookie contracts, but I realized they were philosophically indefensible.

Our task was to compensate Drew immediately with a sizable

bonus—the only guarantee in pro football—yet make sure he was still earning what he was worth as the years went by. The problem was, to fit under the new cap, a player would have to accept a smaller first-year salary, and each successive salary could only go up a quarter of the original amount. By his third or fourth season, he would most likely be underpaid and have long forgotten about his generous bonus.

After Jeff Moorad, Scott Parker, and I spent hours and hours on the issue, we finally figured out a solution. We called it "voidable years." In essence, we proposed to preserve the right to void the last three years of Drew's six-year contract if he competed in 40 percent of the Patriots offensive plays from 1993 through 1995, or started seven games in 1995. Barring injury, given his talent and the Pats' lack of options at quarterback, that was about as sure a bet as there was in the National Football League. The team accepted, and that was how we beat the rookie salary cap. Drew received a record $4.5 million bonus. It could not have worked out any better as it became clear early on Drew would meet those benchmarks.

As a result, in 1995, we worked with Bob Kraft, the new Pats owner, to land Drew an even more attractive package: $42 million over seven years, with a signing bonus of $11.5 million, the largest in NFL history.

Drew was elated. He and his brother, Adam, used to call the bank and entertain themselves by having a teller tell them the balance in the account. Having that much money seemed a bit surreal.

I was elated, too, by the contract and just as much by the $1 million apiece Drew pledged to his foundation, which assisted in family counseling, and to one set up by Bob Kraft to assist a number of charities in the New England region. Exactly twenty years had passed since I first observed the life-changing impact an athlete can have on his community, with Bart in Atlanta. To me, nothing I achieved as a sports agent meant more.

•   •   •

In each of these communities, large or small, no entity could lift spirits and bring people together for a common purpose like a professional sports franchise. I realized that as a kid going with my grandfather to watch the Hollywood Stars at Gilmore Field. Old and young, white and black, rich and poor, they rooted as one. I saw it again at Dodger Stadium, and in the Bay Area, and at just about every stadium across the country I visited year after year. Fans take on a sense of ownership, and the owners let them. After all, the public address announcer proclaims, "*Your* Los Angeles Dodgers."

This is why they feel so betrayed when a team packs up and leaves town to improve its bottom line. Turns out it was not their team, after all, was it? Such betrayals took place over and over, even in Baltimore and Cleveland, proud cities where professional football was as big as it was anywhere in America, franchises that gave us Johnny Unitas and Jim Brown and many other icons. If it could happen there, it could happen anywhere.

Like in San Francisco, for example.

In 1992, I received a frantic call from the city's mayor, Frank Jordan.

"We are about to lose the [baseball] Giants to an investment group in Tampa in the wake of the vote not to authorize funding for a new stadium," he told me. "Owner Bob Lurie is intent on this deal. My advisers in this area consider it a fait accompli and aren't helping. Could you please help me figure out what to do?"

Absolutely, I assured him. I had loved my home in the Bay Area—Lucy and I lived there till moving to Newport Beach in 1989—and didn't want to see the fans and the economic vitality damaged in any way.

Besides, I had always opposed the concept of a professional team leaving an area and breaking so many hearts unless it had failed in every attempt to build sufficient support. These teams are not like other private businesses. Owners ask for public contributions in building stadiums and arenas and agree to be bound by limitations on franchise movement when they fill out their applications.

Mayor Jordan and I soon devised a strategy on multiple fronts:

- Change public perception that the move was unstoppable. I spent days appearing on local media outlets arguing the team could be saved.
- Convince the National League it was "against the best interests of baseball" to approve the relocation.
- Find local owners willing to buy the team from Lurie.
- Formulate a plan for a new stadium.

I had a close friend from my Berkeley days, Larry Baer, who was in New York working for Larry Tisch, the head of CBS. Larry Baer had grown up in San Francisco and would be the perfect person to assemble an ownership group. He agreed to come home and give it a try.

The first owner we found was George Shinn from Charlotte. George and I toured the stadium, and the fans went wild, but Charlotte was hardly local. A better fit was Safeway CEO Peter Magowan, who agreed to lead a group of billionaires Larry Baer had put together. We then kept up the pressure on the National League to reject the move. I helped rally support when I did the color commentary for one inning on ESPN's "Goodbye to Candlestick" broadcast, which also featured ex-Giants greats Willie Mays, Orlando Cepeda, and Willie McCovey. While on the air, I stressed the point that the whole premise of the broadcast was wrong. We were *not* going to lose the team. It was a good omen when our clients Matt Williams and Will Clark recorded hits in that same inning.

I spent days in Mayor Jordan's office, and without his stalwart leadership, the building of Pac Bell Park, and the eventual World Series victories in 2010 and 2012, would never have happened.

The league delayed the move, Larry Baer and the ownership

group took over the process, and the team stayed put. Mayor Jordan asked if I wanted a "Leigh Steinberg Day" in San Francisco. I told him helping to save the team was enough. There certainly would never be a day to honor me in Tampa. The group there sued me and others for interfering with its contract to purchase the Giants. My friend, attorney Jack Friedman, convinced the court I was legally entitled to express my opinion.

Mayor Elihu Harris of Oakland faced a similar dilemma in 1994. The Haas family was selling the A's, who appeared headed for Sacramento. I helped him assemble a group of businessmen and develop a slogan, "There is no O-kl-nd without the A's." Fortunately, Steve Schott and Ken Hofmann purchased the team and kept it where it belonged, in Oakland.

It was clear to me the problem with attendance in Oakland stemmed from the cold and foreboding nighttime environment at the Coliseum. Daytime games on the weekends would sell out, but the place was practically empty during the week. I proposed that we needed to build a "Sports Town" in the parking area surrounding the stadium with virtual-reality interactive sports-themed rides and retail and a West Coast Hall of Fame. It would be a daytime tourist attraction with hotels and amenities. In that way, there would be continual traffic and use of the land.

I only wish I could have been as successful in saving the Los Angeles Rams.

In the early '90s, owner Georgia Frontiere announced she would move the team to St. Louis. Ironically, Georgia had been the dinner chair for an Anti-Defamation League banquet in Los Angeles where I was honored as Man of the Year and gave me a personalized jersey that hung in my office. I was frequently a guest in her luxury box.

I don't recall if I was more angry or hurt by the possible move. The Rams were why I fell in love with football in the late 1950s: Jon

Arnett running to daylight, Norm Van Brocklin and, later, Roman Gabriel finding receivers. I knew attendance had dropped significantly since the team left the Coliseum in 1980 for Anaheim, but that was no reason for abandoning Southern California and the people who had been so loyal for decades. My anger wasn't enough. As my dad would say, *"They* is you, son."

I assembled a group of 120 businessmen, along with cochairman Jack Lindquist, president of Disneyland. We used a stadium plan based on the Sports Town concept. At a critical NFL meeting in Phoenix, we were thrilled when the NFL voted against the Rams relocating. The joy faded, however, when Orange County declared bankruptcy and justified the move.

I warned publicly over and over that if Southern California were to lose the Rams, we would also lose the Raiders—they left shortly afterwards—and have no NFL team. I said that it would be years before a new franchise came, and the expense of building a stadium in the future would far surpass what the cost was in 1994. I was ridiculed. The NFL, people argued, couldn't exist without the Rams, especially if it hoped to secure a more profitable television contract.

Well, to state the obvious, the NFL has done just fine without a franchise in Los Angeles. It is the city that has been affected the most.

As for ever obtaining a new franchise in L.A., an issue I am asked about constantly, there are several critical factors that must be in place. They include civic leaders determined to bring the project to fruition, one venue, private funding, and a supportive press and public. Virtually every one of those prerequisites has been missing or inadequate in the last twenty years, most notably in 1999 when the NFL awarded an expansion franchise to Houston.

For years, Commissioner Paul Tagliabue desperately wanted a Los Angeles team as part of his legacy. The league offered a deal on a silver platter: They would build a new stadium surrounding the same venue, which would preserve some of the classic features of the old Coliseum, and send the bill to the new owner. Once again, the area failed to deliver and the NFL walked away in disgust. Every city that has received a franchise provides a sense of excitement and determination, but in Southern California, the attitude has been that we don't need the NFL, and they need to prove to *us* why we should make any effort. This view is shortsighted. A professional team would offer jobs and vitality, and due to the high rollers in the entertainment community, luxury boxes and premium seats would be in demand.

The Rams left after the end of the 1994 season. I hope we don't have to wait another twenty years for a team in Los Angeles.

By the mid-1990s, while I was not recruiting players, negotiating contracts, or involved in client maintenance, I was preoccupied with a very serious matter I had recently begun to investigate. The more I learned, the more alarmed I became about the future of the young men I cared about, and the sport they played.

Twenty years have passed since then, and I am more alarmed than ever.

12
TICKING TIME BOMB

There was not just one wake-up call. There were many. They came until I would need no more. The first was during Troy Aikman's rookie season in 1989. I will never forget it. I was in Phoenix on a Sunday in mid-November to watch the Cowboys play the Cardinals. Troy was on fire that afternoon, setting a passing record for a rookie quarterback with 379 yards. The woeful Cowboys lost again, 24–20, falling to 1-9, but the cavalry was coming, at last.

Troy was hit after throwing a touchdown pass and knocked to the ground. Blood came out of his ear. Hits like that occur in every game, if not every *quarter*. The dazed player moves one part of his body at a time, slowly regaining his senses. That wasn't the case here. Troy, flat on his back, didn't move one inch. I was terrified, every fear imaginable racing through my brain. It felt as if Troy were on the ground for an hour. It was perhaps five minutes. I never felt so powerless. I realized that from then on, I would need a pass to gain access to the locker room immediately if another of my players was injured.

Troy finally got up, the crowd at Sun Devil Stadium cheering warmly, and the game proceeded, most people, I suspect, not giving the hit a second thought. This is football. Players get hurt. Here comes the next play.

I thought about it, for the rest of the day, and longer.

Such a severe blow to the head, I assumed, must cause serious damage to a human being's brain, and what is the damage if there is another blow, and another after that?

It was not as if I were naive about the tremendous punishment the sport inflicts on its participants while they are still active, and long into retirement. How could I be after seeing how fate dealt with, ironically enough, three players I represented from the same draft in 1981—Kenny Easley, Curt Marsh, and Neil Lomax, each forced to leave the game before he turned thirty? Or after seeing what happened to Mike Sherrard, the Dallas wide receiver who would not let a coin flip dictate his first contract in 1986?

Observing the pain and frustration Mike went through during a series of freak injuries in the late 1980s led to a different sort of wake-up call.

Doctors make mistakes, too. Big ones.

When I was growing up in the '50s and '60s, like most people, I put doctors on a pedestal, thinking of them as every bit the heroes we saw on TV in shows such as *Dr. Kildare* and *Ben Casey*. Doctors made house calls back then, and their authority was never in question.

During a scrimmage against the San Diego Chargers in August of 1987, Mike's second year with the Cowboys, he fractured his tibia and fibula, the bone in his right leg breaking like a pencil through the skin. Danny White, the Dallas quarterback, was so affected by the gruesome sight he asked to be excused from the rest of practice. The doctors inserted a metal plate and eight screws into his leg, which occurred without any input from me. Mike was gone for the season.

The following March, while jogging on a beach in California,

Mike broke the tibia again in nearly the same spot. A few months earlier, the screws and plate had been removed, but it was too early; the bones were not hardened enough, leaving the leg more susceptible to a second break. Mike would sit out another year, and another after that. He never played for the Cowboys again.

The lesson for me was obvious. From now on, I would strongly urge my clients to always seek a second opinion.

The teams, not surprisingly, did not share this perspective.

For years, they screened agents out of the process, viewing the request for a second opinion as a personal insult to their own medical experts. Those experts, in consultations with team executives, would make the important decisions on how to treat a player's injuries. The inherent conflict the doctors faced was unavoidable. While they'd sworn to the Hippocratic Oath and were extremely competent, they were employed by the teams, which meant they were pressured, subtly or not, to sign off on players returning to the field as fast as possible.

I found myself questioning my role as an agent as never before.

Was I fulfilling my fiduciary responsibility to my clients by simply stacking dollar after dollar in their bank accounts, without regard to the consequences of the game they played? Or did I have a larger obligation to do everything I could to look out for their long-term health? I concluded that if I did not assume a more aggressive role, I was being an enabler facilitating their demise. I did not enter this business to lead young men like cattle to the slaughter.

I put together a list of doctors I would call to provide input when necessary, depending on the extent of injury. I kept a *Physicians' Desk Reference* in my office and learned as much as possible about the ligaments and cartilage in every part of the body. I didn't take human anatomy in law school, at least not in the classroom. Fortunately, as part of the 1993 collective bargaining agreement, players secured the right to a second opinion. It was about time.

As for Marsh, Easley, and Lomax, the toll the game exacted on them could not have been much harsher.

In 1987, Curt Marsh, one of the cheeriest players I represented, retired after six seasons with the Raiders. It was a testament to his remarkable endurance and will that he lasted as long as he did. He underwent twelve operations, including four on his right ankle and right foot.

The pain did not go away once he quit the game. It never does. In September of 1994, his right foot was amputated. I was devastated. Curt, I am relieved to say, was comforted by his strong faith in God and has lived a very productive life.

What happened to Kenny was just as frightening.

In the spring of 1988, as he was taking a routine physical in Phoenix after the Cardinals acquired him for quarterback Kelly Stouffer, doctors discovered a serious kidney ailment. The trade was called off, and Kenny, only twenty-nine, was forced to retire.

When Kenny called to say he flunked the physical and had only about 7 percent function in his kidney, my immediate reaction was, how was it possible the Seattle doctors were not aware of his condition before? Kenny might have died if he hadn't been traded. He went to dialysis three times a week and in 1990 received a kidney transplant. He later sued the Seahawks, claiming his kidneys were damaged by the ibuprofen the doctors recommended he take to cope with any discomfort after ankle surgery. Kenny ingested about thirty a day. Amazingly enough, a wide assortment of pills was kept in large, open containers in the Seattle locker room; players were free to scoop up whatever they wanted.

With Neil Lomax, the problem was a bad hip, misdiagnosed by the Cardinals as a groin injury. Neil started to limp during the 1988 preseason, though he managed to throw that year for nearly 3,500 yards and 20 touchdowns. By the next preseason, the hip was much worse, and the Cardinals put him on the injured reserve list. Perhaps sitting out a whole season would allow the hip to heal. It did not. In 1990, Neil retired, and a year later, he received a new hip.

Watching him in agony one day, the sweat poring down his face, tears in his eyes, as he did a little stretching to break down the adhesions that had developed in his old hip, I asked him, "When does it hurt the most?"

He gave me a puzzled look. "It always hurts," he said.

"How do you deal with it?"

"You do the best you can to tune it out."

Tuning it out is one of a professional athlete's most admirable gifts. It is also what leads to their bodies eventually breaking down. If they had not possessed such a high degree of tolerance for pain, they would have quit the sport long ago, sparing themselves those additional, often decisive, years of devastating hits. They are not like the rest of us, who put long-term health as our No. 1 priority. They are in denial. To them, the next play is all that matters. How it might impact the next game or next season or season after that is often secondary. Plus, they fear that if they don't play in pain, they will lose their place in the lineup and maybe even on the team.

Furthermore, gifted with a rare elasticity in their joints, players are able to avoid injuries, and when they do get hurt, they heal much faster than us mere mortals. Take the Vikings star Adrian Peterson. He tore his ACL in December 2011. That's a crushing injury for an NFL running back. Players used to need a year to recover, at least. He was back on the field in September, and all Peterson did was rush for a near-record 2,097 yards and win the MVP award. Recovering so rapidly, though, is not necessarily a good thing. It blinds the players to the long-term cumulative effect on their bodies as they age, and the aging process is the one reality they cannot avoid.

Yet if you ask any former player who experiences pain every day, some much worse than others, if he would make the sacrifice again, the response is almost always a resounding yes.

That's because the level of camaraderie players established with their teammates, knowing the man next to you will watch your back and come immediately to your aid if you get hit, is unlike any they formed after football—at the workplace, home, anywhere. It is why those who served in combat have so much trouble adjusting to society when they return home. No one understands what they are going through, except other war veterans.

I never knew a single player who willingly retired. Even if, on the surface, they appeared content in their new lives, I'm certain most gave a lot of thought to launching a comeback. What kept them back was being too injured to make a team or accepting the fact that their skills had eroded too much. Troy, during his first year out of the game, while everybody praised him for walking away at the age of thirty-four, was very close to signing with Miami. No doubt, given how well he's done on TV, he made the right choice.

Few players I represented were as determined to compete as Troy Aikman. Perhaps too determined. In June of 1993, he underwent surgery to repair a herniated disk in his lower back. Dr. Robert Watkins, who performed the operation, said the standard recovery period was three months, which meant Troy would not return until the third game of the season.

For Troy, that was unacceptable. I visited him in the hospital several hours after the surgery. He was walking around his room. I couldn't believe it.

"Let me ask you something," I said. "Did Dr. Watkins say you could do any walking?"

"No, but isn't this great?" he asked.

In my view, it was most definitely not great.

"You need to get back in bed," I told him.

As the years went on, the issue of concussions continued to torment me. I would visit physicians treating players who had suffered a concussion and ask a lot of questions. What is the effect of one on the next? How many are too many? What are the long-term effects? They had no answers, most insisting concussions were not a major issue. MRI scans they did to look for brain damage were always negative. Yet since I no longer had complete trust in the medical community due to what happened with my other clients, I did not feel any less troubled.

One night, I visited a client in his darkened hospital room hours after a game. He was alone and looked confused.

"Where am I?" he asked.

"In the hospital," I replied. "You had a concussion."

"Did I play today?" he asked.

"Yes," I responded.

"Did I play well?"

"Yes, you threw three touchdowns," I said.

His face brightened. Five minutes passed as we talked more about the game. He then asked, "Where am I?" and "Did I play today?" and "Did I play well?" I gave the same answers I did the first time. Ten minutes later, it happened once more.

I finally wrote a narrative on a piece of paper so he could glance at it whenever he became confused. It was terrifying to witness how delicate the line was between full consciousness and dementia. This was one of my closest clients. At dinner the night before, he had been his usual witty self. I decided to contact the leading neurologists across the country and ask them to conduct a seminar on concussions for my athletes, though I wasn't sure they would come.

Older players were in denial just like their younger brethren, and if they recognized they were suffering symptoms from head injuries, they certainly were not about to share that information. The way they viewed it, if they were to worry about the risk of long-term consequences to their health, it might impact the mental toughness required to excel in a dangerous game. Most, in fact, wished I would drop the whole matter. I couldn't. An injury to the brain is in a whole different dimension than other injuries. It is one thing to know that every joint of the human body is impacted by football, and that at age forty, an ex-player might have aches and pains that make it difficult to pick up his child. It is another to not be able to recognize that child.

The brain, I learned, is the last frontier of medical research. Instrumentation has long existed to allow comprehensive knowledge of the knee, shoulder, hip, and elbow. Yet most of what has been discovered about brain function has emerged in the last ten years due to miniaturization and technological breakthroughs. New discoveries are happening all the time, thanks to neurologists such as Dr. Robert Cantu, Dr. Julian Bailes, and Dr. Mark Lovell.

The first seminar I helped put together was held in Newport Beach and included helmet and turf manufacturers. There was press from across the country, as well. I was most comforted to see a number of my players attend, such as Warren Moon, Steve Young, Troy Aikman, Rob Johnson, and Gary Plummer. At least our clients would find out how serious the problem was.

After it was over, we issued a white paper with a set of recommendations. They focused on awareness, education, prevention, and treatment. The paper called for organized football and other sports to ban blocking or tackling with the head or neck and for playing surfaces to be reevaluated and hard turfs eliminated. It also called for a neurologist on the sideline at every game, and a standardized regimen of diagnosis and treatment that would rate the hits and mandate when returning to the field was safe. We asked for research into supplements, helmets, and mouth guards. Our feeling was that if society had the technology to send a probe to Mars, why couldn't we develop better ways to protect players? There were three conferences in all, the last in Los Angeles led by Dr. Keith Feder and Senator Barbara Boxer.

From these sessions, I learned a great deal, such as the danger of second concussion syndrome, which is when the first diminishes reaction time and sets the brain up for a second. Thus, an athlete who returns to play too quickly after the first has a higher risk of a second concussion, and two in close proximity can cause even more severe consequences.

Dr. Lovell designed a program for baseline testing that checked the cognitive skills in athletes prior to a season. If the athlete was concussed, a second test was given that determined how much damage had occurred. For the first time, there was an objective way for a trainer, doctor, or coach to judge whether a player was asymptomatic at rest, on an exercise bike, and at practice before being cleared to play. Players told me they intentionally answered questions incorrectly when they took the original test so that if they were to suffer a concussion, any similar responses the second time would not raise concerns about their mental state.

In another series of conferences held in 2006 and 2007, we learned even more. Doctors concluded that three concussions appeared to be a marker for exponentially higher rates of ALS, Parkinson's disease, Alzheimer's disease, premature senility, dementia, and depression. Their research uncovered a condition called chronic traumatic encephalopathy, which stems from concussions and can lead to depression and suicide. I called these developments "a ticking time bomb" and an "undiagnosed health epidemic" and predicted we would have an outbreak of symptoms that would be unprecedented.

A big obstacle we faced early on in dealing with concussions is fighting a culture that has long celebrated the glory of a hard hit. For years, the opening of *Monday Night Football* presented a logo of two helmets crashing together. Hot-selling DVDs featured the best knockout blows. ESPN ran a regular segment of monumental tackles; the effects of such hits were minimized with familiar expressions along the lines of "He got his bell rung." Players who returned to film study were highly praised by their coaches and teammates for the most vicious blows.

Another hurdle was the league itself, which released a finding in which lead physician Dr. Elliot Pellman stated that concussions were not a problem. He said there was no data suggesting long-term impact and that one did not necessarily lead to another. No one, however, charted concussions for the longest time, and we had no idea of the damage that was being done to players. My colleagues in the medical community preached to me that being knocked out was not required to suffer a concussion. The official definition is a blow to the head or body triggering a change in brain function.

I once asked Steve Young how many concussions he had in his career. "You mean official ones?" he responded.

"What's an official one?" I asked.

"That's when you get knocked out and carried off the field. But I have many times every game where I get hit and am woozy for a while. I still knew what plays to call."

On a number of those occasions, Steve would keep his distance from the coach so he couldn't be pulled from the game.

It became clear to me that the phenomenon of subconcussive hits must be endemic to the game. When an offensive lineman hits a defensive lineman, the force of that collision has a stunning effect that alters brain chemistry. No one talks about the damage that occurs play by play, game by game. If a player starts in high school, continues in college, and then practices and plays sixteen games a season in a long NFL career, with an average of 70 offensive snaps a game, it is possible he will leave football with 10,000 subconcussive hits. None of those hits might knock him out, or even be recorded as a concussion, but the cumulative impact must be staggering. More frightening is the fact that this danger exists in any sport that has collisions: hockey, baseball, field hockey, boxing, MMA, cycling, even youth soccer.

It is not simply a professional football issue but a challenge to all of society. The adolescent brain is especially vulnerable as it is still forming and takes much longer to recover from the symptoms than an older person's brain. Students need to attend classes on the issue. The risk is everywhere.

When I became an agent in the '70s, Jack Youngblood played defensive end for the Los Angeles Rams at 245 pounds, while offensive tackles weighed around the same. They had big bellies and ran a 5.5 forty on their best days. Today, it is difficult to play tackle at less than 310 pounds, and an offensive lineman ran a 4.65 forty at last year's scouting combine. We also now understand nutrition as a science and body chemistry as never before, allowing athletes to adopt a diet and use supplements designed to increase their size and speed. The training techniques are revolutionary.

Since our conferences in 2006, the NFL, to its credit, has mandated baseline testing, passed rules limiting contact with the head and neck in tackling, and placed a high priority on education. Commissioner Roger Goodell has been very involved. He convened a physicians conference to discuss the issue and issued a whistle-blower edict asking players to identify any of their peers who seemed to be suffering from concussive symptoms.

Yet can enough really be done to minimize concussion risk in football and other collision sports, or is it inherent in their structure? If the basic play that starts at the line of scrimmage produces a low-level concussion over and over, is the game simply too dangerous? I believe diagnosed concussions are just the tiny tip of the iceberg. The long-term effect of the undiagnosed low-level concussions will create an enormous amount of suffering in coming years.

When Tom Brady's father publicly said he would be "very hesitant" to let his son play football if he were to start today, it showed the real threat the sport is facing. If it can't find a way at the youth level to teach safer techniques, many parents will reach the same conclusion. The NFL should fund research and development into every possible protective device.

We need to develop a protocol to diagnose and chart low-level concussions and find a way to get nutrients into the cells to have a greater effect. I have consulted with medical researchers working with veterans of the war in Iraq on curative medicines, and I hope to find a sports drink that can help. I've also set up a foundation, Athletes Speak, comprised of current and retired players, to focus on concussion prevention and research.

As dire as the situation remains, I will never give up. Too many lives are at stake.

13

BIG DADDY AND BIG DEALS

In early 1994, I met Dan Wilkinson, or "Big Daddy," as he was known. Dan was a 315-pound defensive tackle from Ohio State. The early projections had him as a top 5 pick, but after missing the opportunity to represent Trent Dilfer and Heath Shuler, the two highest-rated quarterbacks, I set out to make Dan the No. 1 pick. Two of the prior three No. 1s—Russell Maryland in 1991 and Steve Emtman in 1992 from the University of Washington—were defensive linemen. Why not a third?

The first step was to generate as much coverage as possible about Dan. I had no illusions that any one article would suddenly elevate him in the eyes of scouts and general managers who had spent months evaluating the crop coming out of college. I only wanted to make it more acceptable for the club in the top spot, the Bengals, to pick him without the fans in Cincinnati ridiculing the decision.

Several days before the draft, *Sports Illustrated* came through with a cover story on Dan.

Dan made for good copy, no doubt. The tenth of eleven children, he grew up in a five-bedroom house in Dayton crammed with bunk beds. On the day his dad, Oliver, died of a heart attack in 1987, Dan, a freshman at Dunbar High, quit football. He was back on the team a few weeks later, as his remarkable mother, Veronda, found a way to raise the kids and get them through school. Dan kept growing and growing, and by the time he left for Columbus, he weighed close to 350 pounds.

After his junior year at Ohio State, his stock rose, as well. The Patriots, at No. 4, were among the teams interested in moving up to snatch him. Yet it was Mike Brown, who revered Ohio State—he played the Buckeyes fight song constantly on the tape deck in his car—I dealt with once again after the Bengals rejected other offers. The negotiations went smoothly. They always did with Mike when his team had an immediate need for the player, unlike with David Klingler or Jason Buck. Dan received a $14.4 million deal over six years to become the highest-paid Bengal ever. He would play for thirteen years with Cincinnati and three other teams.

We staged draft day at the Marriot in Newport Beach. One room was set up to look like my office, and we had rooms for Dan's extended family and friends. We also had ample space for press, coaches, and anyone else who was interested in attending.

When Dan was selected as the first pick, the room exploded. Draft day is the most emotional day you can imagine for the family and friends who have been involved in helping the young man achieve his hopes and dreams. Dan's proud, loving mother who sacrificed so much broke down in tears. She was like many of the mothers I knew, believing in their children every day, helping them believe in themselves.

Another was Kathy Carter, mother of Ki-Jana, the Penn State running back who rushed for 1,539 yards as a junior to lead his squad to a 12-0 season. Carter was so ready for the NFL that Nittany Lions coach Joe Paterno, who felt every student-athlete should stay until he received his degree, gave him his blessing to leave State College a year early.

I flew to Columbus, Ohio, to recruit him, but had to wait for almost two hours while a group, similar to the businessmen who advised Troy, met with Kathy Carter. It gave me a chance to thaw out. I had left 70-degree sunshine in Southern California to land in a bone-chilling 15 degrees. I didn't necessarily mind waiting, being under the impression the group was advising the Carter family as a courtesy—until I received reports from my office in California that these men hoped to be Ki-Jana's agent themselves, and if I didn't act fast, I would lose him.

My chance came when someone left the room for a short break. I handed the person a note to give Kathy.

"I'm not quite sure what's going on in there," I wrote Kathy, "but I am sitting here ready to make my presentation, which I know will create the best situation for your son." Five minutes later, the door opened and Kathy Carter pulled me into the room. By the end of the day, I was her son's new agent.

In that 1995 class, I also represented the other standout from the Penn State backfield, Kerry Collins.

Both players were with me in New York, as the NFL had promised our group our own room. Carolina enjoyed the first pick, and team president Mike McCormack had told me they were going to take Kerry. Jacksonville owned the No. 2 choice and was prepared to choose Ki-Jana. It would be like 1991 all over again. Then Carolina swapped places with Cincinnati, slotted at No. 5. The Bengals had traded up to snatch Ki-Jana, giving us our third top overall pick in a row, and sixth in the last seven years. Kerry wound up going to Carolina.

In that same draft, I also represented Rob Johnson, the USC quarterback, who was sitting in our Newport Beach office feeling a bit apprehensive as the day unfolded.

As usual, there was a constant exchange of information before the draft between me and the teams, who often asked how a player felt about joining their particular franchise. These contacts knew I would share what they told me only with clients, which helped me predict when a player would be taken, and in which slot. Buffalo definitely had interest in Rob. So did Jacksonville—until they traded for quarterback Mark Brunell, who would be their new starter. Mark later became a wonderful client. When Buffalo passed on Rob and took another QB in the second round, Michigan's Todd Collins, things looked grim. Thankfully, Jacksonville used its fourth-rounder on Rob, who went in with a tremendous attitude and played well enough for us to eventually negotiate a $25 million package for him to start in Buffalo. Rob would go on to win a Super Bowl in 2003 as the backup quarterback for the Bucs.

In July 1995, three months after the draft—remember, nothing happens in the NFL till the last minute—I went out on the road to get Kerry and Ki-Jana signed, along with Colorado quarterback Kordell Stewart, who went in the second round to the Steelers.

Spending time with Kordell was always uplifting. He was so cheerful and positive. He was determined to play QB and didn't waver during the scouting season. Although he naturally created a sensation as a "slash," a multipurpose threat, he later started at quarterback for Pittsburgh and made the Pro Bowl.

That year, I also represented tight end Christian Fauria, selected in the second round by Seattle, and worked on the new deal for Drew Bledsoe.

In just four days, flying from Charlotte to Pittsburgh to Cincinnati—I did the negotiations with the Seahawks for Christian over the phone—I secured deals for each of them, except for Drew. Kerry received a record signing bonus, topped a day or two later by Ki-Jana's contract.

For Drew, I went to Boston to see Bob Kraft.

Bob, like Jerry Jones, was part of the new breed of pro football owners who earned their fortunes elsewhere. In Bob's case, it was in the paper and packaging business. "I just bought the team," he told me at our Super Bowl party in 1994. "I don't know what your relationship was with the team's owners before, but I want ours to be a special relationship."

Bob meant every word. No subject was off-limits, and we asked each other for advice. I saw Bob as I saw Jerry, as an ally, not an adversary; the larger the pie, the bigger slices for everyone. He had amazing sons, Jonathan and Robert. I was in awe of Bob's commitment to charity and love of family. He and his wife, Myra, became close friends. In 1999, they showed up at my fiftieth birthday party on a boat in Newport Beach, bringing a Patriots jersey with my name and the number 50 on the back. Bob never missed a Super Bowl party.

We hammered out the extension for Drew in about twelve hours, starting at an Italian restaurant by the water and working into the early morning. Later that same day, Bob and I drove together to celebrate at his house on the Cape. After dinner, we went to his hot tub and toasted the signing with a glass of the most expensive champagne. I can't think of another owner in the NFL I would have rather shared a hot tub with.

Back inside a short time later, we saw a report on ESPN about the agreement with Drew, which ended with this account. "What a week it has been for Leigh Steinberg," the anchorman said. A chart in the background showed every deal I had wrapped up the past week. "First he signs Kerry Collins to the biggest rookie bonus ever. Then he signs Christian Fauria. Then Kordell Stewart. Then Ki-Jana Carter to a bonus higher than Collins's. And now the Drew Bledsoe deal, which ties Troy Aikman for the largest in the NFL. All in the span of just five days. Leigh, it's time to take a rest."

Bob and I laughed, and I went to sleep. Then the phone rang.

Another client needed me, more than ever.

The sound in Warren Moon's voice was unlike anything I had heard before, and it was understandable. He had never faced anything like this. The police were charging him with spousal abuse against his wife, Felicia.

I flew to Houston and drove straight to his house. Getting inside was no easy task. I had never seen so many satellite TV trucks in one place.

The first thing I suggested to him was that he could not appear to be hiding a single bit of information reporters might dig up later to inflame the crisis. He needed to stage a press conference. He was reluctant. Yet when the moment came, Warren was in control, as usual, apologizing for putting his wife and children through the ordeal. Months later, Felicia testified her wounds resulted from him attempting to restrain her, and a jury took less than a half hour to find him not guilty.

Assisting athletes who encountered problems with the law was nothing new for me. I guess you might consider it another form of client maintenance, and every agent does it.

In 1983, I had come to the aid of Mark Gastineau, the eccentric New York Jets defensive end who had been charged with misdemeanor assault in a brawl at the city's posh club Studio 54. I was told by friends who accompanied him he was an innocent bystander. Innocent or not, what was I doing representing *him*? He did not exactly fit my profile, did he? The thing is, I really believed if I could get a tough player like Mark, whom I met through another client, his teammate Ken O'Brien, to give to charities and be a positive role model, the impact would be enormous. It would be difficult today to re-create what Mark Gastineau meant to the game back then with his dramatic sack dance. Walking down the street with him in Manhattan was unlike any other experience I ever had with an athlete; every person greeted him with "Yo, Mark." He embodied what countless middle-aged businessmen dreamed about becoming, even more than the quarterback, a superhero who could demolish anyone in their path.

One night, Jets owner Leon Hess asked me to meet at his lavish penthouse in Manhattan to discuss Mark's future. We talked for hours. At one point, he described the influence owning an oil company can have on the whole world. He took out his Rolodex and showed me the phone numbers for an array of well-known figures, including one for Ayatollah Khomeini. No, we didn't give him a call.

I wasn't as successful with Mark—he was convicted and sentenced to ninety days of community service—as I would later be with Warren and other clients who landed in trouble.

In 1997, for some inexplicable reason, there seemed to be one crisis to deal with after another.

The first was in May, and it involved Arizona Cardinals quarterback Jake Plummer. As charismatic as "Jake the Snake" was on the field—he had taken Arizona State to its first Rose Bowl in ten years—he was the same off the field. Jake also had the good fortune to be drafted by his hometown team, although being a celebrity, as usual, came with a price. A month later, he was involved in an alleged incident at a nightclub in town. A civil case was settled out of court. It never would have gotten that far if his name hadn't been Jake Plummer. I was glad to help him get through the experience.

Then, in July, Bruce Smith was found asleep with his car running around 6:00 A.M. at an intersection in his hometown of Virginia Beach, Virginia. He had been drinking.

Bruce called me right away, sounding very similar to Warren two years before. He and I were especially close. Bruce was an amazing role model. His three-day golf tournament for his foundation brought tons of celebrities to Virginia Beach.

"I've spent all these years making sure I was straight and that I've matured past my early career," Bruce said. "This is so embarrassing. I haven't lived like this. This is not who I am, and now this is how people are going to remember me forever."

I did not agree. "In the cyclical nature of news these days," I told Bruce, "let me assure you something will happen very soon with another athlete to knock your story out of people's consciousness."

"No, Leigh," he insisted. "That's never going to happen."

Sure enough, a few days later, Cowboys coach Barry Switzer was arrested when a loaded .38 caliber revolver was discovered in his carry-on baggage at the airport in Dallas. Bruce, meanwhile, was charged with DUI, but the case was later dismissed. Fans remember Bruce the way he wants to be remembered, as one of the greatest defensive players in NFL history.

In November, the final incident of that crazy year took place in Boston. In a mosh pit, of all places. I didn't even know what a mosh pit was.

At the center of it all was Drew Bledsoe, who dove off the stage into the crowded pit at the Paradise Club on Commonwealth Avenue. As one might imagine, Bob Kraft was livid. Recognizing Drew's penchant for daring pursuits—he loved to heli-ski, for instance—Bob had hoped to insert language forbidding such activities as part of the contract renegotiation in 1995. We refused.

I wasn't overly thrilled with Drew's antics, either, but I defended him. I believed in Drew, and eventually, the story vanished.

Well, not everyone let the story drop.

"Steinberg had another magnificent year," the *Sporting News* wrote in rating me one of the top 20 most powerful people in sports, "but we can't believe he actually stood up for Drew Bledsoe."

14
SHOW ME THE MONEY

In that same year, one day sticks out. For a change, it was not the first day of the draft in April, when I represented 3 of the top 13 picks. The day came a month earlier, when I was mingling with a different group of stars, ones from the silver screen. The scene was a Sony party in Hollywood near the site of the sixty-ninth Academy Awards ceremony. I had been in love with movies since I was a kid, thanks to my mom. Now I was waiting breathlessly to find out if *Jerry Maguire* would win the Oscar for Best Original Screenplay.

It had started with a phone call I received in 1993 from director Cameron Crowe. He asked if he could spend time with me to gather research for a film that would feature a sports agent as the lead character. I admired his work quite a bit, from the pieces he wrote on the grunge rock scene in Seattle for *Rolling Stone,* which I read as thoroughly as *Sports Illustrated,* to the superb job he did directing *Say Anything* and *Singles,* and writing the screenplay for *Fast Times at Ridgemont High*. The character of Spicoli in that film, the druggie played magnificently by Sean Penn, is among the most hilarious in cinema history.

I told Cameron he could spend as much time with me as he'd like. I figured it would be fun, and it was.

He showed up at the 1993 draft when Drew was the first pick and then flew to Boston with us for the press conference. He showed up when writers interviewed me about players, and any changes to the collective-bargaining agreement. He showed up at Super Bowl parties and at games. He showed up at dinner when I spoke to Colts GM Jim Irsay about trading a disgruntled Jeff George. He showed up for Pro Scouting Day on the USC campus. He showed up at my office in Newport Beach to watch me work the phones. He borrowed my legal pads, briefcase, wardrobe, and pictures on the wall of me next to different players, superimposing Tom Cruise's face on mine. For the next couple of years, Cameron Crowe showed up *everywhere*.

It was from one such gathering, in the spring of 1993, that Cameron wrote the most memorable line of the film—one of the most memorable lines of any film in the recent past. We were in Palm Desert, California, for the annual meeting of NFL owners. A major topic that week was free agency. Owners had done everything in their power for decades to prevent this day from ever arriving, but now that it was finally here, they hoped to minimize its damage.

The first client of mine to take advantage, Tim McDonald, was also in town, still deciding between several different teams. Cameron, after observing Tim meet with general managers and coaches, went to his hotel room to interview him. CNN's *Moneyline,* hosted by Lou Dobbs, played on in the background.

Tim claims he said "show me the money" during the interview while Cameron says he came up with the phrase. Either way, the line was recited in the movie by Cuba Gooding Jr., whose portrayal of wide receiver Rod Tidwell earned him the Oscar for Best Supporting Actor. I'll never forget when Cuba came to one of our Super Bowl parties and shouted, "Show me the money. Show me the money."

I spent a fair amount of time with Cuba as he prepared for the film. Cameron sent him down to Phoenix with me for the week leading up to the 1996 Super Bowl between the Cowboys and Steelers, where I represented all six quarterbacks, including starters Troy Aikman and Neil O'Donnell. "I would like Cuba to get some feeling of this world of football off the field," Cameron said, "but, Leigh, remember he is an actor, and I don't want him to get in any trouble with those hard-drinking guys."

Cameron had nothing to fear. Cuba went to every party with me and was a perfect gentleman. I recall seeing everyone from our group at one local establishment, around closing time, in various comatose states—everyone except Cuba. He was dancing on the bar, amazingly nimble with his feet, in total control. I told Cuba to envision himself as a wide receiver who was my client, and not an actor hanging around football players. It helped him immensely to play the part for real. I said to him, "If you get this down right, you could win an Oscar."

Once filming got under way, with Tom Cruise playing Jerry, Cameron asked me to be on the set as much as I could, giving him what's known in the business as notes, essentially how scenes and dialogue should look and sound. If the characters, details, or dialogue don't appear real, the sports fan will think of the film as a spoof instead of a serious work of art. He also asked what I thought of Jerry O'Connell, who portrayed highly coveted quarterback prospect Frank Cushman, Jerry's No. 1 client—his throwing, not acting, ability. I had spent enough years around quarterbacks to recognize proper mechanics. I proceeded to teach O'Connell how to throw a spiral.

As for the script itself, it couldn't have been more authentic. The scene where Bob Sugar, the sleazy agent portrayed by Jay Mohr, stole Jerry's players was eerily reminiscent of Mike Sullivan's coup attempt in 1985. The moment when Dorothy Boyd (Renée Zellweger, in her breakout role), Jerry's new wife, complained after he had been on a long road trip it wasn't the marriage she wanted also hit home. Lucy was not pleased.

"Did you have to tell him *everything*?" she asked me.

I told Cameron tons of stories, to be sure, but the movie was most definitely not my life story. As Cameron told me, "Jerry Maguire *aspires* to be Leigh Steinberg."

I kept one scene out, and I am forever grateful. I was set to play Jerry's brother, who, during the bachelor party early in the film, would have given a toast that was pretty damning. While I recited the line, I started to mumble. Cruise came over after Cameron yelled cut.

"You looked really uncomfortable with this," Cruise said. "What can we do to make it easier for you?"

Cameron stopped by to chat, as well.

"When you see a movie and there's a villain, it is difficult not to assume the person is actually a villain, even though it's only make-believe," I told them. "I don't want to be forever known on celluloid as the person who ruined Tom Cruise's bachelor party."

Neither Cameron nor Cruise attempted to change my mind. To this day, I may be the only actor who ever talked his way *out* of a scene with Tom Cruise. I would have played his brother in another scene but missed my opportunity because they shot it while I was on vacation in England with Lucy. The one appearance I did make was in a smaller role, introducing Jerry to Troy Aikman.

My acting career was just getting started.

"I'm going to put you in every movie I do," Cameron told me.

Released in December of 1996, *Jerry Maguire* was a hit with both the critics and the public. I could not go anywhere without hearing someone shout, "Show me the money." I attended the premieres—on a dock in Manhattan and in Westwood—and walked down the long red carpet while photographers shouted my name. For the first time, I knew how my grandfather must have felt attending the galas in Hollywood during the '40s and '50s.

The film collected five Oscar nominations: Best Picture, Best Original Screenplay, Actor in a Leading Role (Cruise), Actor in a

Supporting Role (Gooding Jr.), and Film Editing (Joe Hutshing). The odds of winning for Best Picture weren't very good, but winning for Best Original Screenplay—the other nominees were *Fargo, Lone Star, Secrets & Lies,* and *Shine*—was a distinct possibility.

The big night at the Shrine Auditorium arrived on Monday, March 24.

Finally, midway through the ceremony, came the moment we had had been waiting for. ". . . And the winner for Best Original Screenplay . . . Ethan Coen and Joel Coen for *Fargo.*"

Cameron later said he would have thanked me in his acceptance speech. I had bought an ad in *Variety,* the daily Hollywood trade publication, wishing him good luck. I felt terrible for him. I wanted Cameron to win the Oscar he deserved.

Being involved with *Jerry Maguire* changed my life forever. I could not go on a plane without somebody, recognizing who I was, deciding to talk sports for the entire flight. I was asked to sign autographs on posters from the film, and lunch with me was auctioned off for $15,000. Crazy, I know. Most gratifying of all was landing roles as extras in the movie for friends, such as Warren, Troy, Drew, Tim, Ki-Jana, Christian Fauria, and Jim Irsay, and inviting general managers and owners to the premieres. Athletes can be as star-struck as anyone else.

Several years ago, Cameron spoke highly of me in a magazine article, saying I "helped enormously with access and the details with which we could fill in the character." That's my recollection exactly. I have fond feelings for Cameron and am very grateful for the time we spent together. He did a phenomenal job of showing the world I lived in and presenting a more balanced view of a sports agent.

Not long after the Oscars, I received a call from another prominent director, Oliver Stone. He, too, asked for help with a new project, and I was glad to provide it. Unlike Cameron, who requested cooperation from the NFL, Stone lived up to his reputation as a maverick and didn't want to be constrained in any manner.

The movie was *Any Given Sunday,* and it featured a stellar cast: Al Pacino, Cameron Diaz, James Woods, Dennis Quaid, Jamie Foxx, and Charlton Heston. The plot centered around the up-and-down fortunes of the Miami Sharks, coached by Pacino, who are fighting to qualify for the playoffs after their starting and backup quarterbacks go down with injuries.

I took Oliver to our charitable golf tournament, where he interacted with various players, including Troy. I spent a night with Pacino and shared my insights into what made a successful coach in the NFL. Coaches were psychiatrists, as well as strategists, I told him, aware of how each player needed to be motivated differently.

Pacino was a boxing fan who knew little about pro football, but he understood. Seeing him prepare for the speech he delivered in the locker room before the big game was most illuminating. While the other actors joked around with each other to pass the time, he was slumped against the wall. He seemed almost depressed. He wasn't. He was in character. Five minutes later, he gave one of the most inspiring talks I ever heard, pointing out the parallels between life and football. Rockne could not have fired up his troops any better. That's why he's Al Pacino. For that same scene, I showed players how to pound each other's shoulder pads.

With Cameron Diaz, who played the owner of the team she inherited from her father, I pointed out how she'd encounter sexism wherever she turned in the sport and how, rightly or wrongly, people would always compare her to him. She needed to be charming and yet no pushover, a most delicate balancing act. She pulled it off.

Stone also enlisted my help to assess the throwing ability of a well-known rapper he was going to cast in the role of the third-string quarterback who saves the day.

"Can you take this film to your friends who are general managers and get some objective feedback?" he asked.

I didn't need any general managers to tell me the obvious. The rapper made Jerry O'Connell look like Steve Young.

"Oliver," I said, "I represent half the starting quarterbacks in the NFL and I've been doing this for twenty-five years. This guy throws like a girl."

Stone proceeded to find a couple of former NFL coaches to give the actor some tips on how to release the ball.

"Now what do you think?" he asked.

"He still throws like a girl," I said.

Ultimately, Stone went instead with Jamie Foxx, a relatively unknown comic in those days, and the movie was released in December 1999.

In the late '90s, I also worked on *Arli$$*, the spoof HBO series that featured Robert Wuhl as a loose wheeler-dealer agent, the opposite of Jerry Maguire. As a consultant, I suggested a number of my nefarious fantasies for plotlines. In one, Arliss sleeps with his client's wife. In another, he represents the owners of *both* sides in a franchise relocation. I made sure my name was not on the credits—I didn't want to be seen as endorsing the character's behavior—although I did make a cameo appearance in a scene shot at one of our Super Bowl parties.

On network television, I played myself in an episode of *Beverly Hills 90210,* in which the character portrayed by Tori Spelling asked me to persuade Steve Young to attend her boyfriend's birthday party.

I played myself, as well, in *First Monday*, a TV show about the Supreme Court, sharing the stage with Georgetown basketball coach John Thompson in the episode entitled "Court Date." I also appeared in two episodes of the NBC sitcom *Sports Action Team,* which spoofed an ESPN show.

I was a consultant on *For Love of the Game,* the baseball movie starring Kevin Costner. Kevin did all his own pitching, though when he didn't show on opening night because of a dispute with the studio over the final cut, I filled in for him on the red carpet to do interviews.

For me, meanwhile, in the mid-1990s, there were plenty of captivating plotlines in real, not reel, life.

Take the 1996 Summer Olympics in Atlanta.

As I watched the telecast, one performer stood out. Her name was Kerri Strug.

Kerri, despite an injured ankle, came out for her last vault, which would determine whether the U.S. women's gymnastics team won the gold. She ran down the runway, perfectly executed the vault, and then collapsed in pain. Coach Bela Karolyi carried her up to the stage for the medal presentation. Whatever Kerri lacked in size—she was about 4'10"—she made up in unbelievable courage. She was a true heroine for America.

Several hours later, her father, Dr. Burt Strug, called and asked if I could meet them in Atlanta prior to a major press conference she would hold. The Olympics are a premiere marking event because they transcend the narrow genre of sports to reach a worldwide audience. The difficulty is that once the games end, if a particular sport does not have a high profile, the athletes fade from the spotlight. I was amazed to see that, instead of being supportive, the other members of the gymnastics team were jealous of Kerri because, at least in their view, she was not supposed to be the star. That meant we'd have to chart her path.

To prolong her celebrity and create revenue opportunities, we set up a touring gymnastics show. I was also successful in urging the Ice Capades to have her do vaults on the side of the rink during breaks in their show. She rang the bell on Wall Street, and we enlisted Steve Case, the chairman of AOL, to lift her "Bela like" onto the field at halftime of a Monday night football game. She was a copresenter at the Family Film Awards with Bob Hope and was a good enough sport to allow *Saturday Night Live* to lampoon her high-pitched voice in a skit in which Chris Kattan played her evil twin, "Kippy." Barbara Walters named her one of the Most Fascinating People of 1996.

I was surprised how sheltered Kerri had been throughout her life, with the training regimen consuming almost all her time. The real-world interaction was new to her. We secured a few endorsements, and Kerri wrote a book, and there was no doubt in my mind she would have a most promising future.

Representing Kerri was hardly the first time I ventured away from the more traditional sports. I'd worked in the late 1980s with U.S. figure skater Brian Boitano, connecting him with legendary rock promoter Bill Graham to put together his own skating exhibition instead of being part of an established show. Representing Brian gave me the freedom to be much more creative than I could be for athletes in team sports. He was exciting on the ice, and handsome and charming off it.

Brian, who had won the gold medal at the 1988 Winter Olympics in Calgary, Alberta, secured help, as well, from his good friend, women's gold medalist Katarina Witt, and together they signed up most of the other top skaters. Instead of taking a fee, they acquired ownership. Brian also wanted to do *Carmen on Ice* as a television special. I approached Bob Iger of ABC, and it ended up being an award-winning prime-time hit. To generate endorsements, we staged a special skating exhibition at Rockefeller Center in New York City, and met with potential sponsors at a private reception.

I had also been involved with the world's most popular sport, soccer.

It was a few months before the 1994 World Cup was to be held in the United States when I received a call from Peter Vermes, a member of the American team, which was training in Mission Viejo, California. Peter asked if I could meet with him and others to discuss the idea of representation. Sure I would. It was quite a collection of talent: John Harkes, Cobi Jones, Tony Meola, Alexi Lalas, Tom Dooley, Joe-Max Moore, and Paul Caligiuri. They would comprise the backbone of U.S. soccer for years to come.

The assignment was challenging, to say the least. Representing a group is always more problematic than representing an individual. Instead of one client with a point of view, there were twenty points of view. Plus, each player had his own agent for separate endorsements. The players also worried that if they asserted themselves too much, the Soccer Federation would cut them. Even so, I was able to collectively bargain benefits and bonuses that they thoroughly appreciated. I'll always cherish my experience with those guys.

Needless to say, I remained very busy in the sport that consumed most of my time—pro football.

In 1997, I got a call from the father of Jason Taylor, the gifted defensive end from the University of Akron.

"We are very interested in your services," he said, "but I have one final question. How do you train players?"

I was taken aback. "I'm not sure what you mean," I said, "but from 1989 to 1995, I had the very first player picked in the NFL Draft six out of seven years. You can't go higher than that. They each trained themselves using their schools, weight coaches, and trainers."

The elder Taylor was not appeased. "I need him trained for the combine and for the All-Star games," he said, "and IMG has a great trainer."

Off to IMG Jason went.

The conversation made me think in a deeper way about how much the sport had evolved in the twenty-two years since I took on Bart, then respond accordingly. If I hoped to keep up with the competition, I needed to train my players, hiring the best experts I could find. No doubt it would be fairly expensive—roughly $20,000 per client, I later estimated—and not exactly cost-efficient for anyone

drafted lower than the second round, but we dove right in, bene-
fiting greatly from our close contacts with scouts, coaches, and
general managers. I knew what teams liked about my players and,
more importantly, what they did not like, and that's what we set
out to improve as much as possible in the two or three months
leading to the scouting combine. The results were dramatic.

The highest-rated prospects, from O. J. Simpson to Andrew Luck,
all had knocks against them. When reading an official team scouting
report, the correct reaction isn't to say, defensively, "They don't
know what they are talking about." The approach is to change the
perception before it's too late. The draft is not a merit award for
conspicuous college performance. It is a projection of how an individual will perform over the next decade. Many outstanding college
players do not possess the size, strength, and speed to be successful
pros. The "Second Season" of scouting, which consists of bowl games,
All-Star games, the combine, and campus pro scouting days, often
determines draft position. Thus, using state-of-the-art nutrition
and training technology is critical.

In the spring of 2004, for example, scouts worried how Ben
Roethlisberger, who operated mostly out of the shotgun at Miami
of Ohio, would handle the short snap directly from the center. Any
quarterback from a shotgun system will stir similar doubts. To put
those concerns to rest, we hired Steve Clarkson, an expert in tutor-
ing quarterbacks, to train Ben to take the ball from center in drills
open to every team. Case closed.

The All-Star games are held in January; the two most important are the Senior Bowl in Alabama and the East-West Shrine Game
in Florida. Owners, directors of player personnel, head coaches, and
assistant coaches show up. Players can't afford to hold anything
back in the practices or games.

Even before making training clients a priority, I recognized the
importance of quick fixes. In '95, when I received word at the

Senior Bowl that a couple of teams were concerned about a hitch they spotted in Kerry Collins's delivery, I took action. With representatives from every team mingling in the same hotel bar, the rumor spread in a hurry.

Bill Walsh came to the rescue. I paid Bill, who was out of coaching by then, $20,000 to rid Kerry of the hitch. Soon afterward, Bill certified Kerry as "de-hitched," and everybody believed him. Was the hitch truly gone? I'm not sure it was ever there.

Preparing my clients for the scouting combine was essential, both physically and mentally. We brought them to Newport Beach and created a set of training, practice, and chalkboard facilities, allowing us to supervise their nutrition and hire doctors to perform thorough examinations to identify any problem areas before teams conducted their own. The goal was for their bodies to be as cut and athletic looking as possible. We used two trainers: Chuck Williams, who had won worldwide weightlifting contests, and Doug Hix, a former track star. No longer busy in practices or games, players made dramatic improvements in speed, strength, and flexibility.

In a sport obsessed with speed, especially at wide receiver, running back, and defensive back, too often at the expense of less skilled athletes who just know how to play the game, knocking one or two tenths of a second off a player's time in the forty-yard dash can mean a huge difference in where a player is drafted. In 2000, R. Jay Soward, a wideout from USC, vaulted to the first round—he was picked by the Jags at No. 29—after we took a chance and coached him up. He ran the fastest forty in the combine. There is no other way besides improving speed to rise that far in the opinion of scouts.

As for a player's mental preparation, we administered the Wonderlic IQ test and then hired a former general manager to conduct mock interviews. The interviews they'd have for real at the combine, with the entire coaching staff or GM, would be the first impression teams would receive of an athlete's personality and character, and if the session did not go well, quite possibly the last. The costs of choosing the wrong individual, one with off-the-field issues resulting in his eventual release, were more severe than ever. Besides losing the player, teams would also lose the bonus money and would not have the salary-cap room to replace him.

Normally, with our profiling, there was no record of dubious behavior. On the occasions there was, our goal in rehearsals was to get players to the point where the phrases they used didn't transport them back in time to the horror of the event. That would make them appear defensive and ward off potential suitors. They also needed to explain why they stumbled, and what they'd learned about themselves to avoid similar mistakes in the future.

When our draftees left for the combine, their trainers went for any last-minute tweaks or support. Agents weren't allowed to attend the workouts, and that was fine with me. It was up to the players now. I couldn't run the forty for them. Yet some agents showed up anyway, mostly to protect their relationship with clients by convincing them they were vital. I never felt that was necessary.

As usual, the closer we got to draft day in '97, I gained a better indication of which teams were interested in which clients of mine. It wasn't necessarily the same information the press gathered. The word most people received on Warrick Dunn, for example, who rushed for over 1,000 yards in three straight years for Florida State, was he was too small and would slip into the second round. The word I received, though, was that Tampa, picking twelfth, adored Warrick, and that's where he ended up. Whatever he lacked in size he made up for in speed and determination. To elevate his profile, I put together an exhibit that showed how many of the defensive linemen and linebackers he ran past in the ACC made it to the NFL.

The future for Cal's standout tight end Tony Gonzalez seemed just as clear. I was told that the Chiefs, picking immediately after the Bucs, liked him, and what wasn't there to like? There weren't many players who could compete in the NCAA basketball tournament—he was a power forward—*and* be a star on the football team.

Still, about a half hour before the Chiefs would be on the clock, I took a call from Carl Peterson, the club's general manager and president.

"We're inclined to take Tony with our pick," Peterson told me, "but we want you to agree to this contract."

With the minutes ticking away, he quickly spelled out the terms. They were not terribly unfair, but that wasn't the point.

"Carl," I responded, "I am not prepared to negotiate a contract in fifteen minutes."

"Well, you better," he said, "because if you don't, we're going to pass on Tony."

It was similar to Jerry Jones threatening to take Tony Mandarich instead of Troy Aikman in 1989. I called Carl's bluff just as I called Jerry's.

"Dallas isn't too far behind you," I said, "and Dallas is a pretty good place to go. So do whatever you need to do. Tony will be just fine."

The Chiefs picked Tony, and good thing they did. Over twelve seasons in Kansas City, Tony, a lock for Canton, caught 916 passes, 76 for scores, and was just getting started. He added 326 receptions and 27 touchdowns the next four years in Atlanta.

Tony is an exception. Most players never come close to competing for that long. The average tenure is about three and a half years, and when the end arrives, as it does for so many with a summons to the coach's office—"bring your playbook"—no words can soften the blow.

Some take the news better than others. Among those who take

it poorly, many blame the agent if other teams don't scoop them up. If only the agent had worked the phones, they tell themselves, there'd be no shortage of options. I was extremely careful in what I said to these players about their prospects, especially if they had been in the NFL only a short time. I didn't have a right to dash anyone's dreams. My job was to fulfill them.

In the case of Darrell Russell, the third of my three first-rounders in 1997, my job was more challenging than ever.

Darrell, a defensive tackle from USC, should have been the No. 1 pick without question. He had that much talent. However, he also allegedly smoked marijuana, which scared off Bill Parcells and the Jets, who traded the choice to the Rams. Darrell went instead at No. 2 to the Raiders, which seemed a perfect fit given how the team, run by Al Davis, relished its well-deserved reputation as the league's outcasts. Only Darrell went too far, even for the Raiders. He was late to practices and meetings and argued with coaches. I never represented a player who had more of an issue with authority than Darrell Russell.

Bruce Allen, an Oakland executive, asked me to intervene, which I was glad to do.

"You are so bright," I told Darrell. "Let's find a way to get you back on track."

For a week or two we did, and Darrell was as funny and charming as ever, but soon the rebel in him resurfaced. His problem was he didn't buy into the concept of what is expected from a professional football player. Not everyone does. He was too intelligent and posed too many questions for his own good.

Darrell loved playing on Sundays. Who doesn't? Sundays are when heroes are made, and he certainly was one, receiving All-Pro honors in 1998 and 1999. The rest of the week was where he had trouble. Football, he never quite understood, is not a democracy. Never has been, never will be. Fight the system and you will not last. He was suspended several times for violating the NFL's drug policy. His career ended in 2004, way too soon.

I felt awful for Darrell. There was much to admire in him. His heart was in the right place, and he was fun to be around.

I had high hopes for another young man I met in the late 1990s. Little did I imagine Ryan Leaf would turn out the way he did.

15
THE WRONG CHOICES

Leaf or Manning, that was the great debate of '98. Which star quarterback, Washington State's Ryan Leaf or Tennessee's Peyton Manning, would go No. 1 in the draft? Manning, the son of an NFL quarterback—Archie played fourteen years—was more polished and adept at reading defenses. Ryan possessed more raw ability. Both were can't-miss prospects.

I faced a debate of my own: Which quarterback should I try to sign? I couldn't represent both, not two quarterbacks as highly rated as these two.

I met Ryan at his family's home in Great Falls, Montana. Any concerns I might have harbored about him being arrogant, as was his reputation in college, soon went away. His parents, John and Marcia, asked the right questions about the new world he would be entering, and so did their son. When we watched football together in his basement, he showed tremendous respect for the game's veterans, and that wasn't always the case with the younger generation. Too often they act as if they invented the sport. When I gave Troy Aikman's phone number to Ryan, he could not contain his excitement.

My meeting with Peyton and his father also went very well. I was always a big fan of Archie Manning. He played for a lot of poor teams, but he was an amazing quarterback and a true gentleman.

It was a difficult decision, but I went for the sure thing in Ryan. Because he was a junior, he had to declare for the draft in January, while Team Manning could wait months to select its representation. I didn't want to risk losing both. For another, when facing a similar choice in 1993, I chose the quarterback with more natural talent, Drew Bledsoe, over the more accomplished Rick Mirer, and that decision could not have worked out any better. In fact, Drew and Mike Price, the coach at Washington State, both spoke quite highly of Ryan.

It was not until several months before the draft that I realized Ryan might present challenges I didn't anticipate. By then, it was too late.

"No way do I want to play in Indianapolis," he told me, referring to the Colts, who owned the No. 1 pick. Instead, because of the exceptional weather and the more laid-back lifestyle, he preferred the San Diego Chargers, who would go second.

"That's fine," I warned him, "but the way to achieve this is not exactly going to help your image. You'll get a lot of criticism." Ryan didn't care about his image, though, only his destination.

Making his wish come true would not be easy. The Colts leaned toward choosing Ryan. Many scouts also saw him as a better prospect than Peyton Manning. Hard to believe now, isn't it?

I told Ryan it would do no good to approach Colts GM Jim Irsay. Irsay saw the sport the same way he viewed his other passion, rock 'n' roll. Just as musicians tended to be a bit eccentric, so did football players, and that did not stop him from drafting Jeff George or trading for Eric Dickerson. "Leigh," he used to say, "it's about the freaking talent." If someone is that gifted, in Irsay's opinion, you simply find a way to deal with his personality.

Instead, the case needed to be made to the Indianapolis coach,

Jim Mora, and it couldn't come from anything Ryan said. It had to come from what he did, or, rather, did not do.

"If you go to the combine," I told Ryan, "but fail to show up for a meeting with Mora, that should do it. Jim is a real prideful person who has a tendency to explode. I am not recommending you do this, but if you are desperate to go to San Diego, this is the way."

Ryan approved, but I first cleared the idea with Chargers general manager Bobby Beathard, lest San Diego also question my client's reliability. Beathard went along with the ruse. If he'd had a problem, Ryan would've shown up for his meeting with Mora. Some purists argue players should not have the right to dictate where they start their pro career, but aren't college graduates who don't play football allowed to choose where they want to work and live? The draft was not handed down by Moses as part of the Ten Commandments. The draft, let's be honest, is a control mechanism designed to prevent college athletes from exercising the same freedoms everyone else takes for granted and to limit their leverage in contract negotiations. It is important to separate the honor of being selected from the concept of not being given the freedom of choice. Just because athletes are well compensated doesn't change the underlying principle.

Once Ryan was a no-show, Mora, as anticipated, went ballistic. I defended my player, naturally, dismissing the coach's response as another Mora meltdown. As I'd anticipated, Ryan was criticized, but the plan achieved its purpose. The Colts took Manning. Something tells me the folks in Indianapolis have never regretted that decision.

Neither did Ryan, who received an $11.25 million signing bonus. It was a superb deal—even if it didn't appear that way shortly afterward when Manning's agent landed his client an $11.6 million bonus. The fact remains, Manning would never have reached that figure if we hadn't put together Ryan's deal first. Manning's representative could say to the front-office personnel in Indianapolis, "Look at what San Diego just paid Ryan Leaf, and Peyton was picked ahead of him."

No one, of course, will ever remember the amount of their bonuses.

All people will remember is that Peyton Manning became an icon and Ryan Leaf a bust. The ramifications for the two proud franchises, and cities, one uplifted, the other demoralized, would be felt for years.

It did not start poorly for Ryan in the NFL. He was charming at his first press conference and calm throughout training camp. The Chargers won the first two games he started. Not till his third game, in Kansas City, did Ryan become unraveled, on and off the field. Facing one of the top defensive lines in the league, he completed only 1 of 15 passes for 4 yards and fumbled 3 times in a 23–7 defeat.

That was disappointing enough, but what really made people cringe was what occurred in a locker room the day after. Ryan screamed an obscenity at a reporter, which still would have been no big deal if the TV cameras had not been rolling, but they were. Players have often yelled at writers. It's understandable. After giving everything they had, and more, for sixty agonizing minutes and coming up short, their emotions were still raw and intense when the press filed in a few minutes later, ready to assign blame. Things could spiral out of control in a flash. Usually, once everybody cooled off, apologies would be made, and all would be forgotten.

Not this time. While I watched the videotape of Ryan's outburst, two words came to mind: Rodney King. King was the black motorist whose merciless beating by the police in March of 1991 led to the deadly riots a year later in Los Angeles. The tape of King was played over and over on TV, just as I knew the tape of Ryan would be, branding him as the villain he was not. Instead of viewers realizing that this was just one single incident, the effect of seeing the same footage repeatedly created the false impression the L.A. Police Department beat up helpless blacks on a daily basis.

My first task was to limit the damage as much as possible. I had gone through difficult experiences with Warren and Jake and Bruce and Drew, and the crisis eventually passed, as long as no new information surfaced.

In this case, however, there was one major difference. Instead of Ryan being accessible to the media, he withdrew into himself because he felt unfairly attacked, which made the situation even worse for him. If only he had issued a formal apology, the fans in San Diego would have forgiven him, and so would the press. He was still a rookie.

The other problem was Bobby Beathard. He did not back up Ryan where it mattered most: in public. Bobby was charming and youthful, a surfer, casual dresser, and health food devotee who once grabbed my hand when I reached for the salt shaker at lunch to warn me, "Salt, the silent killer." Yet when it came to football, Bobby was old school. He was embarrassed by how Ryan acted and was unable to treat it as one mistake by a young player dealing with the type of adversity he had never encountered at any other level of football.

Even so, a few sympathetic words from him in Ryan's defense, sincere or not, would have gone a long way. Instead, Ryan felt like an outcast on his own team, and as the season wore on and the Chargers went nowhere—they finished at 5-11—his fate was sealed. Ryan spent three years in San Diego and one in Dallas, and that was it for his career in the National Football League.

Could the situation have played out differently for Ryan? No question, and believe me, we tried everything we could to get him the help he needed, including therapy, but he kept withdrawing more and more. Ryan saw the battle as himself against the world, and he would not allow anyone to get through that barrier.

To this day, I remain convinced Ryan had the talent to be a

very successful pro quarterback, but talent is not enough. The margin between success and failure in professional football is thinner than people realize. The wrong coach, the wrong system, the wrong city—pick one—can send a young man down the wrong path, and he might never find his way back.

Take the quarterback class of 1999. Five of them were drafted among the top 12, including the first three, Tim Couch to Cleveland, Donovan McNabb to Philadelphia, and Akili Smith to Cincinnati. The others were Daunte Culpepper, at No. 11 to Minnesota, and Cade McNown, at No. 12 to Chicago. Yet none of the five won a Super Bowl. McNabb was the only to take his team to one, losing to the Pats in 2005. Three of the other four—Couch, Smith, and McNown—did not throw a pass in the league after 2003.

What happened? All three could not have been scouting mistakes . . . could they? It's unlikely. Their difficulties came as a result of how they were developed, or, rather, not developed. The care and feeding of young quarterbacks—when they play, how often they play, what they are taught in film study—usually determines whether they will make it in the pros. I've always thought that, given the critical nature of the position and the money teams invest, further study of the ways to best develop a quarterback is needed. It helps, of course, to have a solid offensive line and a reliable running attack to put less pressure on the rookie behind center. Many quarterbacks aren't that fortunate, as Bart and Jeff George could testify.

For years, before the salary cap took effect, quarterbacks were brought along slowly with care, given time to learn how to better read the defenses and become familiar with their receivers. Four or five years would pass before anyone judged them.

In today's NFL, however, due to the salary cap—most teams can't afford two highly paid quarterbacks—rookies are forced to play too soon, and for every Andrew Luck or Russell Wilson or RG III, who propel their teams into the playoffs, countless others are vilified, in blogs and on talk radio and on analysis and highlight shows, as busts if they don't succeed in four of five *games*. One generation ago, there were just a handful of games on TV each week, and nowhere near the amount of "insiders" weighing in. There was *Sports Illustrated* and the beat writers on daily newspapers, and that was about it.

Such instant analysis is premature, to say the least. Their early performance is no indication of the player they may become one day, if only given the opportunity. They are not like running backs or wide receivers, who burst through holes or run routes just as they did in high school and college. The pro game for quarterbacks, played at a much faster tempo and with more complicated offensive formations and defensive schemes, is a giant step up from the college version.

In that 1999 class, perhaps the most highly touted collection of QBs since the 1983 class, I reached out to Akili Smith from the University of Oregon. Akili didn't have the reputation of the other quarterbacks. What he had was a cannon for a throwing arm, perhaps second to Jeff George among the QBs I handled. At his pro day it was akin to watching a machine release the ball. In his senior year, he threw 32 touchdowns in leading the Ducks to an 8-4 record. Akili did not require any training—well, except for the Wonderlic test, which he hadn't taken seriously the first time, when he scored a 9. We had an SAT specialist work with him, and he scored a 27. He possessed so much innate ability that the Browns, who were on the clock, considered drafting him instead of the more-publicized Couch. This was one of the most meteoric rises in draft history. It hadn't been that long since Akili would have been ecstatic just to be signed as a free agent. Our plan was aggressive, and to his credit, Akili seized every opportunity to showcase his skills.

The evening before the draft, after speaking to team officials, we still didn't know which way Cleveland would go, and wouldn't find out till the next morning. I met constantly with Akili and his family to lay out the various scenarios.

"If we don't end up signing with the Browns," I said, "there is Cincinnati, who has the third pick (the Eagles weren't interested), and Cincinnati, I must tell you, has been a death knell for my quarterbacks before. Steve Young didn't sign there. David Klingler, a great prospect, didn't flourish. I can assure you it will be a tough negotiation, because when Mike Brown has a need, he can be reasonable, but if he doesn't, all bets are off."

Everyone then formed a prayer circle led by Akili's father, Ray, a preacher.

"We received guidance," Ray said, "and believe God is approving of Cincinnati."

Cincinnati it was, the Browns having adopted the safer route in Couch. This time, at least, I didn't offend Mike Brown on national television.

The negotiations were even tougher than I anticipated. Soon it was time for training camp to start, and the gap between us and the Bengals was still significant—more like a chasm.

Akili now was officially a holdout. I have never thought that term was fair to players. Players are *freezeouts* more than holdouts, because of the NFL rules that don't allow them into camp until they have signed a contract. I could do nothing but wait, and there is no greater frustration for a dedicated professional football player anxious to secure his spot. He has to remain at home while his teammates practice and bond without him. Little wonder players holding out are constantly on edge.

Typically, if informed in the morning of the latest substandard offer from management, they are defiant. "Screw them," a disgruntled player says. "I never want to play for those guys." At 3:00 P.M., he calls back. The defiance is gone, replaced by a desperate sound in his voice. "Do you think they will ever improve their offer?" he wonders. "It's still a lot of money. Shouldn't I be taking this?"

Finally, in late August, the Bengals agreed to pay Akili $58 million over seven years.

Was the holdout worth it? Only in terms of an enhanced first contract. Anytime a quarterback misses twenty-seven days of camp, it is a failure on both my part and the team's. Those first days in camp are when a young quarterback takes the most snaps, visualizing the whole field over and over. If he gets too far behind, as Akili did, there isn't enough time to catch up before the season starts, and once it does, he won't work in practice with the first unit unless the starter gets hurt. Akili was let go in 2003.

I can't help but wonder, and I accept my share of the blame, how different Akili's career might have unfolded if he had been in training camp from the start. I prided myself on having precious few holdouts, always contending it would be far better if teams signed players for the short term to get them into camp while both sides kept working on a long-term agreement. Teams would never go for that idea. They want as much leverage as they can get. Either way, I should have found a way for Akili to sign much sooner.

Akili Smith wasn't my only rookie holdout in 1999. The other was Edgerrin James, a running back from the University of Miami, selected by the Colts one pick later.

Edgerrin was taken ahead of a more accomplished runner, Heisman Trophy winner Ricky Williams from Texas, a choice some questioned. Edgerrin had everything teams look for in a running back: speed, power, elusiveness, and a great ability to score. He could catch the ball out of the backfield and turn a nothing play into three or four yards. Edgerrin was also brighter and more analytical than people who didn't see behind the dreadlocks and the gold teeth gave him credit for. He kept the incentives in his contract on a flow sheet on his computer. No doubt he would be a valuable asset to the Colts, who won just three games in the first year of the Peyton Manning era and had traded their marquee runner, Marshall Faulk, to the Rams.

Bill Polian, the Colts president, conducted the negotiations. Jim Irsay, my kindred sprit in our love affair with rock 'n' roll, was now the owner, taking over after his father passed away. Polian was a football genius and would not be won over by an *agent's* assessment of the player's talent. Jeff Moorad tried that approach with Polian during the Kerry Collins negotiations in Carolina and received a lecture in return.

Complicating matters was that we didn't have to simply satisfy Edgerrin. We needed to satisfy *Team* Edgerrin, a sophisticated group that included his brother (a med student), an attorney, and a lobbyist for the school system in Miami. They served him well.

Once the holdout entered its second or third week, Team Edgerrin grew increasingly restless.

"We'd like to see first-hand what's happening," they told me.

"Okay, we'll go to camp in Terre Haute [Indiana]," I said. "I'll take you to meet with Polian."

I wasn't too optimistic the meeting would resolve our differences. There was not, after all, the same sense of urgency in doing a deal, and getting Edgerrin his reps in camp, as there is with rookie quarterbacks. I was also concerned Polian might not reveal his true feelings in front of people he didn't know. Or if his responses were too combative, Team Edgerrin might take offense. It wouldn't be the first time.

In fact, Polian may deny it, but I am quite sure he had a calendar in his office marking the date when he needed to sign Edgerrin, and the deadline had little to do with the beginning of training camp. Running backs, he knew, learn the playbook in a hurry, and actually spare themselves a lot of needless punishment if they show up a few weeks late.

Some players delayed their arrival in training camp for as long as possible for that very reason. A perfect example was offensive tackle David Williams, who played for the Houston Oilers during the '90s. I knew he hated camp, so I waited until four or five days into it to finish negotiating a new contract for him early in his career. I just didn't realize how much David hated camp.

"David, I have great news for you," I said. "The Oilers have accepted our proposal."

"I don't want it," he responded.

"David, maybe I didn't explain this very well," I went on, "but they are giving us exactly what we asked for and more money than either of us thought you would get. We should accept this right away."

"I don't want it," he reiterated.

"David, can you please explain to me what the problem is?"

"Leigh, I told you not to get me into the first three weeks of camp. I am not signing."

A fairly mellow guy, David had been at the center of a controversy when he didn't leave his wife, Debi, in Houston after she had given birth on the night before a game in New England. When he called me for advice before the baby was born, I said, "David, there will be many games but only one Debi and one first child." The Oilers docked him a game check, and the ensuing controversy became known as "Babygate."

"This is like World War II, when guys were going to war and something would come up but they had to go," one of his coaches said.

The issue became a national debate that went on for weeks, with editorial writers and cartoonists weighing in. Vice President Al Gore led a discussion on the floor of the U.S. Senate. Pampers even offered to have David and Debi, as two loving parents, do an endorsement. We didn't go for it.

•   •   •

Dave signed his contract extension, eventually, although the distaste for camp he shared with many of his peers was understandable. Camps were held in the dustiest, dankest, most obscure towns, in close to 100 percent humidity, with unreliable air-conditioning. Players slept on tiny beds in college dorms. Such Spartan surroundings are no longer the case, thank goodness, as teams spare no expense to offer the players the luxury they have come to expect wherever they travel.

Also different in today's NFL is the purpose of training camp. Years ago, offensive linemen arrived in camp with huge potbellies. Plenty of players smoked. They used camp to get in shape, although you would never know it by what they ate once they arrived, the most unhealthy food one could imagine. The training tables now list the grams of fat and carbs and the number of calories in every appetizer, main course, and dessert, and with the money they could lose, few players risk reporting in poor condition. They rest for a week or two after the season ends and go back to their private gym or the team's indoor facility. There is no off-season.

In just a few minutes, it became clear that meeting with Bill Polian was a waste of time for Team Edgerrin. If anything, our presence made a tense situation even more stressful.

"Why are you here? We have nothing to talk about," he said. "I already made you our best offer."

Polian didn't deter me. I always believed there was something to talk about.

"I understand your position," I said, "but if we spend more time on this, we can get this done today."

That was all Polian needed to hear.

"You have five minutes to get out of camp," he ordered.

He wasn't kidding. Moments later, a few security guards escorted Team Edgerrin and me off the premises. I had certainly impressed Team Edgerrin with my negotiating prowess.

The next day I was on a flight to San Francisco, although I did not stay there for long. When I called Jeff from the airport, he said he and Polian had reached a deal as I was in the air. Maybe, for the good of my clients, I should have spent more time at 35,000 feet. I took the next plane back to Indianapolis.

The deal for Edgerrin was worth the extra travel: $49 million over seven years, including a $9.5 million signing bonus and a series of eminently attainable performance-based incentives known as escalator clauses.

For example, if Edgerrin were to gain at least 701 yards in his rookie season, his salary would go up another $1 million in each of the ensuing six years. Given his talent, and the Colts' need at running back, it would be a major upset if he did not reach that threshold.

He reached 701 yards, all right, in just the eighth game of the year. He finished with more than twice that total, 1,553 yards, and scored 17 TDs. Yes, missing all those days in camp definitely set him back. Because of the numbers he put up, Edgerrin earned about $20 million his first two years, an all-time record.

Too bad I couldn't enjoy his success more than I did. Few players ever started out like Edgerrin James. However, I was preoccupied that fall of 1999 with two other matters, one dealing with a client's future, the other my own.

The client was Steve Young, and his future was in serious jeopardy as a result of a hit he received during a Monday night game in September—on the same field, ironically, in Arizona where Troy had been knocked unconscious ten years earlier. Steve was taken to the ground by Cardinals defensive back Aeneas Williams, who got through on a blitz after running back Lawrence Phillips missed his blocking assignment. Just like Troy, Steve did not move, and watching on television, I was as terrified as I was the first time, perhaps more, knowing what I did about concussions and their impact on the brain. Once Steve came to, he left the field under his own power, replaced by backup quarterback Jeff Garcia.

Steve had suffered another concussion, an official one, his fourth in three years and the seventh of his career. He wasn't naive about the potential risks to his long-term health—he went to those conferences with neurologists and might have had the highest IQ of any player I represented—but, bright or not, he was like every other player: in denial. Nothing meant more to him than the next play or next game. That's how badly he wanted to play, which I'd known about him since the first meeting at the airport in Salt Lake City, and which led him to choose the USFL over the Bengals.

I, however, did not want to see him in the next play or the next game. I didn't want to see him on the field ever again. He was thirty-eight. He had his Super Bowl ring. The monkey was off his back, forever. Besides, he could look forward to a bright future off the field. Politics, law, business, Steve would thrive in any profession he chose.

Steve missed the rest of the 1999 season, but he could not bring himself to quit, despite the wishes of his wife, parents, and doctors. He was reluctant to give up the only life he had ever known. He had not become a starting quarterback in San Francisco until the age of twenty-nine, and he aimed to make up for lost time. Steve also knew he was still one of the best quarterbacks in the game. At the very least, he needed to go through a process, with a timetable only he could set, before reaching a decision on his own terms.

He wanted to see how he might feel in the months ahead and how the 49ers might feel. The 49ers felt uneasy, and with good reason, though finishing his career somewhere else was not out of the question. His former offensive coordinator, Mike Shanahan, whom he loved working with, was now the head coach in Denver and very interested in acquiring Steve.

By the spring of 2000, Steve had yet to make up his mind. This presented me with a dilemma: If I pushed him too hard to quit, he would resist and perhaps resent me for the rest of his life. Conversely, if I didn't push him hard enough, he might play again, and if he were further hurt, I would never be able to forgive myself. In hoping to find a middle ground, I went public with my misgivings. I'm not sure Steve was very happy I made my sentiments known, and I always tried to fulfill his goals, as he defined them. In this situation, though, I felt a higher duty to preserve his health and future.

That June, he finally let go. I was as happy for Steve as I was when he won the Super Bowl.

As for the decision related to my own future, the result would not be nearly as gratifying. In 1999, with the decade coming to a close, our football practice was thriving. We represented eighty-six players, a number I did not advertise. Why would it make sense to destabilize our own clients or challenge owners by flaunting power? Using that power is what matters. A high percentage of those we represented were superstars, Pro Bowl players, and quarterbacks. Our baseball practice, meanwhile, was among the top 3 in the sport, and the NBA side of the business was growing, as well. Our roster of television newscasters and announcers had grown to more than forty, and I had recently written the bestselling *Winning with Integrity*. Most gratifying of all was that our players were doing an outstanding job with their charitable and community projects. There seemed no reason we could not sustain the same level of success forever.

Yet I was looking to have a broader impact on sports and entertainment. I'd always had the ability to envision future markets, anticipate technology, and try to keep us on the cutting edge. I felt no different as the new century was about to dawn.

We decided to set up a special projects unit to explore technologies and new companies that could utilize sports in different ways. The Internet was still in its embryonic stage, with AOL as the gatekeeper. I felt if we could put athletes into a Web site format, it would increase their exposure and opportunities. They would write weekly diaries and discuss their charities, and we could set up an e-commerce application to allow fans to purchase memorabilia directly from them.

I hired a brilliant young attorney, Tyler Goldman, to work on special projects. He brought on board Ross Schaufelberger from STATS, Inc., and that's when we created the Web site, which we called Athlete Direct.

The concept was a hit, drawing fans and fan clubs. Eventually Jeff Moorad and I, who sold part of our share for $20 million, realized how the benefits from such projects could dwarf the representation side of our business. Tyler and I worked, as well, on bringing the Tampa Bay Buccaneers to Hollywood Park and thought the deal was done, only to have the track owner pull out at the last second. We also marketed a process called Motion Vision, which could put fifteen frames of film on a flat surface like a trading card. When it turned, it captured a complete motion such as a pitcher throwing to a batter who then hits a home run. We used it as a promotion for the film *Striptease* in which Demi Moore walks down a runway while gradually unclothing.

Jeff and I also became minority partners in a firm called Integrated Sports International run by Frank Vuono, Fred Fried, and Steve Rosner. The firm was able to do marketing for players, leagues, teams, conferences, corporations, and any high-profile individuals in sports. It could also offer any independent agent the same access to high-quality marketing for his clients that the mega-agencies did. Our investment multiplied when ISI was sold to the entertainment outfit SFX. We realized that by combining representation of athletes with marketing and content supply and technologies, we were creating synergies that could be much larger than the parts.

Besides, Jeff sensed, and rightfully so, that at the rate we were going in our core agency, we'd burn out sooner or later, probably sooner. He also understood that this new focus would bring him closer to his ultimate goal of owning a Major League Baseball franchise, which he fulfilled years later with the San Diego Padres.

Jeff's solution was to sell the firm. My friend David Falk, who represented Michael Jordan and other basketball stars, sold his practice to SFX in 1998 for $100 million, becoming CEO of SFX Sports. SFX went on to collect about a dozen smaller companies. We could do the same.

Yet I still did not want to sell. I was concerned about losing the autonomy I had craved from the day I took on Bart.

Whether working from the small card room in my parents' house in West Los Angeles or the four-level dream house in Berkeley, I had always been my own boss and saw no reason to change. I relished my freedom so much I resisted offers to join larger firms, including one from Michael Ovitz, head of Creative Artists Agency and one of the most powerful people in Hollywood. Ovitz took me to a Lakers game, and I was tempted for sure, mostly by the chance to affect a broader audience with positive role models in entertainment, as well as sports.

When it came time to decide, though, I could not imagine being unable to set my own schedule and dedicate a percentage of my time to community and charity programs, or if I wanted to appear in a movie or give a speech or take part in any other endeavors that did not necessarily contribute to the bottom line. I did not believe in bottom lines. Our business, in any case, would always be profitable because of the areas we picked. Only with great reluctance, in 1989, after the move to Newport Beach, did I work for the first time in a traditional office.

Selling the firm could very well mean the loss of my autonomy, and I was not the only person who was wary of the idea.

"You have as unique a brand as there is in professional sports," Bob Kraft assured me. "I don't think you should sell it. I think you'll end up being sorry."

On the other hand, I recognized there would be a serious consequence to not selling: the likely end of my partnership with Jeff Moorad. We had worked wonderfully together ever since those difficult weeks in the spring of 1985, when we scrambled to keep and sign our clients. Losing Jeff was as threatening as losing my autonomy, maybe more. It was unacceptable.

So with my great reservations, in October of '99, the sale went through, to Assante, a financial management corporation based in Winnipeg, Canada. The final settlement was for $120 million, the largest deal ever for the acquisition of a sports firm.

My portion in cash and stock amounted to between $30 million and $40 million after taxes, but we had more money already than I ever dreamed of. More appealing was the fact that I had become CEO of a new sports empire where we could buy agencies and build an entertainment company and marketing arm. Our goal was to build a studio to create the new standard in movies, TV, video games, and mobile apps.

I had high hopes, as there seemed no limit to what we could achieve. Little did I know how soon it would all crumble.

16

THE BEGINNING OF THE END

I began the new millennium in a new role, spending the majority of my time as an executive, assessing how to best apply our resources to move the firm forward as never before. That didn't mean, of course, I stopped working with clients. I couldn't see myself ever giving that up entirely.

We enjoyed another exceptional year, signing three players who were picked in the first round: wideout Plaxico Burress, tight end Bubba Franks, and wide receiver R. Jay Soward, elevated by his faster time in the forty. Plaxico and Bubba would go on to register outstanding careers. To visit with Bubba's mother, who resided in West Texas, I flew on a small airline. I felt as if I were on a roller coaster at Disneyland. A friend I brought with me was so scared he turned white. He was convinced the plane was going to crash. Such is life on the road, never a dull moment. I traveled so much I logged enough frequent flyer miles for a free trip to Mars.

As for no dull moments, that goes double for another player I took on in 2000, Ricky Williams.

There was a duality to Ricky. One part was the person who chose running back, the most punishing position in the game, and a hard-core program, the University of Texas. He possessed impeccable work habits and never complained. Nick Saban, who later coached him in Miami, told me Ricky was as good a practice player as he ever had, and Nick is one of the sternest disciplinarians around.

The other Ricky was a sensitive soul in search of a higher truth and a natural way to live his life in peace and harmony. Both sides coexisted, which made him a fascinating client. However, when the more sensitive side surfaced, he clearly could not abide by the rules and structure of football.

Ricky asked me to represent him after his rookie season. In a departure from my usual policy, I didn't suggest he try to fix the situation with his current agent, then get back to me if he deemed it hopeless. I knew it was hopeless. Everybody did.

His contract was the most obvious blunder. Ricky, drafted by the Saints one pick after Edgerrin, received a decent enough signing bonus, $8.8 million, but the majority of his $68 million package revolved around incentives, and they were not easy goals to attain. Ricky needed to run for at least 6,400 yards during his first four years for most of them to kick in, which was something that only a few players in the history of the NFL had done. The first season, he was held to 884 yards. Injuries hindered his chances, and so did the franchise he played for. The Saints, who traded practically the entire roster to draft Ricky, were terrible—they would finish the season 3-13—and were forced to pass on almost every down to overcome double-digit deficits, depriving him of the precious carries he needed. The attention the media placed on his yardage total did not help, either. Ricky already felt enough pressure.

Agreeing to a long-term contract with too many uncertainties was not the only example of poor judgment in his camp. Prior to the season, Ricky, standing next to his coach, Mike Ditka, posed in a white wedding gown for a cover photo in *ESPN Magazine,* the headline reading FOR BETTER OR WORSE.

Ricky didn't see the problem, and there wasn't any, really, except that it created the image of him as a total eccentric. This was harmful and unnecessary, especially given how much his teammates and opponents respected him.

"What you do not want to see as a safety is Ricky Williams breaking through the line and coming toward you," Tim McDonald said. "You are just hoping somebody else will tackle him because you certainly don't want to have to do it."

As grossly unfair as his contract with the Saints was, I advised him he would have to wait a while for a new one. We needed to work on a new image first. During an interview with *Sports Illustrated,* Ricky had made a number of unfortunate comments about his coach, teammates, and city. They didn't go over too well.

"New Orleans is a great place to hang out," he said, "but not a great place to live and work."

That was the last thing a client of mine would ever say. I always felt that rookies, long before they came to terms with their new teams, needed to embrace their new communities. They would win over the fans in no time, and the press, too. You can't overstate how critical such support can be for a young player's development. Ricky did the opposite. He alienated everyone. Now it was essential he win them back.

He needed to do another interview, and this time come across like a member of the New Orleans Chamber of Commerce. Ricky did just that, and more, pledging to assist local charities, and even moved into an apartment in the center of town, which most players would never consider. Most players lived in the suburbs. Over time, his image improved, and so did his production. Ricky rushed for 1,000 yards in 2000 in leading the Saints to a 10-6 record and first place in the NFC West. Which is why it was so devastating when the Saints took Deuce McAllister, a running back from Ole Miss, in the first round of the 2001 draft.

A year later, Ricky was traded to Miami, where he rushed for a league-high 1,853 yards in his first season as a Dolphin. The next year he gained 1,372 yards. He became a big star.

We had restructured portions of his contract when he got to the Dolphins with a series of incentives, which rolled over into the base of his following year. The team refused to totally renegotiate because he had been stopped in front of the *Fort Lauderdale Sun-Sentinel* building with no driver's license, no shirt, and no shoes in his car. The pictures of him sitting in handcuffs on the curb ran everywhere, causing owner Wayne Huizenga to have serious doubts about Ricky's character.

Two years later, the Dolphins were finally prepared to negotiate a new deal. I was sure it would work out to Ricky's satisfaction, yet he became increasingly frustrated. He was worried his body couldn't take the amount of pounding it received when he carried the ball 383 times in 2002 and 392 times a year later.

As training camp approached, he told me he was going to retire.

I was stunned.

"Ricky, it is too late," I said. "They have built their whole offense around you. It will destroy their season. Your teammates are counting on you, as well as the coach, the organization, and the fans."

"Leigh, I have this one life to live, and I am done with football and need to focus on things that are really important. Don't worry."

Worry? I was aghast. I completely support the right of anyone to live according to whatever values and lifestyle he or she chooses—as long as it doesn't hurt others, and this would definitely be the case. He explained he was adopting a more spiritual lifestyle and the temporal world was not for him. He told me he would go to Hawaii and think about it and call me. I was sitting in my front room watching television one night when sportswriter Dan Le Batard announced on ESPN that Ricky had told him he was retiring. I could think of many better ways to get the official word. We were bombarded the next day with calls from team officials, coaches, teammates, and reporters. I had very little to tell them.

Ricky then did another interview with Le Batard, in which he was open about his use of marijuana. I was not offended, but it was against the law in most parts of the country and definitely against NFL policy. Furthermore, given how strongly I felt about athletes being role models, I was disappointed a player of mine had walked out on his contract and was promoting drug use. Many people urged me to cut ties with Ricky, but I had no idea what was going on in his life and didn't want to abandon him.

He soon called from Australia. He was living in a pup tent in the middle of nowhere overlooking a beach, and he wasn't communicating with anybody but me. The Dolphins suspended him and filed a lawsuit. I kept trying to get Ricky to return to the United States, but he was quite content and the season was already under way.

I finally thought of a way to get Ricky out of his pup tent. I had set up a business in China to help develop sports in that country. I met with the Chinese minister of culture and the head of CCTV, the country's main television network, lectured at Beijing University, and had a luncheon thrown for me by the sons and daughters of every Chinese leader after World War II. We had the only foreign office in the Forbidden City and were producing one of the first foreign concerts ever at the Great Wall. Alicia Keys was headlining along with Boys-II Men. I invited Ricky to join us.

He said he would, flying to Bangkok on the way to Beijing. Only there was one problem. The picture on his passport was upside down—don't ask me—and they wouldn't let him on the flight. Instead he went to a bar and watched a preseason Raiders game, which was where, he later told me, he had an epiphany.

"My destiny is to play for the Raiders," he said when he arrived barefoot at my office in California. "And for my new team, I need a new identity."

"Okay," I said, "and what would that be?"

"I want to change my number from 34 to 21, and I want my new name to be Rio Don," he said.

I handed him about a dozen footballs to sign for charities, which we did whenever athletes stopped by the office.

Before I left for the day, I looked at the footballs. Each was signed "Rio Don, number 21." That was Ricky Williams. The next day he took off to become a yoga instructor at the College of Ayurveda, which teaches the traditional Indian medical system, in the California Gold Rush town of—I kid you not—Grass Valley.

Eventually we negotiated his return, and by then Nick Saban was coaching the Dolphins.

Nick was a godsend for Ricky. He had researched everything he could about his condition. When people ask how the University of Alabama is so successful these days, I recall how Nick treated Ricky as an individual. After Ricky later encountered more difficulties, I landed him a deal with the Toronto Argonauts for a year. He loved playing in Canada, where there were many less demands. He finished his career with the Baltimore Ravens.

Whether or not selling to Assante was the right move for me, I was intent on making the best of it. I purchased Maximum Sports Management, a football practice run by agent Eugene Parker, whose clients included future Hall of Famers Deion Sanders and Rod Woodson, a hockey agency, and a basketball firm operated by Dan Fagan, who represented the No. 1 pick in the 2000 NBA Draft, Cincinnati forward Kenyon Martin. Basketball is a tougher sport for agents, as recruits are identified at a younger age—twelve or thirteen years old in some cases—and many of them draw entourages that do not always have a player's best interests in mind. Shocking, I know. Still, I had loved the sport for as long as I could remember, going with my father to watch the Bruins, a dynasty in the making.

I was also a die-hard Lakers fan, listening each night on the radio to the one and only Chick Hearn.

Our firm had represented basketball players in the past and had been very successful. One player who stood out was Greg Anthony, a point guard for the UNLV Runnin' Rebels during the school's glory days in the early 1990s under coach Jerry Tarkanian.

The basketball gods could not have designed a better first NBA draft pick for us than Greg. He had a high IQ and an engaging personality, and he was ambitious on and off the court. He'd already set up his own memorabilia company, turning a profit as an undergraduate, and had attended a world economic summit the previous summer in Houston. We interviewed Greg at the law firm of Las Vegas mayor Oscar Goodman. Greg's success in television is no surprise. He could be a big-time CEO or politician if that's what he wanted.

We were almost desperate to persuade the New York Knicks, who held the twelfth pick in the '91 NBA Draft, to select Greg, who was perfect for the grand stage of New York City. The problem was that the Cleveland Cavaliers, picking one spot ahead of the Knicks, were also interested. We informed Cleveland that Greg would not be comfortable there. The Cavs got the message and took Terrell Brandon, a point guard from the University of Oregon. Greg wound up in New York, which led us to signing his backcourt mate, John Starks.

The Knicks, coached by Pat Riley, whom I knew from his Laker days, were a talented team specializing in tough defense. Greg and John were subject to discipline for overly aggressive fouls so often that I became a regular phone pal of NBA executive Rod Thorn. I did my best to convince him Greg and John were simply following Pat's directive to guard their man as closely as possible. I went to the finals in Houston and stayed at the team hotel. The fans kept me and the Knicks up all night before one game by honking horns and exploding firecrackers.

Securing a new contract for John in the fall of 1994, a few months after the Knicks lost that series to the Rockets, turned out to be quite an adventure.

We finally reached an agreement with the team on a new deal but needed to file the paperwork by 5:00 P.M. on the day a moratorium on contract extensions was slated to begin. With time running out, John called on his cell to say he was stuck in traffic. He arrived at Madison Square Garden at about 4:40 P.M. and ran upstairs to the Knicks' offices to sign. The contract arrived via fax at NBA headquarters with two minutes to spare.

John Starks was a study in tenacity, having gone from being a boxboy in a Tulsa supermarket to a star in the NBA. He never forgot his hometown, where he retrofitted high school athletic equipment through his foundation. A poster of him blocking a Jordan shot still hangs in my office.

Speaking of pictures, I grew up with one of Jerry West on the wall over my bed. So it was quite a challenge when I met with West decades later, when he was the Lakers general manager, to negotiate a contract for guard Byron Scott. To perform as a pro, I needed to put my emotions aside, which I managed to do—well, for the most part.

"This is the hardest thing I've ever done," I told Jerry. "You were one of my boyhood heroes."

I faced a similar situation when I represented Providence's Austin Croshere, a lottery pick with the Indiana Pacers in 1997. The new coach was none other than Larry Bird. Spending time with a legend like that was quite a thrill.

My saddest experience in representing basketball players involved Wayne Simien, an All-American forward from Kansas. Wayne, the epitome of wholesome midwestern values, was drafted in the first round in 2005 by the Miami Heat. A series of injuries, however, forced him to retire without ever playing regularly. There is no doubt he would have enjoyed an outstanding career.

•   •   •

Another man I greatly admired was June Jones, whom I met when he was Bart's roommate with the Falcons in 1976. He possessed strong faith, unshakable values, and a most creative mind. He was also a scratch golfer who could have easily competed on the PGA Tour. His best talent, though, was as a football coach, which was how I came to represent him. I was slow to work with coaches, but it didn't take me long to realize they could be tremendous clients. Unlike players, they receive guaranteed contracts and, if successful, have much longer career spans.

June took over the Falcons in 1994 and then, in 1998, became the interim coach of the San Diego Chargers. One year later, he was offered the head job at the University of Hawaii, where he had played in the '70s. It was not an easy decision. Hawaii was offering him only a third of what he'd been paid in San Diego, and the team was coming off an 0-12 season. He asked for advice.

"No one will understand, but follow your heart," I told him.

That's precisely what he did, and with his innovative "run and shoot" offense, the team went 9-4 in his first year with a bowl win over Oregon State. That set the NCAA record for biggest turnaround in a single season.

Representing coaches, I soon discovered, also offered another opportunity to give back to communities that needed as much assistance as they could get. June, for example, set up a charitable foundation to help kids in Dallas and Samoa.

In 2000, June continued to work his magic, but in February of 2001, while driving on the freeway one night, he fell asleep and crashed into a concrete stanchion. His aorta ruptured, and he suffered multiple broken bones. He should never have survived. The hospital was deluged with visitors, and June's condition became a central focus on the Hawaiian islands. Miraculously, he healed—and surprisingly fast, becoming well enough to stand on the sidelines for the first game in the fall. His recovery was another example of an athlete's amazing recuperative powers.

In 2007, the Warriors were the only team in Division I to go undefeated in the regular season; they lost to Georgia in the Sugar Bowl. Nothing like that had ever happened before on the islands. No wonder Oahu was in a frenzy. Too bad the school's facilities and recruiting budget were substandard. Thus, when Southern Methodist University came in with a handsome offer to hire June, we flew to Dallas to seal the deal.

That night the countercampaign was intense. Hawaii governor Linda Lingle called and said June's departure would have a devastating impact on the state's morale and economy. Calls came from military figures who said it might demoralize the troops. The president of the university called me and matched SMU'S offer.

Knowing June, and how much he cared about the people in Hawaii, I was not surprised he was having such a difficult time deciding between the two schools. He told me that he needed to pray on it and would return to my hotel room to give his answer. I assumed he would be right back. He wasn't. Soon it was midnight, and the hours kept rolling on. At 4:00 A.M., he still had not returned and no one was answering his phone. Finally, at eight, he knocked on the door. He was at peace. He had decided on SMU.

In the end, June simply could not justify to himself taking that much money from the University of Hawaii and becoming the state's highest-paid employee. I can't think of many people in any profession who would have displayed so much character under that type of pressure.

Fortunately, I was blessed to represent a lot of clients with character, and that included two star prizefighters: Oscar De la Hoya and Lennox Lewis.

I'd been fascinated by the sweet science since I won my first bet by backing Muhummad Ali, then known as Cassius Clay, when he upset Sonny Liston to capture the world heavyweight crown in February 1964. In an individual sport, fighters can assume a unique profile in American culture. Ali, for example, at the height of his career, was the most recognizable person on the planet. The macho aspect of boxing also made it a powerful tool to deliver positive messages to young people who otherwise would have been resistant to authority figures.

I first worked with Oscar, a handsome, engaging Latino who would win world titles in six different weight classes.

We helped Oscar with marketing and image building and were able to land some good endorsements, in both the English and Spanish markets. Yet as I looked around the sport, I saw how boxers were generally uneducated and exploited. I thought Oscar could become the head of his own promotion company instead of having to fork over a large percentage of each purse to someone else.

He did just that, putting together a talented team to establish Golden Boy Productions. Oscar was a tremendous inspiration to young Latinos, as when he appeared with Steve Young on a poster for the Anti-Defamation League with the slogan "Prejudice Is Foul Play."

I then took on Lennox Lewis.

Lennox was brilliant, well read, funny, and good-looking and he also had an appealing British accent. Coming after Ricky Williams and Edgerrin James, Lennox made me the official agent for athletes with dreadlocks. We agreed to raise his profile and market him as much as possible. It was a challenge because he was in America for only half the year for tax reasons, and much of that time was taken up by training.

Part of the mission with Lennox was to give him entrée into the entertainment community. I threw him two parties with studio heads, producers, actors, writers, and television executives. The first one, at the Buffalo Club in Santa Monica, included Arnold Schwarzenegger and CBS president Les Moonves. The second featured the cast of the film *Ocean's 11*, including Matt Damon and George Clooney. We walked the red carpet for the premiere of *Ray,* and for Lennox's rematch in late 2001 against Hasim Rahman, I chartered a plane, which carried Leonardo DiCaprio, Tobey Maguire, Jeremy Piven, Chris Connelly, and my son Jon.

During the fight, which was held in Las Vegas, Leo sat on one side of me, Tobey on the other. Leo was mobbed, Tobey hardly recognized. We chartered another plane about six months later for Lennox's fight against Mike Tyson in Memphis. Except this time, with *Spider-Man* now a smash hit, Tobey was mobbed while Leo was the one ignored, though he was full of pride for his good friend.

Not surprisingly, in boxing, as in other sports, I received my share of criticism.

Several months before the first Lewis-Rahman fight, set for South Africa, Jerry Weintraub, a longtime friend, called me to inquire about Lennox's willingness to participate in a fight scene for *Ocean's 11,* which he was producing. Jerry wanted Lennox and Tyson to come to the Mandalay Bay in Vegas.

"Are you crazy?" Lennox responded. "He'll think it is a real fight and bite me."

Jerry settled for another heavyweight, Wladimir Klitschko, instead of Tyson. To be in the film, Lennox trained in Vegas instead of his usual spot, the Poconos outside of New York. Once the shooting was completed—my wife and I played reporters—Lennox went to South Africa, where he was knocked out in the fifth round. Lo and behold, I was blamed for messing with his training regimen. Typical.

As time went on, Lennox began to trust me more to guide his future. He appreciated the reaction to the public service announcement he appeared in, "Real Men Don't Hit Women," and was eager to do more. Like Oscar, he created his own production company, which would afford him more profitability, as well as the ability to educate and promote young boxers. Lennox asked me to negotiate his fight with Tyson, set originally for Vegas. The difficulty in working with boxers, however, is that they have such huge entourages that the politics become treacherous. I was not used to having lawyers, managers, PR people, promoters, and camp followers all vying for control. It was much more simple in team sports—me, a financial planner, and the athlete.

The highest profit margin comes in the pay-per-view market. I sat in a room with Ross Greenburg, the head of HBO Sports, and a large group around Lennox and negotiated the terms.

We couldn't have done any better. The deal was likely to earn Lennox the most lucrative purse in boxing history. Lennox was thrilled. We celebrated in Miami at a nightclub called B.E.D., where guests were seated not at tables but on, yes, beds. At one point, Lennox and I had Britney Spears on one side and P. Diddy on the other.

Lennox and I went to a hotel in New York for a press conference to officially announce the fight. Things usually went pretty much as planned at similar press conferences I attended over the years. Not this time.

We were standing toward the side of the stage while Tyson gesticulated wildly. I had talked with him at times when he was stable and found him to be bright and sensitive. He got wilder and wilder on the podium, jumped off, and then ran toward Lennox and tackled him. The two rolled around the floor. Finally, the fight was broken up. We retreated to Lennox's hotel room. He rolled up his pant leg and blood was pouring down.

"Oh my God, the geezer bit me!" he said.

A hotel doctor was called, who administered a tetanus shot.

Lennox's manager warned everyone, "No one say a thing publicly about this or Tyson's license will be yanked and we'll lose the fight."

No one did. His license was yanked anyway, and that's how the fight ended up in Memphis. Lennox knocked Tyson out in the eighth round. I wasn't involved in that promotion.

• • •

In 2001, I also represented Leonard Davis, a 6'6", 370-pound offensive tackle from the University of Texas. His nickname was "Big." Leonard was as kindhearted as he was imposing, and there would be no lack of interest from teams requiring size up front. With each performance in the All-Star games and at the combine, his stock kept rising, although we had to coach him up on his lateral drill—the agility a player demonstrates moving from side to side— after the Bengals, slotted fourth, complained he wasn't quick enough.

In the days leading up to the draft, I was pretty sure we were locked in with the Browns at No. 3. Still, I felt we could do better. So I approached the Arizona Cardinals, who possessed the second pick. I knew it would not be an easy sell. The Cardinals had just signed a bunch of free-agent offensive tackles and seemed more interested in shoring up the other side of the ball. Florida defensive tackle Gerard Warren was the perfect fit.

I made my case anyway. I asked their executives which team they aspired to be like. The Cowboys, they told me.

"Well, look how they win," I said. "They have a big, smashmouth offensive line that triggers everything, so you can't overload the line too much. With Leonard, you start him at right tackle and later move him to left tackle."

Leonard aided his own cause by telling reporters he'd love to go to Arizona. Gerard Warren did his part, as well, conveniently pointing out how the Cardinals rarely signed their draft choices early enough for them to start camp on time. The Cardinals picked Leonard. They knew they could deal with me, and, as it turned out, Leonard received a larger signing bonus than Michael Vick.

I was in no mood to celebrate, however. The spring and summer of 2001 were the worst months of my life, personally and professionally. I did not realize it at the time, but the period spelled the beginning of the end of what I spent a quarter of a century building.

The arrangement with Assante, as I initially feared, did not work out very well. Due to changes in upper management or a shift in corporate strategy—I was never sure which—they lost interest and stopped funding new investments into other firms, as well as our efforts to build a marketing and production company. In June, David Dunn, the third partner with Jeff Moorad and me, walked away. He was spurred on by a young attorney, Brian Murphy, who, it was later proven in court, had hatched an elaborate plan to break up the firm. They told Assante that they would negotiate a return. In the meantime, they convinced Assante to let them be "sole stewards" over half the practice, forbidding me to talk to those players. Dunn and Murphy assured Assante that this was temporary, but they had already sought financing for a new firm while putting out the word to those clients that I had retired.

My clients did not leave me. They were taken from me. Dunn and his associates staged a coup. I had seen a lot of dubious behavior among other agents, and I had dealt with it in my own firm when Mike Sullivan solicited clients at my wedding in 1985. Yet David Dunn was like a younger brother, and it stunned me. These were people I carefully tutored on role modeling and the concept that there was a lot more to representing professional athletes than the bottom line. I was oblivious to who they really were. To them, the bottom line was the *only* line.

A series of lawsuits ensued. Assante blamed me for the mess, which led to the company pulling back even further. Dunn and Murphy used the most venal and false of all defenses, "hostile environment." I was not even allowed to defend myself in the press, as any calls to my office were transferred immediately to Assante's public relations people.

In court, we won a stunning $44 million verdict. The jury ruled Dunn and Murphy were guilty of violating a contract that had prohibited them from enticing clients to leave while the two still worked for Assante, had dealt fraudulently in inducing the clients, and had falsely maligned me. As punishment for slandering my reputation, the foreman declared, "Mr. Steinberg is a man of honor and we want to punish this conduct." I was awarded an additional $22 million in punitive damages. However, since I'd already transferred my interest to Assante, the money meant nothing to me, and though I was grateful for the ruling, it didn't make up for the months of negative publicity. Dunn received a two-year suspension by the NFLPA. Murphy escaped any sanctions because he wasn't certified.

On the personal side, Lucy and my son Matt began to feel sick. The problem, we discovered, was toxic levels of mold, which had entered the house through the air-conditioning system. A few weeks earlier, when the El Niño rains slammed Southern California, our Olympic-sized swimming pool flooded; the water overflowed into our house on a double lot in Newport Beach. We thought we captured it all when we put in a new floor. We did not. Once tests confirmed the mold, we took off immediately, leaving every piece of furniture behind. The house was later demolished because we did not want anyone else to live there.

Luckily, my financial planner let us stay in a home she owned under the flight pattern near John Wayne Airport in Orange County till we could find a place to rent while we looked to buy a new home. The stress the move put on my marriage cannot be minimized, and if that weren't unsettling enough, we weren't there more than a few weeks when September 11 happened. The sound of every plane circling overhead only added to our anxieties.

There was more. Around the same time, Matt and our older son, Jon, both started to experience problems with their vision. Watching them try to cope with new limitations broke my heart.

I felt powerless in every area of my life—a firm that was no longer mine, a disease I couldn't prevent, a wife I couldn't make happy. I saw no answers, and that was new for me. I'd always assumed I could solve any problem, whether getting a player more money or finding him a new team. I was wrong. I felt like the fictional character Gulliver, tethered on my back with Lilliputians sticking forks in me.

I turned to alcohol to check out and escape. Not until many years later, after the damage was done, did I realize it was no escape at all. It was a trap, and I couldn't get out.

I did not drink as a teenager. There was never alcohol in our home. Even at Cal, I got drunk only on occasion. My friends called me "One-Beer Steinberg." They would order a pitcher of beer at Kip's restaurant across the street from our dorm and pour me a glass. I rarely finished it, and if I did, I certainly did not need another. I was too engaged in the conversation. I didn't like feeling as if I weren't in control.

Little changed over the years. During dinner one evening at Mastro's in Westwood with my friend Tommy Lasorda, the energetic L.A. Dodgers manager, and others, the wine kept flowing as they shared their stories. At one point, Frank Sinatra came by to say hello. I kept looking for more inventive ways to dump the wine without anyone noticing. I hid one glass under the table. I took another into the bathroom. Anything to stay in their company. The stories were priceless.

On some occasions, however, One-Beer Steinberg had one too many, like the time I got drunk at Drew Bledsoe's wedding in May 1996, though, as I recall, everybody got drunk. Or later that same year, when I made the mistake of getting in my Mercedes after a few drinks and was arrested.

In March of 2002, I checked into McLean Hospital in Belmont, Massachusetts. Lucy and the children flew back east with me. Maybe now I would receive the treatment I needed and the nightmare would end.

It was not the case. When Lucy returned to California, she told me she wanted a separation. I knew there was no way to change her mind.

I found an apartment in Newport Beach, living on my own for the first time since the mid-1980s. I missed the kids. I missed Lucy. I missed my clients. I missed everything about my old life.

I made an important decision. I would fight to get it back.

Lucy was first, agreeing to reconcile with me in 2003. Finding a way to make our marriage work would take time and energy from both of us, and there were no guarantees, but at least there was a chance now.

There was no chance, though, of reconciling with some of my former clients, such as Drew Bledsoe and Tony Gonzalez. The hurt was deeper than I could ever express.

No player I represented was more grateful than Drew. Someone put together a poster listing "Six Reasons Why Drew Bledsoe Is Great." Drew cut one of the panels out, inserted my face, and sent it to me. He paid our firm 5 percent of his earnings instead of the standard 4 because he was so happy. No wonder he was so angry with my drinking. Drew depended on me, and now he couldn't. He wasn't alone. Some clients put me on a pedestal. I was one of the few people who was a source of unending support in difficult times. We traveled from college through retirement together.

Tony also took it hard when our relationship ended. I was close to him and his parents. I wished him well. I wished all my former clients well. They did not ask to be put in the middle of a nasty battle between dueling agents. They had their own careers to be concerned with, and those careers did not last long.

There were other ex-clients, thirty or so current and former NFL players, who still belonged to Assante. I decided to buy back the rights to them. Lucy advised me against the idea. Quite a few were past their prime, and the ones who were not, disturbed by the uncertainty, would likely search for more stable representation in the not-too-distant future. For me, though, $4 million for the football portion of the firm was worth restoring the autonomy I cherished. I also felt a deep sense of loyalty to the players and their families, dating back many years. I moved into new offices in Newport Beach; despite some heavy losses in the stock market, I was still well-off enough to afford the $50,000 a month in rent. I was optimistic again, just as Dad taught me to be.

The financial losses, however, continued to mount.

Commissioner Tagliabue held up a deal I negotiated for Sirius Radio with eight franchises to carry their games, which would have netted us about $2.5 million. The income alone would have kept our firm in decent shape during a very difficult transition period. The commissioner decided no team could sign a deal with Sirius; only the league as a whole could. The road back would be more treacherous than I anticipated.

Still, it was not the loss in the bottom line that set me back yet again. A much greater loss was coming. I wasn't prepared for it, though I don't know how I could have been. My father was diagnosed with esophageal cancer.

It is impossible to exaggerate how much Dad meant to me, as a boy and as a man. Outside of my kids, he was my one source of unconditional love. He was a rock. I always knew how much he cared, and I cannot overstate how much that helped me cope, even in the worst of times. Especially in the worst of times.

"You know we don't need newspaper clippings to be proud of you," he once said.

Dad underwent surgery in the summer of 2003, and for three or four months, we believed he just might beat the odds. He believed it, too. He was even back on the golf course and playing tennis. Then the cancer entered his liver, and any hope was gone. The toll the chemotherapy took on him, when his weight dropped from 210 to 120 pounds, was almost unbearable. Dad had always had so much physical vitality. Yet this remarkable man who spent his life in education wasn't done teaching those close to him just yet. He had taught us how to live, and through the love he showed for everyone except himself, even when he could barely speak, he taught us how to die.

My father passed away on July 8, 2004. As the oldest son, I took care of most of the arrangements and delivered the eulogy.

I didn't cry, just as I didn't with the other losses. I kept the pain inside, which wasn't the best thing. I just soldiered on. I was busy recognizing every important person in Dad's life and making sure Mom and the kids were okay. I didn't cry later, either, when I was alone.

Yet I was devastated, and a full decade later, I still miss him every day. He always knew what to say, and I can't help but wonder how much his faith and strength could have served me as the years rolled on, one disappointment followed by another, no relief in sight.

17
THE END

He didn't come from one of the elite programs in college football and didn't receive nearly as much attention as more celebrated peers such as Eli Manning and Philip Rivers, but the first time I saw him, I was certain Ben Roethlisberger would be a franchise quarterback in the NFL. He combined a powerful arm with an ability to anticipate the rush and keep a play alive longer than anyone I'd seen since Steve Young. He had the ability a quarterback needs to tune out all distractions and focus on the moment. I actually thought Ben would be better in the pros than in college. He was a natural leader. There aren't many of them.

Ryan Tollner, one of the agents working with me, established a good rapport with Ben from the start; the two spoke often over the phone. After a few months, I sent Ryan to visit Ben in person. Ben loved a beanbag game called cornhole, which we installed for him in our office.

In the summer of 2003, I went to Oxford, Ohio, to see Ben and I also met with his coach at Miami of Ohio, Terry Hoeppner, and Ben's parents, Ken and Brenda, whom I adored. Terry and I got along wonderfully. He later asked me to represent him, but he died of complications from a brain tumor in 2007.

I checked in with Ben every week or two, Ryan more often than that. Near the end of the recruitment process, Ben and his parents visited us, and we walked on the beach in Corona del Mar to plot his future.

The timing could not have been more pivotal. In 2003, after paying the $4 million to get my clients back, I had signed Kwame Harris, a Stanford offensive tackle, who went in the first round to the 49ers, and Lance Briggs, selected in the third round by the Bears, who remains one of the premier linebackers in the NFL. I was eager to represent another franchise quarterback and Ben was just the man.

As with any quarterback coming out of college, there were doubts.

With Ben, after we resolved the concern over him not taking enough direct snaps from center, our next assignment was to satisfy those who felt his competition in college—Miami of Ohio was in the Mid-American Conference—wasn't stiff enough. I came up with a list of defensive standouts Ben faced in the MAC who made the NFL, as well as small-college QBs, such as Phil Simms (Morehead State) and Neil Lomax (Portland State), who performed exceptionally at the next level.

"I have made a career out of representing franchise quarterbacks," I told the scouts. "I know exactly what a franchise quarterback looks like. He looks like Ben Roethlisberger."

The scouts seemed to get the message. Only time would tell.

The suspense in the hours leading up to the draft was greater than usual. In most drafts, the identity and destination of the top pick are known well ahead of time, and the player has often agreed in principle to the club's offer. Not in 2004. Not with Manning, the consensus No. 1, averse to playing for the Chargers, who were on the clock.

So where would Ben go? I briefed Ben in New York with ESPN cameras chronicling it the night before and told him the Steelers

(No. 11) and the Bills (No. 22) were the most likely spots for him to land. They both needed quarterbacks.

Ben, though, was excited about the possibility of going at No. 4 to the Giants. Coach Tom Coughlin called Terry Hoeppner the night before the draft to indicate his team would pick Ben if San Diego took Eli Manning, Oakland chose Iowa offensive tackle Robert Gallery, and the Cardinals selected Pittsburgh wide receiver Larry Fitzgerald. I advised Ben and his family not to get too excited, as I was sure the Giants would trade up to get Manning. The team's GM, Ernie Acorsi, had told me that he considered Manning a once-in-a-lifetime player. I also knew the Chargers coaches had fallen in love with Philip Rivers when they worked with him at the Senior Bowl.

Ben still kept his hopes up of going to New York. Nothing I said could change that.

On draft day, Ben, his family, Coach Hoeppner, and I sat backstage at Madison Square Garden at a table crowded near other prospective draft picks and their families.

The draft, at last, got under way. San Diego took Manning, the Raiders chose Gallery, and the Cardinals picked Fitzgerald. Now it was New York's turn. Ben was more pumped than ever, the cameras recording his every expression. Even the press figured it was done.

"It's going to be fun dealing with you in your negotiations with the Giants," one reporter texted me.

Yet I still knew Ben wouldn't be a Giant, and the seconds couldn't go by fast enough. Draft time is not like real time. It is water torture time.

Tick. Tick. Tick.

Seconds seem like minutes. Minutes seem like hours.

Tick. Tick. Tick.

The Giants were down to a minute left. The tension was almost unbearable.

Finally, with only seconds remaining, the commissioner arrived at the podium to announce the Giants had, indeed, traded Rivers, whom they chose, in a package to obtain Manning. As much as I had prepared Ben, he was quite deflated.

Now the vigil began, a torturous one for those who come to the ceremony in New York with high expectations. Based on my conversations with GMs and scouts, I knew no team was likely to pick Ben before the Steelers, and if they were to pass on him at No. 11, the wait would grow even more agonizing. The Bills, the other strong possibility, wouldn't be on the clock for several hours.

Pittsburgh was where he ended up, of course, and it couldn't have worked out any better, for Ben and for the Steelers. Ben had grown up in Findlay, Ohio, which was close to Pittsburgh. It did not matter how mediocre the Steelers had been in 2003—they finished 6-10—because they were, well, *the Steelers,* the team that gave us Terry Bradshaw and Lynn Swann and Franco Harris and a defense filled with future Hall of Famers. The Steelers won four Super Bowls in six years during the '70s. They would surely be an elite franchise again, and soon. The Steelers featured a strong running attack anchored by Jerome Bettis, a gifted offensive line, topnotch receivers, and a stellar defense. They also enjoyed perhaps the most passionate fans in the sport. What more could a rookie quarterback ask for?

Meanwhile, I enjoyed a close relationship with Dan Rooney, the owner, the two of us having bonded over the unsuccessful Save the Rams campaign in the 1990s. A true steward of the game, he understood that stability and consistency were the keys to a successful franchise, and he constantly nurtured players to help them fulfill their potential. They came to believe they were better by simply wearing the Pittsburgh uniform. Once, when Ben was recovering from an injury and there was tremendous public pressure to get him back on the field, I called Dan, and he told me he had little concern over whether Ben played in that next game, or even the rest of the season, as long as he would be healthy in the long term. His son, Art, has run the franchise with the same values and traditions.

Based on my prior dealings with Dan, I was quite confident of reaching an agreement that would benefit both the franchise and Ben.

So, naturally, when camp started in late July, we still didn't have a contract. We weren't close. I flew to Pittsburgh. I always felt that being on the premises greatly enhanced the chance to find a consensus. Reporters used to say, "If Leigh makes the trip, he will sign the player." Approximately 90 percent of the time, that was certainly the case.

Ben needed his reps. Each throwing session or film study he missed lessened the possibility of him being ready to step in at some point for the starter, Tommy Maddox. If Ben didn't suit up soon, a whole season might be sacrificed, and who knew how that could affect the rest of his career.

I stated my case in no uncertain terms. "Dan, I'm going to remain here until we sign Ben," I told him. "You have not had a quarterback you picked this high up the draft in years. This is your most critical position. We somehow have to find a way to get this done."

We did, and it was the rapport we had established long before that made the difference. He agreed to pay a quarterback premium, and Ben received a $9 million bonus, more than cornerback Dunta Robinson, who was picked by the Texans a spot ahead of him. We were able to structure the contract to achieve our goals while still abiding by the organization's policy against offering escalator clauses.

Toward the end of our talks, as I pushed for a five-year contract, Dan asked for a favor. "You could really help me if you would agree to do six years," he said, "and I promise you if the player performs the way we think he will, we'll rip the contract up after three or four years and do a new one."

I would have been suspicious if just about any other owner had asked for an oral agreement on such a significant issue, but I could think of no one I knew in pro football whose word I trusted more than Dan Rooney's. We closed the deal.

Ben took the reps he needed and was soon the face of this glorious franchise. He made his first start in just his third game, against Miami. The Steelers prevailed, 13–3. He won the next thirteen in a row, and Pittsburgh ended the regular season 15-1. His team fell to New England in the AFC championship game, but few rookie QBs ever made more of an impact on a team and city.

Nobody was tougher than Ben. If anything, he might have been too tough. In October of 2006, after he suffered a concussion, I advised him not to play the following week. "Ben, when you get a concussion," I said, "your reactions are slower, and it will take much less force for you to get a second, which is what knocked Steve Young out of football."

He listened politely and said he would seriously consider sitting out a game. I did not believe him for a minute. I knew as long as he could walk, he'd take the field on Sunday afternoon. I phoned his parents, who agreed with my concerns and made a similar appeal. He played, of course. That's Ben.

He was also the most superstitious player I'd ever been around. In 2005, I was at the game when the Steelers lost the AFC title to the Patriots. The next year, a couple of days before Pittsburgh was to face the Broncos in Denver for the right to go to the Super Bowl, I called to get him to leave a ticket for me at Will Call, as clients did whenever I asked.

There was a long silence.

"Last year, you were at the title game in Pittsburgh and we lost," he finally said.

"Ben, there were 60,000 other people in the stands," I said.

That was not the point. For some reason, he was convinced it was me. I could show up at Will Call, he said, "but it will be a long, long wait."

I watched the game on television from Newport Beach. Two weeks later, I was at the Super Bowl in the Motor City when the Steelers beat the Seahawks 21–10 for their first crown since 1980. I sat next to Ben on the bus back to the hotel.

"Ben, you just won the Super Bowl and guess what? I was there," I told him. "Does that mean I get to come to more Super Bowls?"

"Yes," he said, with a straight face, pausing for maximum effect, "but never to an AFC championship game."

There was even more riding on that Super Bowl than usual. Ben had refused to shave as long as the Steelers kept winning, and by now he had grown a Grizzly Adams–type beard. We negotiated with Gillette for Ben to receive $100,000 to shave his beard if the Steelers prevailed, similar to when Joe Namath shaved his Fu Manchu mustache for the famous Schick ad in 1968.

Everything was set, or so I assumed. As we sat in the stands during the game, one of our agents received a text from a Gillette official. Because Ben, due to other commitments, would not make a press conference it had set up, the company was dropping its offer by $25,000. I could not believe it, and was in no mood to negotiate. Besides, Ben would shave it off live on the Letterman show. That would be much more impactful than a press conference.

I told our agent to text him back this message: "Surely you do not expect me to run down to the bench in the middle of the game and tell him that you have rescinded your offer. When Joe Namath shaved off his mustache on national television, the ad executive who was in charge of that deal received so much adulation that he has a prominent bust in the Public Relations and Marketing Hall of Fame. If you get this deal done, you'll have your own bust. Sign the deal."

Fifteen minutes later, the Gillette representative texted back, "We accept."

. . .

Ben's performance against the Seahawks in Super Bowl XL capped a weekend I will never forget.

The day before, I was at our Super Bowl party and a technician was showing me how to operate a new ESPN phone when Warren walked in. He had just been elected to the Hall of Fame. The moment I saw him, I broke down. Yes, me, the person who never cried, in public or private, even when I lost my father. I was crying now, and I didn't care.

Why here? Why now?

I felt exhilaration for Warren and the remarkable journey he and I took together for almost thirty years—with one more stop to go, the best yet, Canton. I represented well over a hundred athletes. No one meant more to me than Warren Moon. On the same day, Troy also stopped by our party, and he was just as excited as Warren at making the Hall. I was overjoyed. Troy and I had shared his journey from overcoming a quarterback controversy as a rookie with the worst team in the NFL to his three Super Bowl victories.

The weekend in Canton gave me hope. It didn't last long. In the fall, heavy rains came to Southern California, causing a leak in the deck over our living room. The tests revealed mold yet again. The odds of that happening to us twice in five years were hard to calculate. We moved out, the stress worse than ever.

At work, another client, Chad Morton, a former wide receiver from Southern Cal, who later played for the Jets, fired me, but he did more than that. He sued me. I had never been sued before. In 2003, Morton, without my knowledge, loaned about $350,000 to a firm, SLL Enterprises, run by an employee of mine in China. I was a minority partner. I tried to pay him back, but he fired us and went to David Dunn's firm, and they upped the figure. The legal battle would go on for years. The most disheartening aspect was that I had carefully stressed to my employees how critical it was to follow regulations. I didn't care whether every negotiation went smoothly or if we signed every recruit, but breaking rules was unacceptable. That's how to lose your reputation, and in many cases, your business.

What else could go wrong? Plenty.

A new group of investors I thought I had secured backed out. I wasn't sure how much longer we could stay afloat.

Then came the most distressing news of all. Lucy and I separated for the second time. We would never be a couple again, and I would lose daily contact with my children.

I moved into another apartment, the loneliness more than I could bear—at least, not without a drink or two, or too many to count. I used to drink only late at night, when the kids were asleep. I could now drink anytime I wanted, including in the middle of the day. That felt like a new discovery for me, one I wish I had never made.

Recognizing I had a real problem, I joined a 12-step program, where I was able to benefit from the support of a unique fellowship. However, recognizing and truly dealing with the problem are two different things.

In February of 2007, back in California after the Super Bowl in Miami, worn out, as usual, from the whole experience, I figured one drink couldn't hurt, and might even help me fall asleep. I fell asleep, all right, and did not get up. Needless to say, I'd had more than one. Next thing I knew, there was a group from the program at the door. It was time for my intervention. They took me to the Chemical Dependency Recovery Center at Hoag Hospital in Newport Beach. I stayed there for a month.

Hoag was an excellent facility, but about a month later, I was arrested for drunk driving after my Mercedes ML 500 crashed into three parked cars and a fire hydrant shortly after midnight on Pacific Coast Highway. Local camera crews showed up, and the news ran nationwide.

I started to miss work on occasion, which I had never done, not even in the bleakest days of 2001 and 2002.

Soon there was even less reason to come to work.

I decided not to renew my certification with the NFL Players Association until I could clear up the Chad Morton situation. It was yet another blow, one of the cruelest, and it removed, at least for the next several years, any chance of me staying sober. Being an agent had been my identity since 1975, and now that was gone, too.

From 2008 to 2010, I went through a series of embarrassing episodes, hurting myself and the people who still cared about me. I went to rehab facilities, and each one was excellent. I was one of the best students they ever had, understanding dysfunctional alcoholic families and everything else they taught us about the disease. The problem was I still wasn't ready to stop drinking. It's difficult enough if you are ready. Consuming alcohol became a form of Russian roulette for me. I could never tell when I took that first drink whether it would be followed by just a couple more or whether it would lead to a blackout.

In February 2010, I went back to Miami for another Super Bowl, the Saints facing the Colts. We hosted our twenty-fourth annual party, the one part of my old life that hadn't been taken away. One of our goals that year was to aid victims of the recent 7.0 earthquake in Haiti. We shipped a water purification system from Miami to Haiti that helped save many lives. People were dying of cholera by the thousands. Dad would be proud. *They* is you.

Meanwhile, on the personal side, there was a special woman in my life. Her name was Amy, and I had been seeing her for about three years. She and I were so alike it was eerie. Films, books, sports, politics, there was nothing we didn't share. I was deeply in love with her, and marriage was definitely in my plans.

But I couldn't remain sober. When I returned from Miami, I was exhausted. I figured a little vodka could help me get to sleep.

Next thing I knew, I was kicked out of sober living and in a local hospital for detox. That I could handle. What I could not handle was Amy leaving me to protect herself. She offered me plenty of chances. I wasted every one of them.

I moved into my parents' home, where I spent much of the time sitting on my father's bed, consuming bottle after bottle of vodka. Yet even that wasn't the bottom. The bottom came when my brother Jim took me to Charle Street, a detox facility in Orange County for indigent people and they wouldn't admit me. I didn't fulfill the most basic requirement. I wasn't drunk.

That was easy to fix. I bought a bottle of vodka at the nearest store. Yet they still did not have a bed for me. I wound up instead at another sober-living house in Orange County.

I will never forget the date, March 20, 2010. I haven't had a drink since.

What finally made me stop?

I had a moment of clarity. I asked myself: Was this really my purpose in life at age sixty-one? To lie in my late father's old bedroom, drinking vodka like a baby from a giant plastic bottle?

There had to be another way.

18

A NEW BEGINNING

The other way was turning again to that unique fellowship and this time, following its program. It was the *only* way. I surrendered to the reality that I was powerless over alcohol and that my life had become unmanageable. I discovered a higher power and started working with a remarkably understanding sponsor. Most importantly, I slowly worked the 12 steps and read the relevant literature. I attended meetings, retreats, and conventions and reached out to those who were still struggling, which is why I have decided to open up about my experiences. I did none of this alone. I was surrounded by layer after layer of unwavering support. There is no cure, but as long as I keep sobriety as my top priority and do the work to sustain it, there is a solution, one day at a time.

It is quite a decline to go from chauffeur-driven limousines and private planes to having your car repossessed and not having enough to eat. Yet, through it all, I never questioned for one moment that the way I had chosen to live my life, the idea of serving the community, was the right one then, and remains so today.

For me, that means spending whatever energy I can muster on the causes that are most dear to me. Near the top of the list, as always, is the concussion problem, the "ticking time bomb," as I labeled it nearly a decade ago. As much as the sport, and society, have finally come to terms with the magnitude of the crisis, so much more needs to be done. The discovery that subconcussive hits causing minor brain damage occur on every football play amplifies the danger.

The same sense of urgency must be applied to the issue of steroids.

I realized steroids were a major problem long before many others in the sport did. I could tell by how enormous the players' bodies became and their alarming mood swings between hyperaggression and depression. One of our clients, Oakland Raiders defensive lineman Mike Wise, became so distraught he killed himself in 1992, which was why I campaigned as forcefully as I could to ban steroids from the league forever.

Yet banning them from professional football was not nearly enough. I also worked closely with California state senator Jackie Speier on a bill to ban steroids, along with harmful supplements, in high school and provide education funding. Athletes at that most impressionable age are pushed to become bigger, stronger, and faster without having any idea of what's in the substance they put in their bodies. They, too, like many of the icons they aspire to be someday, are in denial.

With stirring testimony in Sacramento from Bill Walsh, Warren Moon, Kwame Harris, and ex-49er Ken Dorsey, we got the bill through the State Senate and Assembly, but, unfortunately, Governor Arnold Schwarzenegger vetoed the funding part. The bill wasn't as effective without the funding.

I am also heavily involved in dealing with the broader matter of health, nutrition, and longevity. The breakthroughs in understanding how cells work, why we age, and how to stimulate energy and performance without using drugs are remarkable, to say the least. I'm working with a medical researcher who is using clustered water to reenergize the body. Just imagine the possibilities.

I've also been convinced for some time that we remain in denial about the imminent danger of climate change. Let's face it: Melting ice caps, rising oceans, toxic carbons, and aberrational weather patterns are here, and that's not going to change unless we do something about it, and soon. I don't want to be part of the first generation to hand a degraded quality of life down to our children. We all must come up with innovative solutions, and that includes those of us in the world of sports.

In recent years, I have met with companies and environmental leaders from throughout the world who have assembled a package of sustainable technologies under the banner of the Sporting Green Alliance to be incorporated into arenas and practice fields at the high school, collegiate, and professional levels. The goal is to reduce carbon emissions and energy costs in these venues and enable them to sell energy back to the grid.

It will also transform these structures into educational platforms, with hundreds of millions of spectators observing a waterless urinal or a solar panel for the first time and then reflecting on how to integrate these systems into their own homes or businesses, putting sports at the forefront of changing attitudes toward climate change. Imagine Saturday morning cartoon shows with green athletic superheroes fighting for the environment.

As far as my future as an agent, I envision possibilities I could have never imagined when I took on Bart almost forty years ago. In 1975, the universe was dominated by small television sets with three major networks controlling the programming, and remote controls were a luxury. There were no VCRs or PCs. Phones had rotary dials and no call waiting.

Today we have big-screen television monitors that can deliver three hundred regular networks and endless content through smart technology. This content can flow on multiple platforms: computer screen, television monitor, cell phone, or tablet. Consumers can create their own content, and the infinite capabilities of the

Internet provide widespread sources of input on a moment-by-moment basis.

The impact on sports has been explosive. More games are telecast, along with highlight shows, analysis and issue shows, interview formats, and news, documentaries, and films. Many all-sports television and radio networks are being introduced. This is obviously a financial bonanza.

At the same time, however, other factors have greatly narrowed the niche of sports representation.

The players associations, for example, have negotiated rookie salary caps in the NBA and NFL, which destroys the value of imaginative contract construction and skillful negotiations. The unions have put cap limits on what an agent can charge a player. In the NBA, it is 4 percent of a minor portion of the contract, and many agents don't even charge for that service. In the NFL, it is 3 percent of severely capped contracts, and the agent might have to pay about $20,000 for a rookie to train for the scouting process. For most agents, unless a practice is filled with many starters and major stars, it is difficult to make a real living.

Thankfully, involvement in representation can lead to the more profitable areas of marketing, advising, and owning projects in sports technology and content supply. That's what we did with Athlete Direct. It requires imagination to predict where the world of sports business is heading. Imagine fans in a stadium with a monitor in front of them. On one side of the screen, they can keep track of his fantasy team; on another, the bets they made that day. They can vote with other fans on one play each game that the coach must call and for a mandatory official call reversal. They can text other fans in the stadium and around the league.

That's only a start. They could also replay any play at any time, watch live broadcasts of other games, purchase tickets to future games, and receive advertising and promotional information. They could sit wearing a wired helmet and experience any level of virtual sensation they desired, such as a blow a quarterback receives or the thrill of a stolen base. Modern agentry must master all these possibilities for the benefits of individual clients, as well as the prosperity of a firm. Each of these technologies offers advertisers a more accurate way to precisely track the demographics and tastes of their audience. It allows them to target advertising, for example, to female football fans. There is an Oklahoma Land Rush under way to see which technologies, Web sites, and apps will be the next niche businesses to take off.

I have embarked on rebuilding a new company that will be innovative in sports and entertainment. It starts with a core of superstar athletic talent. Football, basketball, baseball, hockey, and soccer are team sports which will continue to flourish. Golf, tennis, boxing, UFC, action sports, Olympic competition, and motor racing are growing, as well. I will also represent coaches, television and radio anchors, and expert commentators, and continue to teach sports law at Chapman Law School in California.

Then there is the matter of building a marketing arm to promote athletes, corporations, colleges, teams, leagues, and other entities. My goal is to create a virtual studio that could facilitate or originate sports-themed content. I've seen the profound effect that motion pictures can have if they have stories of fulfilled aspirations. Sports is also a rich source for TV competitions, reality shows, and scripted projects.

The question is: Why, at sixty-four, should I expend all this energy to build a practice all over again? The answer is simple. For me, work is a passion, and my belief in making the world a better place is at the core of everything I do.

I'm still convinced the most impact I can have comes through working with athletes. I can prepare them to have more fulfilling careers—and lives. Helping them in their journey toward maturity and happiness has always been incredibly rewarding, and when they apply their creativity for service, it brings out the best in them.

An example is the issue of domestic violence. When Lennox Lewis recorded the public service announcement that said "Real Men Don't Hit Women," it had the potential to reach more young rebellious athletes than endless authority figures ever could. It emphasized that domestic violence is not just a women's issue. Every man has women in his life—mother, sister, wife, daughter, lover, or friend—and needs to see the danger through their eyes.

Another is race relations. We are a multiracial society that must operate with mutual respect and harmony. My father spent his life fighting for that cause. Sports is one of the few real models for how whites, blacks, Latinos, and Asians can interact peacefully. They shower together, bleed together, watch each other's back, and work for a common goal with few difficulties. When Oscar De La Hoya and Steve Young posed for "Prejudice Is Foul Play," they reinforced the message.

In 1996, I became so concerned in the wake of the Oklahoma City bombing, with the rise of skinheads and racism, that I approached Abe Foxman, head of the Anti-Defamation League of B'nai Brith, and agreed to fund a program called Steinberg Leadership Institute that would create thousands of young leaders in the fight against hate throughout the country. I did the same with young student leaders in California through the Orange County Human Relations Commission. Athletes can help reverse the scourge of bullying on middle school and high school campuses. They are on top of the status chain, set the trends, and too often are the perpetrators of the harassment. They can be models for tolerance.

Even international issues can be dealt with, from AIDS to global hunger. Along these lines, I helped Secretary of State Madeleine Albright establish Adopt a Minefield, which allowed donors to fund the removal of land mines in postwar countries such as Angola, Mozambique, and Cambodia.

•   •   •

For me, on a personal level, the goal is just as important—to be the best brother and father I can be to the people I love so dearly.

I remain closer than ever to my brothers, Jim and Don. Jim has been an important leader in the spiritual community and an author. Don, meanwhile, has had a distinguished career specializing in aiding distressed countries. He was the United States ambassador to Angola and the president's special representative for humanitarian demining. He is currently the president and CEO of World Learning, a nonprofit which advances leadership in dozens of countries.

My greatest source of joy, of course, is my three amazing kids: Jon, Matt, and Katie. When Jon, the oldest, was born in June of 1986, the transcendent feeling of wonder and joy at watching him come into the world was like no other.

I felt the same incredible sensation when Matt, and then Katie, joined our family. Having grown up with two brothers and raising two boys, I was a bit apprehensive when we had a girl, but when she head-butted me, I knew everything would be fine. Katie, who is attending Michigan State, has an amazing capacity to charm people and is the most likely to take over the business.

Matt, meanwhile, is a creative and exceptionally bright. He recently graduated from USC Film School and is pursuing a master's in education. Jon, who graduated from the University of Arizona, is brilliant and a tremendous writer who finished his first novel at the age of twelve. I am so proud of each one of them.

From Corinth Avenue to Hamilton High to the University of California to becoming an agent to who I am today, there is, however, one voice that has remained the most soothing of all. The example he set as an educator and father has been more inspiring than anything I ever witnessed on the playing field.

Dad never quit, and neither will I.

INDEX